Antiquity Matters

Antiquity Matters

FREDERIC RAPHAEL

Yale UNIVERSITY PRESS

New Haven and London

Published with assistance from the foundation established in memory of Amasa Stone Mather of the Class of 1907, Yale College.

Yale University Press books may be purchased in quantity for educational, business, or promotional use. For information, please e-mail sales.press@yale.edu (U.S. office) or sales@yaleup.co.uk (U.K. office).

Set in Minion type by IDS Infotech Ltd.
Printed in the United States of America.

Library of Congress Control Number: 2017933336
ISBN 978-0-300-21537-3 (hardcover : alk. paper)

A catalogue record for this book is available from the British Library.

This paper meets the requirements of ANSI/NISO Z39.48–1992 (Permanence of Paper).

10 9 8 7 6 5 4 3 2 1

For the wise man, Greece is *everywhere*.
—PHILOSTRATUS (3rd century C.E.)

You never step into the same past twice.
—FEDERICO GARCIA LORCA (20th century C.E.)

Oh those Greeks! They knew how to *live:* what is needed for
that is to stop bravely at the surface, the fold, the skin: to
worship appearance, to believe in shapes, tones, words—in
the whole Olympus of appearance!
—FRIEDRICH NIETZSCHE (19th century C.E.)

Skammenous dromous xanaskavo.
(Ways already excavated, I dig up again.)
—GEORGE SEFERIS (20th century C.E.)

Contents

Introduction

I am an accidental classicist. Born in Chicago, Illinois, in 1931, with every expectation of growing up in America, chance dictated that I should become a pupil at an English "preparatory" school in September 1939. My father had been transferred to London from the Rockefeller Center offices of Shell Oil, in New York City, just over a year earlier. The plan was that we remain in England for a year, during which he would qualify for a more important position, and then return to the U.S. My place at the Ethical Culture School, on Central Park West, was waiting for me. When, with great reluctance, the British prime minister, Neville Chamberlain, declared war on Hitler's Germany, my father, who was a British subject, was asked to stay in London and apply his expertise to the war effort. Of course he agreed.

It was never intended that I should go to boarding school, but my parents thought I would be safer in the countryside than in the capital, which, within a few months, became the target of Hermann Goering's bombers. As France fell and Britain retreated, defiantly, on itself, I was set to learn *amo, amas, amat* (I love, thou lovest, he or she loves) from Kennedy's *Latin Primer*. Had I not left New York City, I should never have been introduced at so young an age, if at all, to the "dead languages" of European civilization just as the continent was being overrun by what Greeks and Romans, for all their differences, would both have regarded as the forces of barbarism.

I began to learn Greek, with its arcane script, when I was eleven years old. Its grammar was even more complicated than Latin (its formal texts were dressed with a sprinkle of accents, *perispomenon* and otherwise, none authentically ancient); its mythology was superbly rich, improbable, dramatic, and bloody. By the time I was fourteen, I was writing iambic verses in the style of Sophocles (the most "English," because the most restrained, of the three great Attic dramatists) and Greek prose that mimicked Demosthenes, the Athenian leader whose brave speeches against Philip of Macedon had something in orotund common with Winston Churchill's diatribes against Adolf Hitler.

The British academic cursus honorum would take me first to Charterhouse "public" school and then to St. John's College, Cambridge. On the way, I learned, with increasing proficiency, to write Latin elegiacs and hexameters in the style of Virgil and Ovid, Latin prose in that of Cicero and Julius Caesar. By the time the war was won, in August 1945, I had been converted from a small American boy to an English adolescent, a properly accented (with long Boston-style *a*'s) collector of scholarships. My father, who had read "Greats"—Latin and Greek literature and philosophy—at Oxford, decided that it would be unfair to transport me back to the U.S.A., where mastery of ancient irregular verbs would do me little good.

Happiness was not the first concern of middle-class British males in the first half of the twentieth century; practical utility plays little part in an aspiring gentleman's education. The study of Latin and Greek was held to inculcate a sense of perfect pitch, in language and logic. The first-class mind (almost always male) could be relied on to have an infallible sense of when people were talking "rot." Culture, in Matthew Arnold's sense, supplied the groundwork of common decency.

The classicist was advised to be modest in conduct and appetite. "Nothing in excess" was the Delphic motto that marked the stylish. The authors whom we were advised not to study, even at university, were those who by their unsavory content and intemperate vocabulary set a Bad Example: writers such as Suetonius, Archilochus, and Martial (not to mention gross chunks of Catullus) were particularly deplorable. We were incited to imitate Ovid's flawless technique, even though, when it came to shamelessly erotic verses, He Should Have Known Better. Passages deemed obscene were left untranslated in the Loeb editions (of *en regard* translations from Latin and Greek). It was, of course, our early ambition to be able to decipher "the dirty bits."

When I went up to Cambridge, in the autumn of 1950, I had had a full decade of the classics in their exemplary and, mostly, unamusing aspects. I had won several scholarships but soon realized that I was never going to be as good a scholar as my contemporary at St. John's College, John Patrick Sullivan. The son of a Liverpool dock worker, John Patrick had had Latin and Greek grammar beaten into him, very memorably, by the Jesuits. Like Doctor Johnson, the bookseller's son who came from a provincial Lichfield to become the Grand Cham of Regency London letters, Sullivan was living proof that "the classics" could be the means by which clever outsiders rose to intellectual eminence. Unable to match him in philology, I veered away into ancient history and philosophy, ancient and modern. I soon became an earnest convert to Ludwig Wittgenstein's "therapeutic positivism." I was also quick to follow Karl

Popper's lead in regarding Plato as the prime source of totalitarian absolutism.

Since my unwavering ambition was to be a novelist, I was also happily seduced by classical anthropologists such as George Thomson and by the manifold versatility of Robert Graves, who went to Charterhouse and was at Oxford with my father. The author of *I, Claudius* and *Claudius the God* (based on the wicked Suetonius) indicated that the classics had more juice in them than the Old School cared to advertise. He relied on Suetonius for the delightfully salacious details of the imperial household, from which Claudius's wife Messalina absented herself in order to enjoy playing the common prostitute in a Roman brothel.

Greece and Rome did not become three-dimensional realities until several years after I had abandoned their formal study. In the second half of the 1950s, I published three novels and wrote TV plays and films. In 1961, my wife and our two small children and I went to live first in Spain, then in Rome. I found that the ancient world was still three-dimensional. Its monuments and its modernized language charged me with an interest I had never felt before. Spanish and Italian came easily to me, thanks to Cicero and Tacitus.

In 1962, we drove from Rome to Brindisi (along the road that had taken Cicero into sorry exile two millennia before) and embarked for Greece. By chance, we were advised to go to Ios, a quite large island in the Cyclades which was, at that time, depopulated. We rented a peasant's *spiti* (cottage) for five dollars a week and I wrote a novel, *Lindmann,* which had nothing to do with Greece, with a liberty that had everything to do with a sense, however fanciful, of living among the muses. As the time approached to return to England, we bought a ruined *spiti* and an adjacent parcel of land on an unspoiled golden beach on the far side of Ios village. Conquered Greece (as the Romans called it) had conquered me, as it did Cicero and Catullus, all those years ago.

I resumed reading the classics, with new eyes. They were opened even wider by the Parisian Hellenists whose works I first happened on in the Librairie La Hune, in St. Germain-des-Prés. Louis Gernet and his epigoni (Jean-Pierre Vernant, Marcel Detienne, Pierre Vidal-Naquet in particular) were careful readers of texts who were also resourceful, not to say inventive, anthropologists. I returned with particular keenness to the Greeks and have stayed with them ever since. When in doubt about what to read next, I repair to the ancient world and its ever-increasing number of commentators and revisionists. Over the years, I have accumulated a scrapbook of fragments, references, memories.

I lack the private treasury of texts which enabled Hugh Lloyd-Jones, for instance, in his finest days, to recite long passages from Greek tragedy; but when our beautiful artist daughter Sarah died, at the age of forty, two lines from Sophocles, learned more than 60 years earlier, came to my mind as cruel comfort: "odos d'odon pason aniasasa dee, malista toumon splanchnon, heen dee nun ebeen" (road more painful than all others, especially to my heart, is the one that now I tread).

Antiquity Matters is more a montage than any kind of a textbook. If it serves the reader as a primer, in the sense of both a place to start from and what might cause an explosion of interest (even of exasperation), then it will not have been composed in vain. I should like to think that its value lies not least in all the signposts it offers to go this way or that, preferably both, or more, in search of intelligence and—why not?—entertainment. Wittgenstein once compared language to one of those great hawsers that tether ocean liners to the dock. The strength and utility of the cable depend on the flexibility that comes of it being composed of thousands upon thousands of complicated elements. None of them reaches from the beginning of the hawser to the end, but they are so tightly interwoven that each makes a contribution to the tenacity of the whole. So it is that the "dead" languages and culture are alive in what we say and think, whether we know it or not.

Not the least of the pleasures of a lifetime among the classics has been the recurrent generosity of academic friends. I have been fortunate indeed to be able to rely on the great Peter Green (who was, as it happened, at Charterhouse a few years before me). He accepted my first short story for publication, back in 1952, and he has again and again marked my card, as they say, when it comes to the classics. More than anyone of his time, Peter has enlivened classical studies with iconoclastic accuracy. Now in his early nineties, he is completing a new translation of Homer's *Odyssey*. His brilliant new version of the *Iliad* was published two years ago. Like Theophrastus, in the fourth century B.C.E., Peter's life will never be sufficiently long for him to think that he has done enough. Paul Cartledge, who has recently retired as Leventis Professor of Greek Culture at Cambridge, has helped me, as so often before, to avoid sorry mistakes both in this book and elsewhere. Richard Seaford, until recently a professor at Exeter University in the west of England, has been tactful and tireless in annotating my stuff. William Lyons, recently retired as a professor of philosophy at Trinity College Dublin, has been as charming as he was implacable in questioning my more reckless opinions and, no less helpfully, pointing out even the smallest errors in my orthography. I am lucky to have known such men, to whom I dedicate this work with great gratitude. Its quality owes much to all of them; its errors are mine.

1.

Among the principal tourist attractions of ancient Athens was the hull of an antique ship beached on the foreshore at Phaleron, the city's main port before the construction of Piraeus.[1] Guides promised that the vessel was the very one on which the mythical Theseus sailed home after he had threaded the maze at Knossos and killed the man-eating Minotaur. His exploit released his father's kingdom of Attica from vassalage to its Cretan overlord, King Minos. Previously, the Athenians had been bound every year to deliver seven maidens and seven youths to the palace at Knossos as tasty atonement for the death of the king's son, Androgeos, while he was on Attic soil. According to one legend, Theseus's father, Aegeus, ordered the assassination of the Cretan prince because his virile charisma (Androgeos was a star wrestler) trumped the old man's popularity. In a variant version, the grandstanding prince elected to go to the mat with a wild bull on the rampage in the fields of Marathon. When he was gored to death, on the plain where today's Venizelos airport stretches, Minos demanded bloody recompense from his Attic

1. In the late 5th century B.C.E., Piraeus was built on the one-size-fits-all grid pattern designed by Hippodamus of Miletus, the prototype of modern city planners such as Le Corbusier and Oscar Niemeyer. According to Aristotle's *Politics,* Hippodamus was the archetypal self-advertising maestro: he had long hair and wore the same trademark robes, made of clever stuff—warm in winter, cool in summer—all year long.

satellite. A third account had the Cretan monarch engaged in a protracted siege of Athens. When he induced Zeus, his divine father, to send a plague on the city, the Athenians were forced to submit, on terms which included that cruel annual tax. Antiquity is copious with rewrites.

Myth prefigured history: in 430 B.C.E., plague struck Athens, at the height of its power, early in the Peloponnesian War, and killed between a quarter and a third of the population.[2] Few blamed the gods; more blamed their elected "Olympian" leader Pericles, in whom they had long vested their trust.[3] Tomorrow-we-die panic and recriminations ruptured the complacent solidarity of the Athenians. To revive morale, Pericles mounted a large military expedition, without clear objective, and cruised it along the coast of the Peloponnese. No

2. The exact nature of the Athenian plague is undiagnosed, but over the centuries maritime cities have been likely to import alien contagions. Venice was repeatedly affected in this way. So was Constantinople/Istanbul. Marcel Proust's father pioneered the use of the cordon sanitaire to avert such infections reaching western Europe via Mediterranean ports.

3. However ironic Pericles' nickname may have been, the intrusion of the gods in human genealogies is at the root of Hellenism; it has no place in Jewish scripture. The word "Christ," which appears only in the Greek New Testament, is essentially Hellenic; as a translation of the Hebrew for "messiah," it means no more than "anointed." The supposed Davidic origin of Jesus bonds him with Judaic royalty; that bloodline, if valid, does nothing to imply divinity. The Pauline savior and the Trinity come, as did the Three Kings, from outside Hebrew tradition (three was a magic number among the Pythagoreans and elsewhere). The Holy One of the Jews does not, as the Olympians did, have personal characteristics or carnal appetites, although He is said, grammatically, to be male. In Exodus 33.17, it is reported that, during Moses's ascent of Mt. Sinai, the recipient of the Commandments was granted a sight of the back of the Holy One, as if to confirm His validity. As Semele discovered when she demanded to see her lover, Zeus, to be faced by a divinity in all his glory could have lethal consequences.

land was occupied, no known Spartan killed. At least and at
best, the sortie served to remove a large body of men from the
risk of infection. Pericles died of the plague in the following
year. The epidemic receded; the war went on.

No subsequent leader matched the Olympian's ascendancy.
Under Alcibiades, Cleon, and others, the democratic Athenians
gambled away their treasure and missed several chances to make
an advantageous peace. A quarter of a century after Pericles'
death, their own miscalculations, no less than Spartan muscle,
led to the end of their city's paramount status. In 404 B.C.E.,
the once impregnable long walls were pulled down, to the sneering music of pipers (*auletai*) commissioned by the Spartan
admiral Lysander. For all the previous arrogance of the Athenians, even their enemies conceded that "the spring had gone
out of the year." The whole city was not destroyed, the story
goes, only because, in Milton's words, "The repeated air / Of
sad Electra's poet had the power / To save Athenian walls from
ruin bare." Lysander was moved when he overheard a Phocian
singing a chorus from Euripides' *Electra*. A few months earlier,
at Lampsacus in Asia Minor, he had ordered the slaughter of
3,000 Athenian prisoners of war.

Fifth-century Athens has neither lost its afterglow nor
silenced its critics. Its self-conscious literary culture prompted
Plato to become the most influential of them. Historians, scholars, and mountebanks[4] have measured the shortcomings of
defeated Athenian democracy on a scale against which the
oligarchies of Sparta, Corinth, and Thebes are rarely graded.

---

4. Taking his cue from Plato, the proto-fascist Gabriele d'Annunzio
(1863–1938) denounced "this grey flood of democratic mud."

Plato and Xenophon, both native Athenians, considered the Spartan constitution to be exemplary.[5] These indictments of Athenian democracy have been taken to prove the folly of conceding power to the votes of a fickle majority. The readiness of the *demos,* the common people, to yield to oratorical blandishment (*peitho*) impelled Plato to advocate a republic (the routine, scarcely exact translation of *politeia*) governed by a caste of experts. His "guardians" would be certified, both by the rigor of their higher education and by the propagation of a *gennaion pseudos* (noble/genetic falsehood), to be entitled to rule. State religion and, no doubt, "faith schools" would inculcate the gospel that the ruling class was guaranteed, genetically, never to be wrong.[6] With summary justice and immutable standards in the place of majority rule, there would be no sides to take: opposition became treason.

Plato sought influence, never election. An aristocrat with private means, he deplored Sophists—professional pundits— who marketed a repertoire of prose and cons and who (provided they got their fees) cared nothing for the merits of a cause. To replace the opportunism of democratic hucksters and plausible prattlers, Plato advocated a serene board of elders with

5. In the 1930s, the English socialist theoreticians Beatrice and Sidney Webb took a similarly admiring view of the advertised constitution of Stalinist Russia while remaining willfully blinkered with regard to that state's murderous practices.

6. Papal infallibility, on matters of doctrine, was not formally asserted, by Pope Pius IX, until 1870, when the authority of the Church was threatened by the rise of liberalism and, locally, by Giuseppe Garibaldi's secularized Risorgimento. "Faith schools" were instituted by Tony Blair's government in the UK in the early 2000s. They have, in more than a few cases, sanctioned the indoctrination of Muslim pupils with undemocratic ideas allegedly rooted in the Qu'ran.

access to a pantheon of unquestionable values. Their rectitude was to be enforced by a secret service, based on the Spartan "nocturnal council."[7] To deserve celebration in the ideal, inflexible city, Homer's disorderly gods were required to renounce their wanton ways. In Plato's moral *logos* (conceptual scheme), deities too were subject to education.

While often united in contempt of democracy, ideologists have long relied on its facilities.[8] Where did Plato found the Academy, in which he advocated a classified, docile, and unsmiling society, but in the one city in Greece where individuality, argument, and comedy were at a premium? Despite Aristophanes' caricature of Socrates, in *The Clouds*, the ribald dramatist is given a star part in Plato's *Symposium* (a modern translator might call it *The Drinks Party*). Wine-cup in hand, Aristophanes amuses the company with the image of lovers, of whatever sexual inclination, as the severed halves of a single original egg. Each couple's greatest ambition is to be reunited in a seamless embrace. Did this pretty idea actually come from

7. The Austrian-British philosopher Karl Popper argued that Nazi Germany's Gestapo and the Soviet Union's NKVD derived their totalitarian warrants from Plato.

8. Karl Marx researched his indictment of capital in the British Museum, where an alien revolutionary was as safe as the Bank of England. Popper's *The Open Society and Its Enemies* (1945) was a vigorous attack on Plato and his "historicist" successors, including Marx, who validated their totalitarian plans by a biased account of society. George Grote (1794–1871) had been the first scholar to redeem democratic Athens from its critics. Popper learned Greek to avert charges of inaccuracy, but such accusations were still made. Most students now do classical studies without learning Greek or Latin. Popper advocated tolerance and would not tolerate those who did not. Herbert Marcuse's *Repressive Tolerance* (1965) was the most brazen of the meta-Marxist manifestos that somewhat glamorized the one-party state and the singlemindedness of political absolutism.

Aristophanes? Plato may well have wished his own conceit onto the fanciest wit in the city. Nietzsche said that the novel began with Platonic dialogues and their multiplicity of voices. The spokesman for immutable Truth took freehand liberties with history, character, and chronology.

Comic playwrights in the scatological, bantering Aristophanic style had no precedent outside Athens. There were jesters in early oriental courts; none made a blend of scorn and ingratiation into entertainment for a citizen audience. Belligerent pacifist, phallocratic feminist, progressive conservative, Aristophanes was a more popular and more stinging gadfly than Socrates, who claimed the title. At once innovator and reactionary, the playwright made a joke of star-gazing philosophers; he also derided Pericles' brash successor, Cleon, for having been a tanner (his father made a fortune in that smelly trade). In *Lysistrata*, Aristophanes imagines the women of Athens mounting a sexual strike which they will end only if their men abandon the city's vain war with Sparta. No naughty suggestion is made that the men might ease their aching erections[9] by having sex with boys. The probably all-male audience enjoyed the words (and the music we can never hear) and the naked slave girls who garnished the comic stage;[10] the war went on to its sorry conclusion.

Aristophanes' last play, *Ploutos,* rewritten 20 years after his city's defeat, was about wealth, which recognized no value but its own and had no shame. Economically, Athens recovered

9. Large phallic appendages were stock items of the comic wardrobe.
10. The lascivious dance known as *cordax* was too gross even for Aristophanes' proto-Rabelaisian taste. He banned it from almost all his productions; *Wasps,* however, ends in a revel of similar shamelessness.

quite quickly from defeat, but its citizens never retrieved the pride of those who once ruled the waves. Almost 40 years later, Athenians would applaud Demosthenes' oratory, but failed to take its cue to march in step against Philip of Macedon. The New Comedy of post-imperial Attica lacked Aristophanic venom. Menander, the most successful and prolific of its writers,[11] made fun of the intrigues and humbug of city life, in which slaves were often smarter than their masters,[12] but his plays carried little satirical charge. The prime ambition was for audiences that would come back for more. Award-winning, socially critical theater flourished in the fifth century B.C.E.; the fourth inaugurated the primacy of the box office and the advent of "no-brainers" (Hollywood's term for hit movies requiring no intelligent response).

The swaggering Alcibiades, whose braggadocio enchanted the demos into the disastrous Sicilian expedition of 415, makes a late, sozzled entrance in Plato's *Symposium* and delights the party with his winsome confessions. Plato himself was too shy, or too sly, to figure in any but his last work, *Laws,* in which he is rendered anonymous as "the Athenian Stranger." He could not bring himself to be among the company in the condemned cell where, according to the *Phaedo,* Socrates pronounced his famous last words, "We owe a cock to Asclepius."[13] The Oxford

11. He was a quarry of material for the Latin playwrights Plautus and Terence, and for subsequent boulevard comedy.

12. Aristophanes' Xanthias, in *Frogs,* was the prototype of the savvy servant who culminated in Beaumarchais' and Mozart's Figaro, if not in P. G. Wodehouse's Jeeves.

13. Deputed by his father Apollo as the god of healing. Can it be that—as some modern glossers would have it—"cock," in this context, referred to an erect penis? Larky to the last, Socrates quaffed his tumbler of hemlock as if it

philosopher Gilbert Ryle depicted Plato as a dramatist manqué who dreamed of prize-winning public success[14] but lacked Aristophanes' capacity to parade challenging ideas in a form more enjoyable than sarcasm. As if to mock him, there was a successful fifth-century Athenian comic poet also called Plato.

2.

Shipped to Crete, the mythical Athenian hostages had to take part in the local rite of bull leaping: the vital trick was to spring and grab the horns, as the bull charged, and vault up and over, like a gymnast. Before Theseus's expedition, even the most agile participants were fated to figure on the menu of the Minotaur. Half-man, half-bull, its carnivorous appetite must have owed more to human than to herbivore genes. The taurine hybrid was stalled at the center of a labyrinth devised by Daedalus, the first artist to make an emblematic name for himself. Adjacent to the royal palace, the Minotaur's basement maze had an easy way in, none out.

On a surviving Minoan mural, a figure who appears to double as Crete's king and its supervising priest is pictured in horny festive costume. Civilized Hellas retained traces of bestial

---

were a cure for the human condition. Ironists have imagined him proposing a toast: "To democracy!" See section 29 below re Phocion. The scene in the condemned cell was made iconic by the painter Jacques-Louis David. Jonathan Miller directed a memorable version of *Phaedo,* in black and white, for BBC Television, with Leo McKern as Socrates.

14. In *Plato's Progress* (1966), Ryle argues with dry wit for considerable changes of view in the course of Plato's intellectual development. Ryle (1900–1976) was also bold, in his day, in declaring the philosopher's sexual desire for young males ("sixteen-year-olders"), an appetite which—according to his pupil A. J. Ayer—Ryle shared, at least in theory.

rites: festivals in Sparta were conducted in animal masks; in Patrai (the modern harbor of Patras, in the northwest of the Peloponnese), animals and birds were bundled alive into great fires on the altars of Artemis;[15] docile throats were cut in large numbers at the altars in front of luridly colorful temples. Stepped pyramids of ash from incinerated victims rose beside them. For centuries, the Spanish bullfight retained the brassy lineaments of sacrificial ceremony, ending—if the bull did not hook his tormentor—with the torero's poised triumph over exhausted force as he sheathed his blade between the bull's shoulders. The cult may have been carried to Iberia, in prehistoric times, by Greek and Phoenician sailors and settlers who traded with silver-rich Tarshish in southern Spain.[16]

In sixth-century B.C.E. Greece, converts swung bull-roaring tambourines as they chanted and stamped in riotous honor of the androgynous oriental god of wine and greenery. A tippling traveler, at once frail and dangerous,[17] Dionysos was too restless for residence on Olympus. The newcomer's claim to divinity, when denied, shattered the peace of his native

15. See Martin P. Nilsson, *Greek Folk Religion* (1972). Artemis was supposedly the protector of the weak, but she was also the "mistress of bloody sacrifices." See Walter Burkert, *Homo Necans* (1972). Aptitude for violence is common among the gods: Marcel Detienne's *Apollon le couteau à la main* (2009) demonstrates that, like Brecht's Mack the Knife, the elegant Apollo could be a smiling killer.

16. Cf. Jeremiah 10.9: "Beaten silver is brought from Tarshish, and gold from Uphaz."

17. When the sailors on a ship in which he was a passenger threatened to rob and then throw him overboard, Dionysos took on the lineaments of the Green Man and caused the timbers and mast to revert to sappy life and burst into vinous leaf. The crew panicked, jumped into the sea, and were turned into dolphins.

Thebes (a city where, according to mythology and its usually Athenian editors, nothing happy ever happened). In Dionysian frenzy, bacchants—wild women and men in disorderly drag—jointed living beasts and gobbled them raw, high on the mountainside. In his last play, *Bacchae,* Euripides, ensconced in self-imposed Macedonian exile, has his raving chorus dismember the unwise young king, Pentheus, who had refused to recognize the hippy stranger's claim to divine honors, despite the fact that Dionysos's mother, Semele, was the daughter of Thebes's founder, Cadmus; Zeus his lightning father.[18] Outsiders' demands for legitimate respect are made by all sorts of bastards and byblows in myth and history: the Spartan *mothakes* (semi-equal citizens) Gylippus and Lysander distinguished themselves in the field, during the Peloponnesian War, as if to atone for and transcend subordinate inheritance in their native city.

18. It was, we may guess, a convenience, if not a convention, for the pregnancies of unmarried girls (or of wives whose husbands were absent) to be attributed to nocturnal visits from divinities. When Semele dared to demand a sight of her divine lover, Zeus revealed himself in a lightning bolt that sizzled her to a crisp. Zeus pouched the embryonic Dionysos in his thigh, from which his offspring emerged, ready for the road, without the obstetric assistance needed by his half-sister Athene before she could be sprung from Zeus's head. Despite the king's seemingly ignominious fate, Pausanias (2.2.7) records that Pentheus was later associated with, if not dignified by, a tree cult at Thebes. Since his death had the effect of restoring the city to stability, Pentheus "returned" as a salvationary figure. Christian artists have often depicted the cross on which Christ was crucified as a pollarded tree. The crucifix itself can be seen as an abstract, arboreal symbol of the possibility of renewal.

3.

Daedalus was the archetypal sculptor in three dimensions. Primitive Greek images of gods were flat *xoana:* limbless wooden totems, planks, or pillars. Draped with accessories or incised with identifying devices, they were taken out, in due season, for ritual ablutions. Orthodox Christianity's icons inherited their flat magic and are given celebratory parades on saints' days. In the *Periegesis,* Pausanias's plodding and invaluable second-century C.E. guide to Greek antiquities, the author claims to have seen a *xoanon* of the naked Heracles, attributed to Daedalus. "All the works of this artist," he remarks, "while somewhat uncouth to look at, nevertheless have a touch of the divine in them." None has survived; but a 1900 B.C.E. chalk image, said to be of the goddess Hera,[19] mimics the primitive form of a xoanon: no arms or legs, a slab for trunk, button head. It can be a relief to find an item of ancient Greek sculpture that fails to be comely.

During his unremitting circuit of Greek sites, Pausanias must have seen many Roman temples and monuments. His inventory ignores them all; he seems to have had no eyes, certainly no words, for Rome's intrusive contributions to the architectural furniture of the Hellenic world. Yet without wide use of the arch and the invention of concrete by Roman engineers, the great post-classical cosmopolitan Greek-speaking cities of the ancient Mediterranean would never have had freestanding theaters as grand as the one at Aspendos in

19. In the Athens Museum of Cycladic Art. Paul Cartledge notes that a few small wooden xoana, not attributed to Daedalus, have survived from archaic Samos.

Pamphylia,[20] or the aqueducts to quench the citizens' thirst and fill their luxurious and cavernous baths. Early Christian aversion to washing owed something to disgust at the this-worldly pleasure of municipal wallowing in ubiquitous pagan *tepidaria* (warm tubs).

Particular divine trees—Hera's willow on the Aegean island of Samos, Pallas Athene's olive[21] on the Acropolis, Zeus's oracular oak at Dodona in the mountains of Epirus in northwestern Greece—were worshipped in archaic cults. Athene inserted a vocal branch from Zeus's oak in the keel of the *Argo,* which was then able, like prototypical sat nav, to prompt Jason's pilot to steer in the right direction, should he lose his way to Colchis, at the eastern end of the Black Sea, in order to filch the Golden Fleece. Dodona's priests, with their divinely dirty feet (it was impious to wash them), read portents in the rustle of oak leaves; so did the biblical King David. Sacrificial bones dangled, in votive piety, on branches in the sacred precinct at Olympia.[22] Since rebirth was identified with fresh spring foliage, evergreens remained without tribute: what never came back to life, like cemetery cypresses, served only as sentinels for the dead.

A palm tree grew where the biblical Deborah dispensed justice at Bethel.[23] At the Mounychia sanctuary of Artemis in

---

20. Forty kilometers east of the Turkish city of Antalya.
21. Athenians hung an olive branch at their front doors to celebrate the birth of male citizens.
22. In today's Athens, lawyers have been known to leave their ties hanging from a large green bush in Syntagma Square, to flag their objection to the government's fiscal policies.
23. Judges 4.7.

Piraeus, young girls raced naked[24] toward a flaming altar and an adjacent tree of the same species. Its fronds served to decorate whoever came first. Winners at the Cannes Film Festival are still presented with the Palme d'Or.[25] In Genesis, an improper appetite for apples primes transgression: when Adam and Eve breach the taboo on eating the fruit of the Tree of Knowledge, they lapse into mortal time and genealogy. All three of the enduring monotheisms contended with earlier tree-worship. In dry regions, greenery flagged the vivifying presence of fresh water.[26]

In the second book of Homer's *Iliad*, Nestor reports that when their ships were stalled by adverse winds, the Achaeans sacrificed on altars around a spring, under a plane tree, in the hope of appeasing the hunter-goddess Artemis, whose favorite stag their overlord, Agamemnon, had stalked and killed. The seer Calchas proclaimed that the king's daughter had to be sacrificed to the goddess before a suitably belligerent wind

24. Nakedness could serve as a rite de passage: at Olympia, competitors stripped off (as modern athletes do their tracksuits) before the race. During the foundation of Athens, Theseus was mocked as effeminate for wearing a long robe. He dumped it and hurled the oxen pulling the builder's cart higher than the roof. In the 6th century B.C.E., the great wrestler Milon of Croton celebrated his unbeaten Olympic career by toting a heifer around the stadium above his head and then, after sacrifice, consumed the whole beast on his own.

25. Laurel too was used to crown victors. Sport begins with the piety which presumes that gods favor winners. The vanity of Olympic victors sprang from their sense of election as much as from sporting achievement. See below for Milon of Croton and Alcibiades.

26. Pindar's first Olympian ode begins "Ariston men hydor . . ." (Best is water . . .). In *The Colossus of Maroussi*, Henry Miller recounts how, in Greece in 1939, the tall glasses of water that café waiters brought with cups of coffee were tasted by connoisseurs who claimed to be able to detect their source.

would blow.[27] In time, the Tree of Life was appropriated as a Christian symbol. In the seventeenth century, Baruch/Benedict Spinoza's insolent equation "deus sive natura" (god and/or nature)[28] revised Hebraic respect for the Creator into a pliable Latin tag for nature-worship. The holism of environmentalists now summons us to venerate the rain forest; the planet is mankind's latest supreme totem. The primitive Greek goddess Gaea (Earth) was one of the first.

Our contemporary atheists too are less original than they advertise: Epicurus of Samos (341–271 B.C.E.) claimed that, if they existed, the gods had scant interest in the doings of mankind. While prefiguring Karl Marx's penchant for the doctrinaire domination of his followers, Epicurus insisted that neither sacrifices nor exemplary behavior could procure divine favor; death was nothing to fear since it had no sequel. Socrates had half agreed: he is said to have told the friends who attended him in his last hours[29] that, logically, either there was nothing after death or whatever there was would be interesting to discover. Epicurus deprecated worldly success; it was wiser to cultivate one's garden and enjoy amiable company.[30] In the first century

27. Homer does not mention Iphigenia by name. Aeschylus was the first poet to do so, presumably to add dramatic and personal poignancy to the ritual of sacrifice.

28. The conceit was anticipated by Ovid in *Metamorphoses* 1.21.

29. Some of which he is said to have spent rendering Aesop's fables into verse. Philosophers cannot philosophize all the time. After a long seminar, Wittgenstein was known to ask a trusted pupil if he had time to go to the "flics." His favorite Hollywood star was Betty Grable.

30. This notion was seconded in 18th-century France by the mordant Voltaire (François-Marie Arouet). After he had retired to the château at Ferney, in addition to his garden he also cultivated his ego by writing and starring in his own unpruned plays.

B.C.E., his disciple, the Latin poet Lucretius, imagined a man going to the "flaming ramparts of the world" and flinging a spear into the void, as if to demonstrate that there were no limits to the universe. Today's posturing powers fire rockets at celestial bodies named by ancient astronomers in honor of divinities no longer worshipped on earth.

In the sixth century B.C.E., Xenophanes of Colophon, in Ionia, had posited a wholly thoughtful deity, without carnal appetites or attributes, prototype of the commanding, incorporeal *nous* (the world's mastermind) postulated by Pericles' counselor Anaxagoras. Aristotle's "unmoved mover" was its ultimate refinement: the uncaused cause of everything. Xenophanes also inferred—from a marine fossil found in a Syracusan quarry[31]—the primal importance of water. Ironizing on mankind's tendency to lend mortal (and parochial) characteristics to its divinities, he observed that Thrace's gods were held to look like Thracians, Ethiopia's like Ethiopians; if horses could draw, he said, they would portray equine divinities. Later wits glossed Xenophanes by adding that if triangles had gods, they would be triangular.[32]

---

31. See the *Oxford Companion to Classical Literature*. It may have been the same quarry in which Athenian prisoners were worked to death after the destruction of the Athenian fleet in 413 B.C.E. It says something for ancient mobility and curiosity that Xenophanes ever saw the place.

32. Quadrilateral might have been wittier: Carl Jung claimed that the Christian Trinity would be improved by the admission of Satan as, as it were, its fourth side.

4.

In the seventh century B.C.E., Thales of Miletus, one of the original "Seven Sages," had already declared water the prime element of Creation.[33] Tradition's First Philosopher conceded that "all things are full of gods," but then elected—in Ludwig Wittgenstein's phrase—to "divide through" by the notion of divine presences: the Milesian's view of natural phenomena discounted, by definition, all supernatural influences. Ancient Greek "science" was solitary, intuitive, and amateur.[34] In time, it supplied a durable vocabulary, but even Aristotle, who did studious fieldwork in many areas of biology, could state, for instance, that males had more teeth than females. He might have known better, Bertrand Russell observed, if his wife had once been allowed to open her mouth in his presence. Medical writers such as Galen, although often blinkered by their own preconceptions, tended to be more observant and empirical.[35]

Whatever Thales' right (which he never claimed) to be labeled a scientist, Plato and Aristotle paid tribute to his practical intelligence. When Cyrus the Great defeated the fabulously

---

33. The idea probably originated in Egypt, where the annual surge of the Nile seemed to bring life out of the new mud. Water has continued to be regarded with reverence in the region. In Constantinople, after its capture by the Ottomans, there was a "hidden Christian world of water" from more holy springs than in any other city. Islam laid no claim to the subterranean: Philip Mansel, *Constantinople* (1995). The Arabian desert had no cavernous basement; Islam no underworld.

34. Prof. William Lyons has reminded me that pre-Socratic philosophy was a speculative hobby, not a profession: it had no defined field or technical terms.

35. See, for examples, G. E. R. Lloyd's *Early Greek Science* (1973). Myth retained a place in medicine: the flower narcissus, which Persephone was picking when she was snatched into the underworld, was said to have narcotic qualities and be likely to induce self-infatuated drowsiness.

rich Lydian Croesus and Persia was poised to dominate the region,[36] the Greeks of Ionia—the western littoral of today's Asia Minor—held a congress in Priene. The council chamber's mini-theater can still be seen, stepped into the dark flank of the city's mountainous site. Thales is said to have proposed that the Ionians form a single assembly, make the coastal city of Teos (north of Ephesus) their administrative capital, and stand together against the barbarian threat. An alternative was to construct a common fleet, sail to Sardinia, and create a unified city. As usual among Greeks, for whom division—democracy would be its uncertain alleviant—habitually trumps solidarity, the Ionians chose to take their separate chances.

The Hellenes of "Asia," like its Jews, Syrians, and, later, Armenians and Kurds, lived in subservient, sometimes subversive, symbiosis with a succession of ruling powers, Persian, Athenian, Macedonian, Roman, Byzantine and Ottoman, French and British. The Fertile Crescent of what came to be called "the Middle (or Near) East" was both rich and accessible to invaders by sea and land. After the defeat of Germany and her allies, including Turkey, in the Great War of 1914–1918, the Greek government in Athens was incited by the British prime minister, David Lloyd-George, to attempt to realize the Big Idea of recovering what had been the territory of the Byzantine Empire.[37]

36. When he conquered Babylon, Cyrus offered the descendants of the exiled Jews the right to return to Jerusalem. By no means all of them accepted his invitation. The descendants of those who remained were the victims of a pogrom at the hands of their pro-Nazi Arab neighbors in Iraq in 1941 C.E. The impartial British authorities on duty in Baghdad turned a blind eye to the massacre. In the 1950s, most surviving Iraqi Jews migrated to Israel.

37. See Michael Llewellyn-Smith, *Ionian Vision: Greece in Asia Minor, 1919–1922* (1973).

Back in the 1780s, Catherine the Great of Russia had already had her own "Greek project." The plan was to divide the Ottoman Empire between herself and the Holy Roman Emperor Joseph II, then to revive a puppet Byzantine Empire under the scepter of her grandson Constantine. The infant was christened with the ingratiation of the Greeks in mind. Russia's annexation of the Crimea, in 1783, was the first step toward access to the Black Sea, and then to the Mediterranean.[38] Vladimir Putin's current expansionist policy is a product of similar ambitions, without any palliative Greek ingredient. For some years, Europeans attempted, with irregular urgency, to beckon Turkey (and what was Byzantium) toward the secularized economic catholicism embodied in the 1958 Treaty of Rome, which lies at the root of what is now the increasingly disunited European Union. President Recep Erdogan's 2016 counterputsch, after the Turkish army tried to stage an anti-Islamist coup, seems to have been calculated to put an end to the westernization of his country.

David Lloyd-George's populism at home did not inhibit him, any more than it had Pericles or Alcibiades, from imperialist long shots abroad. In 1919, British and French diplomats referred, unofficially, to the Middle East as "the booty." In 1922, the Greek military campaign ended—as had the Athenian invasion of Sicily in 415 B.C.E.—in catastrophe (literally, "a turning upside down"). More than a million Greeks were evicted from Anatolia by the resurgent Turks under Kemal Ataturk. The warships of the European powers stood offshore while Ionian Greek civilians were robbed, raped, massacred, or—if they were lucky—

38. Mansel, *Constantinople,* pp. 204 et seq.

evicted.[39] Many of their ancestors had been similarly treated, in 1453, by the forces of the twenty-year-old Sultan Mehmet II. The refugee Ionians were received, with meager generosity, in the mainland that few had ever wished to visit. Tens of thousands of Turks were expelled from northern Greece into Asia. They fared better than the more than a million Armenians whom their Turkish compatriots had murdered during the war.

After Kemal had overthrown the decrepit Ottoman sultanate and triumphed in the war against the Greeks and their fine-weather friends, he determined to westernize his country; women no longer had to wear the veil; Turkish script was transliterated into Roman characters. Drinker and sexual predator, Kemal was at once the great Alexander and the Napoleon of the Turks, an avenging modernizer. He paid lip-service to Islam but was a native of Thessaloniki, the great cosmopolitan port in the lee of the Thracian Chersonese, in northeastern Greece. Until the warring European powers burst in on them in 1914, Greeks, Jews, and Turks had cohabited in the city for centuries in something like a remake of the *convivencia* of Muslims, Christians, and Jews in eleventh-century Al-Andalus (today's Andalusia, in southern Spain). The Sephardic Jews of Thessaloniki continued to speak Ladino, the dialect of the Iberian Jews expelled by Ferdinand and Isabella after the Catholic Reconquista. More than four centuries later, visiting Iberian scholars were able to hear Spanish as it had sounded in the fifteenth century.[40]

39. See *Smyrna, the Destruction of a City* (1972) by Marjorie Housepian. As he records in his notebook, George Seferis returned, decades later, to his family house. The garden gate still creaked as he remembered it from his childhood.

40. Thessaloniki's Jews were deported and murdered in Auschwitz, where their solidarity amazed Ashkenazi deportees. The quarter of Thessaloniki in which they had lived was immediately possessed by Christian Greeks. Vassili

In the course of the siege that preceded the fall of Constantinople[41] in 1453, the leaders of Roman Catholic Europe
failed to help the Greek Orthodox Christians whose city their
forebears had pillaged. During the Fourth Crusade of 1204,
Catholic soldiers took their lead from the octogenarian blind
doge Dandalo of Venice. He had the elderly greed to follow his
nose for treasure up a scaling ladder and over the walls. Today's
Greeks have historical reason to be wary of the good faith of
the signatories of the 1958 Treaty of Rome. They read hypocrisy in the economic piety of those who chose to be outraged
by the Hellenes' bookkeeping duplicity before and during the
economic crisis of 2012. As for the unsmiling Europeans who
claimed that the Greeks had entered the European Union on
false pretenses, had they never heard of the Trojan horse?

According to Aristotle, Thales' speculations were prompted by *thauma,* the Greek for amazement (and later for a mira-
cle[42]); a thauma made you think twice about what you were
seeing. *Thaumadzein* could mean both to look carefully and to
be surprised. Speculator in the sublime and the mundane sense,
Thales is said to have made a fortune in olive oil futures and
also to have fallen down a well while considering the heavens.
The claim that he forecast an eclipse of the sun (in 585 B.C.E.)

Vassilikis (author of the bestselling *Z*) wrote a story on the subject. The largest
square in central Thessaloniki, now named for Aristotle, was in the center
of the flattened Jewish neighborhood. See Mark Mazower, *Salonica, City of
Ghosts: Christians, Muslims and Jews* (2005).

41. Legend has it that the city was first called Istanbul after some of the
conquering Ottomans pointed and asked what "that" was called and were
answered, "Eis teen pol'" (Greek slang for "way to the city"). Istanbul did not
become its official name until the 1930s.

42. The Latin *miraculum* has a similar sense: it suggests something looked
at with amazement.

seems unduly flattering; such a prediction required astro-
nomical finesse that he is unlikely to have possessed. Word of
the imminent eclipse may, however, have reached him from
clever Babylonian sources.

Three centuries later, Thucydides echoed Thales' mundane
"science" when he discounted any divine part in the fortunes of
the Peloponnesian War. Homer had portrayed the immortals
taking sides in the Trojan War; the prosaic Athenian historian
(who had been cashiered for negligence—perhaps compounded
with self-interest—as a general) saw only malice, greed, and all-
too-human vanity as motives for his contemporaries' battles.
After his retreat into Thracian exile, Thucydides' notion of *akri-
beia* (accuracy) was implacably disillusioned; he chose to be
linear and prosaic in contrast with the omnium-gatherum practice of his wide-ranging, good-humored predecessor Herodotus.
Just as Hesiod had to be the rival of Homer, it was, from the
beginning, habitual for historians and philosophers[43] to proclaim
their own trustworthiness as against the credulity of peers or
predecessors. Antagonism and the desire for primacy were implicit in the language: *ariste eris,* the best form of conflict, incited
men to excel; the first meaning of *agon* (from which our word
"agony" is derived) was "a place for competition."

It is fashionable to deplore Thucydides' diagnosis of immutable strains in collective human behavior;[44] but the *stasis*

43. In his 5th-century B.C.E. poetic discourse, Parmenides distinguished
between the immutable Way of Reality or Truth (the domain of Mind, to
which a goddess makes him uniquely privy) and the uncertainties of mundane
experience, which others took for knowledge. René Descartes (1596–1650)
elaborated a not dissimilar dichotomy.

44. In *Thucydides on Politics* (2014), Geoffrey Hawthorn insists on how
different things are today: "there is also an increasing number of media,

(civil war), which turned neighbor against neighbor on the island of Corcyra (modern Corfu) in the prelude to the Peloponnesian War, has recurred, with bloody frequency and small refinement, down the ages: in the Thirty Years' War between Catholics and Protestants in central Europe; in the Spanish Civil War of 1936–1939; in 1940s Greece;[45] in Rwanda in 1994; in today's Iraq and Syria. How obsolete is the notion that no violence is more remorseless than that between people who speak the same language? In 1793, during the French Revolution's reign of terror, Joseph Joubert (a prolifically terse aphorist secluded in Montignac, in the rural southwest) remarked that fear of enemies and their vengeance is redoubled when they also live next door.

5.

As early as the seventh millennium B.C.E., vessels from Tyre are said to have coasted along counterclockwise currents up from Egypt and Crete. Obsidian from the island of Melos,[46] in

---

formal and informal, public and private, through which to praise and shame them [states]." This ignores the use of media rhetoric and website fantasy in rigging and deceiving public opinion. The notion of international law is given exaggerated significance. Powers yield only when they are too weak or irresolute to be able to ignore, in particular, UN resolutions and similar allegedly potent pressures. As for the idea of a New Man unlike his ancient forebears, it is enough to read Theophrastus's *Characters,* drawn from 4th-century B.C.E. observation, to realize that they are still walking the streets and preening themselves in the media.

45. See, for instances, *Greece, the Decade of War* by David Brewer (2016).

46. In his Melian Dialogue, Thucydides makes no mention of the island's mineral wealth as part of the reason for the Athenian expedition, in 416 B.C.E., to coerce Melos into an alliance. Yet part of its purpose was surely to provoke the islanders into a defiance that would excuse the appropriation of their assets, as indeed happened when Athenian colonists were settled on the island.

the Cyclades, was traded in Thessaly to the north and to the south in Crete. At Mycenae, golden Agamemnon's kingdom in the east of the Greek Peloponnese, a shaft grave of 1700 B.C.E. contained elephant tusks from Syria. War chariots carried Dorian tribesmen down from northern Greece, where the plains of Thessaly were grassy enough to nurture and wide enough to exercise fine horses. Bypassing thin-soiled Attica, the Dorians swarmed southward into the wide green valley of the Eurotas in the Peloponnese. In the eighth century B.C.E., after a long war, the newcomers subjugated and reduced the Messenians, the area's previous Greek tenants, to virtual slavery.[47] Perpetual prisoners of war, sentenced to hard rural labor, the so-called helots left the Spartan ruling class free to relish their Orwellian equality. Less city than armed camp, Sparta became the landlocked, laconic antithesis of garrulous, seagoing Athens.

Trade and conquest were at the heart of ancient ambition: the first collectors of written information, Hecataeus of Miletus and Scylax from Caria, were interested more in exploration than in recovering the past. Commissioned by Darius I of Persia, Scylax's voyage around Arabia combined cartographic curiosity with reconnoitering purpose.[48] In a time without copyright, footnotes, or bibliographies, Herodotus helped

---

Vanity remains the prime motive for ruthlessness: it was as insufferable for Athens to be defied by Melos as for Odysseus to endure the insolence of the Greek soldier Thersites in book 2 of the *Iliad*.

47. The specific term "helots," traditionally reserved for the subjugated Messenians, meant, literally, "those taken (prisoner)."

48. Before the Great War of 1914–1918, T. E. Lawrence, later "Lawrence of Arabia," combined academic research into the castles built by the Crusaders, from the 13th century onward, with reconnoitering the defenses and disposition of the Ottoman Turks in the Middle East on behalf of the British government. "Intelligence" has long had a duplicitous sense.

himself to his predecessors' work; thanks to its digestion or disappearance, he has been graced with the title of the First Historian. Scylax is said to have urged the Asiatic Ionian Greeks not to rebel against the Persian "King of Kings." Had he been alive, he would, no doubt, have counseled Alexander the Great against invading Persia merely because, besotted with Homer, the young Macedonian king saw himself as a second Achilles.

"The stories of the Greeks," Hecataeus said, "are many and, in my opinion, ridiculous." Among them was that Heracles went down to Hades to tame the three-headed guard dog Cerberus. Hecataeus claimed that the "hound of hell" was actually a deadly serpent overpowered by Heracles at Taenarum and brought to Eurystheus, for whom the hero was doing twelve penitential labors. Hecataeus does not doubt that the legendary strong man merited punishment for the murder of his Theban wife, Megara,[49] and their children, in a fit of madness brought on by the jealous resentment of Hera, whose husband, Zeus, had fathered Heracles on Alcmena, the queen of Thebes.

Odysseus's prolonged nautical travels and travails, if involuntary, were not entirely unpleasurable. He had, however, to be savvy to survive them. Shipwrecked on his circuitous way home to Ithaca, he was handy enough to construct the raft on which to escape from the delicious nymph Calypso (on the mythical island of Ogygia) and head for the marriage bed which he himself had built and to which he craved, reluctantly,[50] to return. The man whom Homer labeled *polymētis*, "multi-tricky,"

49. Eurystheus's daughter.
50. Constantine Cavafy's 1911 poem "Ithaca" makes clever play with the pleasures of being sidetracked. Nostalgia is not always an accelerant. Tennyson's "Ulysses" (1842) anticipated the Alexandrian's sense of the delights of delay and deviation.

had also had his place in the carpentered horse, designed by Epeius, that the credulous Trojans took to be the Greeks' parting tribute to the successful defense of their city. They dragged it inside their city walls, too smug to guess that its wooden belly was pregnant with a Delta Force of Achaean warriors.

To avoid going soft, the Spartans built no walls around the villages that composed their austere city.[51] Until the late sixth century B.C.E., their arts and crafts were of refined quality. Subsequently, they produced little pottery more elegant than the porridge bowls used in their communal officers' mess. That the city remained formally and implacably at war with defeated Messenia supplied a callous warrant for generations of Spartiates—the élite, pure-blooded Spartan ruling class—when out on night maneuvers to ambush and knife any helot likely to make trouble or to whom they had taken a dislike.[52] Success-

---

51. The Celtic Gauls were regarded by the Romans as uncivilized because they, like the Spartans, lived in *oppida,* small communities, rather than *civitates* (cities). Their life as warriors and herdsmen required few commodities and left them little leisure or reason to abandon rustic life. Gaul's forcible pacification as a Roman province, by Julius Caesar, and the consequent urbanization changed the pattern of Gallic living and religious observation. The Druids quite quickly lost their paramountcy. See Jean-Louis Brumaux, *Nos ancêtres les gaulois* (2015).

52. In 424 B.C.E., when the Peloponnesian War was not going well, the Spartans' fear of a helot rising led them to solicit the helots to choose from their own number those who had best served Sparta on the battlefield. "Two thousand were selected, put garlands on their heads, and went round the temples presuming that they were to be made free. Soon afterward, the Spartans did away with them; no one ever knew exactly how" (Thucydides, book 4, 80). The US civil rights movement grew in confidence after the service of (often segregated) black soldiers in World War II. The demands of returning legionaries often threatened social stability in ancient Italy. War can also be the mother of reform.

ful theft, such as stealing a head of goat cheese (a metaphor for its owner's life?), was a test of manhood. The training manual made a legend of the Spartan youth who hid a fox cub under his shirt. When stopped, he allowed the concealed beast to claw him to death rather than confess to its unwarranted presence. In a less sanguinary ritual of transition to manhood, Athenian ephebes (adolescent males) were required to live rough for a time in the Attic hinterland, where they became inured to fear and to bloodshed by hunting wild beasts.[53]

There was no detectable racial distinction between Dorian and Ionian Greeks. Desire for primacy impelled the Athenians to boast that they were autochthonous, born of the soil in the tight corner where they lived, hence anterior to Doric immigrants—the Spartans in particular—who lacked the deep roots of Attic family trees.[54] The notion of similarity has never discounted difference (a character speaking Greek with a Boeotian accent was always good for a laugh on the Athenian comic stage). The wariness with which Greek met, and meets, Greek was in at the forked foundation of Hellas: Achilles scowled at Agamemnon, Ajax at Odysseus, with whom he wrestled, strength against cunning, in a drawn match at Achilles' funeral games. Even the first team of twelve gods was riven by jealousy—Hera of her husband Zeus, Hephaestus of his wife Aphrodite; Poseidon

---

53. See *The Black Hunter* (1981/1986), by Pierre Vidal-Naquet. Peter Green is disposed to file this interesting work under "fiction." In Macedonia, young men could lounge at dinner with their elders when they had killed a wild boar in face-to-face combat; they were licensed to sport bracelets only after they had killed a man.

54. The Germans, the last Europeans to compose themselves into a major nation, in 1870 C.E., also claimed an autochthonous, homogenous pedigree. See section 79 below.

hated Athene's favorite, Odysseus; spring-heeled Hermes stole Apollo's cattle.[55] Heracles and Dionysos, with their human mothers,[56] resembled Spartan mothakes: they had to strive (and excel) to gain access to divinity. Orpheus, although the son of the god Apollo and of Calliope, the muse of poetry, never made it to the divine mansion on top of Mount Olympus. His chastity frustrated the females whom his music enchanted. They cut off his head and sent it rolling, in Milton's words, "down the swift Hebrus to the Lesbian shore."

In Homer, pride was paired with anger, magnanimity with affront. The Trojan War came about only because Paris, son of the king of Troy, broke the rules of guest-friendship by making off with his host Menelaus's wife, the divinely beautiful Helen. Agamemnon of Mycenae called on the Achaean princes to redeem the vow they had sworn, when they were her suitors, to Helen's nominal father,[57] King Tyndarus of Sparta, to band together to retrieve her from any predatory lover who tried to take her from her chosen husband. Personal pride, never patriotism, was the heart of the matter. If Homer's Menelaus of the loud war-cry had been killed early in the siege of Troy, the call to arms would have lost its raison d'être: the topless towers would never have had to topple.

55. Allegedly, Hermes was one day old on the occasion of his first, famous heist: Norman O. Brown, *Hermes the Thief* (1947). Prosper Mérimée (1803–1870) wore a ring inscribed, in Greek: "Remember to mistrust."

56. Alcmene and Semele, respectively. Zeus was the father of both.

57. Myth has it that Tyndarus was married to Helen's mother Leda, who was made pregnant with her, and with her sister Clytemnestra, by Zeus.

6.

In archaic Greece, *philoxenia* (guest-friendship) put a disarm-
ing face on the reception of strangers, especially of those liable
to render reciprocal favors: the more sumptuous the greeting,
and the parting gifts, the greater the proud obligation to trump
them when previous hosts came calling. The cities, settlements,
and appetites of archaic Greeks extended far beyond the territory now labeled Greece. Plato mocked their pervasive gabble:
Hellenes, he wrote in his *Phaedo,* squatted and croaked around
the Mediterranean and the Black Sea "like frogs around a pond."
Well-heeled visitors had an expectation, suppliants a hope, of
amiable reception. In the *Odyssey,* even the shipwrecked, salt-
caked Odysseus is handsomely received—and, having no other
gift to offer, sings for his supper—at the court of Alcinous, king
of the genial Phaeacians, on the island of Scheria (later Corcyra,
today's Corfu).

Odysseus was never a gung-ho, bounty-seeking warrior
at Troy; he had been tipped off by an oracle that he would receive
no gilded dividend from his inescapable service. On his peripatetic way back home to Ithaca, balked by the seething hostility of Poseidon, Homer's reluctant hero meets all sorts of
dangers. Threatened with solitary drowning, he rates the Danaans who had died at Troy as "three or four times" more fortunate than himself. Had he been of their number, he would have
had the consolation of being booked for lasting celebrity.[58] What

58. Pericles, always the phrase maker, would come to say, "The whole world
is the sepulcher of famous men." When the emperor Vespasian (9–79 C.E.),
an unsentimental arriviste, was dying, he made wry allusion to the by then
established Roman habit of making divinities of dead emperors: "I feel myself
becoming a god." There is no evidence that he found it an elevating prospect.

was life, or death, without an audience? This, it seems, is the briefly self-pitiful point at which Seferis chooses to call Odysseus "red-eyed." In apocryphal, meta-Homeric epic, Odysseus is said to have died at the hands of his own bastard son by the sorceress Circe.

In the *Odyssey*, civilized philoxenia was contrasted with its loutish parody when the cave-dwelling cyclops Polyphemus offers his captive "guest" the cruel grace of being the last of his crew to be eaten alive. The nothing-if-not-wily Odysseus heats a stake in the giant's fire and thrusts the red-hot lance into the monster's single, central eye. He then eludes his unsighted captor's empty grasp, by hanging under one of the Cyclops's fat sheep as it is let out to go to pasture. Odysseus sails away, lingering only to tease the brute he has blinded. When the wounded monster demands his name, the hero replies, "Outis," Greek for "nobody," an untranslatable pun on the dual uses of the word *mētis*, cunning intelligence, the quality that Odysseus shares with his patron goddess Athene; in certain grammatical circumstances, *mētis* can be a synonym for *outis*. When Polyphemus's brothers hear him moaning and call into the cave to ask who has hurt him, he replies, "Outis." Presuming that he is playing games, and no one has in truth done him a mischief, they go away, leaving him unconsoled in the dark.

In the third century B.C.E., the Alexandrian poet Theocritus imagined[59] the Cyclops, on a good day, looking at his own reflection in calm sea water and saying, "And my beard was beautiful, and just as beautiful my one round eye; as for

---

59. *Idylls* 6. Self-admiration is, by definition, in the eye, or eyes, of the beholder. A fanciful modern writer alludes to "Narcissus, that plain boy."

my teeth, their gleam was whiter than Parian marble! To avoid falling in love with myself, I spat three times on my breast!"[60]

Desire for primacy and vindication of personal pride are determining motives among Homer's principal players. The catalogue of ships that carried the variously named Achaeans, Danaans, and Argives (they are never called Hellenes/Greeks) to Troy seems to align national solidarity and promise princely fealty; but the *Iliad* begins with the anger (*mēnis*) of Achilles against his own commander in chief and bristles with resentful personalities on both sides. Deprived of the beautiful Briseis by Agamemnon, Achilles pulls out of the battle. Since he was never among Helen's suitors, he had—unlike the other Achaean princes—sworn no oath to retrieve her, if she were abducted. He returns only to avenge his (older) friend and—some say, though Homer does not—lover Patroklos, after he has been killed by Hector. Unselfish purposes have small claim on heroic warriors. On the other hand, when Glaucus and Diomedes, whose families had enjoyed reciprocal hospitality, recognize each other's blazons, as it were, on opposing sides, hostility yields, briefly, to competitive generosity: Glaucus exchanges his own golden armor for Diomedes' bronze. After the advent of mercantile values, Glaucus's flashy gesture became proverbial for a bad deal.

Glaucus is later killed by Aias/Ajax, whose vanity eventually impels him to madness: as soon as the arms of the fallen Achilles are allotted to the smooth-talking Odysseus by Agamemnon and Menelaus, the frenzied Ajax slaughters a flock of sheep under the illusion that they are the duplicitous kings

---

60. A gesture that has an increasingly obsolete modern counterpart in the Greek use of "po, po, po" as a deprecating adversative.

who have cheated him of his heroic due. When he wakes to his folly, he falls on his sword in frustration and shame.[61] Agamemnon denies heroic burial to the suicide until Odysseus obtains due funeral honors for his mortified rival, if only for the pleasure of making the commander in chief and his stentorian brother, Menelaus, look cheap.

Although no one is sure whether Homer was one man or several, or—as Samuel Butler claimed, with a British straight face—a woman, scholars tend to agree that the text evolved, was emended and amplified, in the period between the eighth and the sixth centuries B.C.E. An authorized version was established under the aegis of the Athenian Pisistratus, who probably winked at, if he did not solicit, the insertion of lines listing an Attic contingent in the *Iliad*'s catalogue of ships. Who knows how many improvising rhapsodes contributed to what is now established as "Homer"? Easy-to-pick-up traditional epithets and recurrent standard phrases are likely to have incited mendicant players to rap out supplementary lines: as long as they scanned, the heroic narrative could be extended without any definition of individual authorship.[62]

61. Unusually in tragedy, where bloodshed is often described but rarely depicted, Sophocles in his *Aias* has the suicide take place on stage.

62. A paradigm of the fugitive nature of individuality is unpacked in I. T. Ramsey's article, in the *Philosophical Quarterly* of July 1955, "The Systematic Elusiveness of 'I.'" The notion of the disappearing/nonexistent author is resumed by Roland Barthes in, e.g., *Le degré zéro de l'écriture suivi de nouveaux essais critiques* (1972). Ingenious arguments for the nonexistence of the self are set out in Derek Parfit's protracted *Reasons and Persons* (1984). The text is, however, copyright in his name. The notion that art should conceal the individual artist ("ars est celare artem" is a bogus Latin tag to lend it dignity) came to be seconded by the impersonal, ownerless nature of logic and mathematics.

In post-heroic warfare, the individual is reduced to the regimented ranks: for the uniform, red-cloaked Spartans, any display of outstanding personal glory was antisocial. In 479 B.C.E., the Spartiate Aristodemus—one of two absentees (supposedly owing to an eye infection) from the regiment of 300 who had died a year before defending the pass at Thermopylae—sought at the battle of Plataea to retrieve his honor by a show of kamikaze heroism. Herodotus rated him the bravest man on the field; in the eyes of his fellow Spartiates, however, his exploit failed to efface his reputation as "The Trembler." They refused him honors not because "he had in effect committed suicide, but rather because of the manner of his doing so—breaking ranks and losing self-control."[63]

Arnaldo Momigliano maintained that the celebration of individual lives had little place in classical historiography.[64] In breach with the ethos of communal politics, biography singles out and, usually, exalts its subject. The first (brief) extant instance of autobiography is the *Vita* of the Jew Joseph ben-Mattathias, alias Titus Flavius Josephus, written, in Greek, in the first century C.E. A century earlier, Julius Caesar had advertised his own exploits in the Gallic Wars in the trim reportorial style of Xenophon's *Anabasis;* with showy modesty he referred to himself, often, in the seemingly self-effacing third person. St. Augustine (353–430 C.E.) dignified self-analysis in 13 volumes of *Confessions,* a form dressed, in his case, if not in the shameless Casanova's, with lashings of boastful remorse.

63. Paul Cartledge's note in the breaking-news-style translation of Herodotus by Tom Holland (2014).
64. Arnaldo Momigliano, *The Development of Biography* (1971). Autobiography was post-Hellenistic; the actual term was first used, perhaps coined, by Robert Southey in 1809.

The *Iliad* showcases the manliness of single combat, culminating in the duel between Hector and Achilles. In the hexametrical mode, hand-to-hand combat between heroes alone
warrants detailed celebration; other ranks, such as Achilles'
"Myrmidons," are mere extras. There was scant honor even for
princes who, like the skulking Trojan Paris, aimed arrows at a
distance. Ajax's bastard brother Teucer was an archer and an
honest fellow, but he was no more than marginal to the first
team of warriors. If Odysseus drew a deadly bow when he served
notice to his wife's suitors that he was back in Ithaca, it was not
a prince's weapon of choice. In ancient warfare, archers are
never front-line heroes;[65] even in Roman military formations,
they serve as (often alien) auxiliaries to legionaries whose virile
weapons are spear and sword. At Troy, however, one particular
archer made all the difference. An oracle had promised that
Priam's city would not fall until the unerring bow in the possession of Philoctetes, passed to him by the dying Heracles, was
leveled against the scoundrel Paris, whose own long shot had
pierced Achilles' single weak spot.[66]

Philoctetes had sat out the first nine years of war on the
flat island of Lemnos. After being bitten by a poisonous snake,

65. The battle of Agincourt in 1415, in which the flower of French chivalry
was unhorsed at a distance by the arrows of low-class English bowmen, signaled the end of a certain convention of upper-class contest. All innovations
in warfare smack of sharp practice to the surprised losers. Napoleon broke
with conventional decorum by crossing through neutral territory to shorten
his march on Milan in 1797. His subsequent victory abated the scandal and
confirmed his future.
66. Achilles' mother, Thetis, was privileged to dangle her infant son in
the waters of Lethe, which procured invulnerability, but failed to immerse
the heel by which she was holding him and which was penetrated by Paris's
lethal arrow.

his purulent foot smelled so repulsive that he was quarantined by the other Achaeans.[67] Odysseus, the persuasive fixer, was sent to lure its owner into lending his unique weapon to the Greek arsenal. With sullen egotism, Philoctetes refused to let go of his prized possession (his name, interpreted etymologically, means "lover of possessions") and insisted on returning to Greece. In Sophocles' play, Odysseus devises an elaborate ruse for Neoptolemos, the honorable young son of Achilles, to trick the bow from its owner's grasp. After several melodramatic twists, it seems that the plan will fail, but the ghost of his benefactor Heracles acts as deus ex machina and impels the mean bowman to honor his fated role.

Mythical elasticity allows Odysseus to be both the messenger of decency in Sophocles' *Aias* and a duplicitous trickster in the same author's *Philoctetes*. In similar refiguration, the conscience-ridden Neoptolemos of *Philoctetes* matures into the heartless butcher of the Trojan princess Polyxena, whom he sacrifices on his father's tomb. He then makes off with Andromache, the widow of Hector, whom Achilles slew in an earlier episode. Homer's Trojans and Achaeans are depicted, with a few courteous exceptions, as pitiless and abusive antagonists. Yet princes on both sides understand each other's speeches and, with regional variants, worship the same gods, which is always said to be the defining characteristic of Hellenes. The Olympian gods could, however, be decked with local distinguishing marks and titles even within Hellas itself (the Romans used "Graecia" to denote the geographic entity, the Greeks rarely, if

67. Another version of the story has it that he inherited his arrows from the dying Heracles, who had dipped them in the poisonous blood of the centaur Nessus. One of them is said to have fallen and pierced Philoctetes' foot.

ever). In the *Iliad,* deep-bosomed Aphrodite (mother of Aeneas) fled the field when slightly wounded and leaking *ichor,* the transparent blood of immortals. While most of her statues were seductive, she was worshipped in Sparta as a martial virago.[68]

The egotism celebrated in epic and in mythology was alien to the ethos of the city-state. The heroes and tyrants whose fates dominated the fifth-century Athenian stage, from Oedipus to Theseus, Creon to Pentheus, were exemplary autocratic anachronisms. A tyrant's subjects (often featured as a playwright's chorus) might sigh or hope, but they had no vote and—lacking the disciplined patriotic pride of the Attic audience, which sighed or gloated at their dramatized distress—no corporate muscle. The tragic chorus consisted almost always of helpless, if sententious, observers. They lacked the self-confident clout of Athenian *hoplites* (heavy infantry who had to supply their own armor and weapons, *hopla*) or the rehearsed pull of the oarsmen who gave the fleet its winning ability to alter course in a tight corner.

Homer's Trojan War was a competition of vanities, exacerbated by what Sigmund Freud (a keen amateur classicist[69]) labeled "the narcissism of small differences." In his history, Thucydides tried to find prosaic reasons for the conflict between Athens and Sparta, but since the former was a naval power, the second pedestrian, during the first ten years of the war they scarcely ever met in important numbers on the battlefield;

68. The Virgin Mary has similar variants: Black Madonnas are found in many parts of the world.

69. With a soft spot for Hannibal, the bane of Rome. See Freud's essay in *The Psychopathology of Everyday Life* (1904) on a forgotten word in Dido's line in Virgil's *Aeneid,* book 4: "Exoriare aliquis nostris ex ossibus ultor" (May some avenger arise from our bones).

without a common frontier, their conceits clashed more than their interests. The war was inevitable only in the sense that it was not avoided. Pride and shame remained stronger motives than patriotic or class interests.[70] In Homer, peace too had its vanities: when Odysseus takes his leave from Phaeacia, his host, the good King Alcinous, gives him a box of presents to which, with generous ostentation, he adds a large tripod and a cauldron, saying, "We'll get repaid by the demos [common people]; it's a heavy price for us to bear alone!"

70. In *The Class Struggle in the Ancient Greek World* (1981), G. E. M. de Ste. Croix (1910–2000) made a copious Marxist diagnosis of the origins and progress of the Peloponnesian War. In Moses Finley's scholarly view, this came of data tendentiously selected to conform to a preconceived dialectic scheme. When Ste. Croix's conviction of perfect moral pitch incited him to call Demosthenes' perennial opponent "the odious Isocrates," Peter Green was provoked to say that "many may feel, as I do, that anyone capable of provoking Ste. Croix to such spluttering vituperation must have some good in him somewhere." In the same spirit, George Thomson's *Aeschylus and Athens* (1941) remains an at once illuminating and dated monument to Marxist preconceptions. The one-time classicist Julien Benda's *La trahison des clercs* (1927) denounced intellectuals, right and left, who accommodated their work to conform to the going ideologies, communism and fascism. Today's "political correctness" embodies a metastasis of what was inspired, sometimes, by high-minded opportunism into selective tendentiousness, notably in sexual matters, e.g., James Davidson's *The Greeks and Greek Love* (2007). Dissenters from Davidson's reading of ancient Greek erotics can find endorsement in the unmitigated scorn for the "pathic" to be found in the 7th-century B.C.E. poetry of Archilochus, and endorsed in, for instance, sections 1840 and 4047 of Giacomo Leopardi's *Zibaldone* (1820). Herodotus (book 5, 95) says that the Greeks called having sex with a dead woman "putting one's bread in a cold oven." No one, I think, has made this into a warrant for necrophilia.

7.

The Fertile Crescent, Syria in particular, was the vortex where tradesmen, invaders, gods, races, and languages swirled, scattered, and spilled into the Greek world. No later than the third millennium B.C.E., copper from Spain had already reached Mesopotamia; lapis lazuli was imported from Afghanistan, carnelian beads from the Indus valley. Phoenicians (biblical Philistines of the same breed as Rome's Carthaginian enemy) battered the Jews in war and bettered them in commerce: a Phoenician salesman, peddling a gold-and-electrum necklace, is let in to shoot a line in Homer's *Odyssey*.

In Ephesus, in the heart of Ionia, Heracleitus observed, with the tart sourness of a disempowered aristocrat, "panta rei": everything is in motion. It was even accelerating:[71] the climate and appearance of the Mediterranean basin have changed markedly over three millennia of aggressive civilization. Ephesus was once a harbor city, surrounded by forested hills that gave the region a much more temperate climate than today's. After their forests were felled for timber, silt from the bare slopes was washed down, clogged the city's harbor, and rolled on to push the sea several kilometers back from the walls. Today's tourists walk along paved quays in the middle of the flat, sandy countryside. The ancient citizens' assault on nature distanced them from the maritime source of their own prosperity.

On the cusp of the sixth and fifth centuries B.C.E., money in the form of coinage came to outflank courts and commercialize courtesies. Carried, as it were, on the same wind,

71. The dread of and desire for progress run together. See *The Great Acceleration* (2016) by Robert Colvile.

money and philosophy supplied practical and sublime curren-
cies that gave men the means to override local ties and hierarchies. Hellenists have been reluctant to advertise that, like the
unsettling Dionysos, coinage and abstract ideas arrived coinci-
dentally in Greece from the mongrel Middle East. Money,
philosophy, and medicine are alike in transcending boundaries.
At once neutral and commanding, their generalities seem to
lend power to the cunning, the prescriptive, and the rootless.
None has anything to do with heroism.

8.

Many of the earliest Hellenic marble sculptures, known as
"Cycladic," date from before the second millennium B.C.E.
Their generic name derives from the archipelago encircling the
sacred Aegean island of Delos, birthplace of the twin gods
Apollo and Artemis. Their mother Leto—a Titan female fancied
by Zeus—eased her labor by leaning on a sacred palm tree. In
the fifth century B.C.E., after the decisive defeat of Xerxes' invasion of mainland Greece, Delos was chosen to house the treasury
of the anti-Persian Delian League. In 454 B.C.E., however, the
Athenians transferred their allies' tribute to their own Acropolis, whence it helped to finance the new Parthenon.[72] After the
Roman conquest, the sacred island, where no one had been
allowed to die for fear of soiling its sanctity, housed the biggest
slave market in the region. The statue of a slave dealer now

---

72. That the Persians had burned their antique temples was said to excuse
the Athenians' diversion of their allies' funds for the glorification of their
city. The solemn maquette of the Parthenon has been imitated in the formal
appearance of any number of intimidating banks. God and Mammon are
liable to be housed in similarly grand premises.

stands, like a head waiter flourishing his bill of fare, at the entrance to its avenue of crouching stone lions.

Some of the (mostly female) figures classed as Cycladic are as thin as plates; others have rounded, three-dimensional grace. All are anonymous. No ancient text alludes to them; no inscriptions announce specific identity. One figure is playing a "twinned oboe," another reaches for a stringless lyre; triangular heads, straight noses, long necks announce no personal distinction, human or divine. Legs and arms (folded across vestigial breasts) are integral to the body. Often with inclined feet, the figures seem designed to lean or rest recumbent, perhaps in tombs, like the conical Egyptian figures known as *ushabtis*.[73] A horde of Cycladic sculpture has been excavated recently by Colin Renfrew and his colleagues on the uninhabited small island of Keros, ten kilometers from Naxos. The quantity of figures suggests that Keros may have been the focal point of a cult to which other islanders contributed in more or less spiritual solidarity.

The anonymous dignity of Cycladic marbles belongs to an age before the ruinous eruption, sometime around 1700 B.C.E., that blew the hot heart out of the island of Thera (modern Santorini) and generated a tsunami that may have ruptured Minoan Crete's dominion over the Aegean. Did the volcano's surging flames and ashen fumes account for the pillar of fire and plume of smoke seen as divine guidance by the Hebrews as they fled from Pharaoh? A blizzard of pumice certainly pelted down and lay thick on neighboring islands till the 1960s, when

---

73. *Ushabtis* were made in large numbers and often carried inscriptions showing them to be the servants of the dead. Hence the fanciful notion that Cycladic females were sexual comforters for the dead.

floods of tourists took almost all the light, grey relics home with them.

Today's Santorini is a hoop of impacted crusts of rock crenellated over scorched black beaches. Multidecked cruise ships loiter in the wide, still warm, sea-filled crater. The ancient city of Akrotiri, excavated[74] from tiers of stiff lava, has been laid open for touristic autopsy under a jaundiced plastic roof. The once blanched and frescoed walls of the intricate archaic houses, untouched half a century ago, have been skinned; only dun-colored husks are still in place. The sloe-eyed, black-tressed, flute-playing females who sported on the polychromatic murals are curated exiles in the island's aseptic museum.

The lost world of Minoan Thera has often been said, mistakenly, to have inspired the fiction of Plato's Atlantis. He placed his lost continent, in the *Timaeus,* "beyond the pillars of Heracles" under what he presumed to be the shallow Atlantic ocean. Plato was the paradigm of reactionary artists who fear—because they so much enjoy?—the innovations of art. He

---

74. By Spyridon Marinatos, who spent many years on site and died when a wall fell on him. Although first appointed inspector general of antiquities by the fascistic dictator Metaxas, Marinatos was fingered as a "liberal" by the right-wing Dimitrios Ioannidis, the driving force behind the oligarchy of colonels who ruled Greece between 1967 and 1974. Papadopoulos and his henchmen, especially Ioannidis, echoed the bloody reaction of the Thirty Tyrants who staged a coup d'état in Athens in 404 B.C.E. under the leadership of Plato's uncle, Critias. Loathing of intellectuals has been as enduring in Greece as the love of wisdom. The 1967 Colonels paid vexed tribute to Aristophanes by banning contemporary all-too-relevant productions of his plays; they also honored the Muses by banning as "Marxist" a small poetry magazine, *Ho kyklos,* founded by employees of the Bank of Greece, to which Kiki Dimoula contributed. After the Colonels' eviction from power, Ioannidis spent his last 25 years in prison. Unlike his softer associates, he never sought parole. See C. M. Woodhouse, *The Rise and Fall of the Greek Colonels* (1985).

postulated the submerged land mass as harboring, 9,000 years before his time, a maritime superpower that was defeated, in a pseudo-epic war, by the army of a noble, mythical, territorially modest Athens. With perverse irony, Plato reconceived his own city as a stolid, prehistoric military power, more like landlocked Sparta than the daring maritime city of Themistocles and Pericles.

Plato's fictional Atlantis has had a long afterlife. At the end of the seventeenth century, Olof Rudbeck, "a real scholar, medical doctor and professor of anatomy," maintained that the Titan Atlas "put down roots in Sweden" and that Atlantis was to be found there; hence Scandinavia "preceded the letters of Phoenicia and Greece." Rudbeck distorted the Greek matrix to suit Nordic dreams of priority; others claimed that it prefigured the New World. Pierre Vidal-Naquet maintains that a Frenchman, A. Audigier, had already insisted on the primacy of Gaul. He happened to know that Noah's authentic name was Gallus. Nazi fantasies of the Aryans as the Chosen People have similarly twisting antique roots. The down-to-earth conclusion is that Atlantis belongs "not to the spatial domain but in that of thought."[75]

9.

Among Daedalus's innovations were wooden sculptures with jointed legs. Not denying their originality, Socrates said that, presented with an example, the contemporaries of Phidias would hold it artless. Daedalus's personal history set the style

75. The quotations are translated from Pierre Vidal-Naquet, *The Atlantis Story* (2007).

for bohemian braggadocio: he is mirrored in Benvenuto Cellini's and Caravaggio's lethal genius. When Daedalus's young nephew Talos invented the potter's wheel, and—inspired by the jagged skeleton of a fish—devised a metal saw, he excited his uncle's envy. Daedalus pushed his precocious rival off the roof of Athene's archaic wooden temple on the Acropolis, lapped the boy's body in a sack, and—before he could be brought to trial—smuggled himself onto a ship to Crete. He secured asylum by hawking his ingenuity to King Minos, the paramount collector, particularly of taxes, in the prehistoric Aegean.

Talos was transformed by the goddess Athene into Perdix, the clever partridge, whose badged plumage mimics the boy's fatal wound. Several historical kings of Macedonia, in the far northeast of Hellas, took the name Perdiccas and claimed Attic descent. During the Peloponnesian War, Perdiccas II was a flighty ally of the Athenians, who, by that stage, did not choose to salute Macedonians as their Ionian kinsmen. In Ottoman times, unwanted women in particular, but also rebellious Janissaries (the sultan's personal army), were stitched into sacks, sometimes in large numbers, while still alive, and flung into adjacent waters. Byron rescued one such female while he was in Athens—not one of the three Macri sisters for whom he wrote, "Maid of Athens, ere we part / Give me, give me back my heart." His keenest, if less advertised, Greek love was Nicolo Giraud, the fifteen-year-old with whom he toured the Peloponnese in 1810.[76]

76. English writers, however wanton, were wary, even in exile, of shocking the public they had gladly left behind: Norman Douglas's *Old Calabria* (1915) is full of local lore, but makes no mention of the twelve-year-old boy whom it was the author's pleasure to take on his southern Italian travels.

The great Phidias himself had to flee fifth-century Athens. The sculptor was first accused of embezzling some of the gold he had been allotted to make armor for the giant figure of Athene. She sat in virgin majesty in the gleaming new Parthenon of Attic marble from Mount Pentelicon. The goddess held a tall image of Nike (Victory) in her extended palm (spoils from the Persian invaders, who had burned the original temple, helped to fund the new one). Provident enough to have made the goddess's accoutrements detachable, Phidias was able to remove and weigh the precious metal to show that he had not shaved an ounce from the allocation. His innocence was not wholly endearing: the smartness of its proof carried a hint of too-clever-by-half premeditation.

Artists were not distinct from artisans. The routine word for art was *technē*, meaning skill, of whatever variety (the French *métier* is similarly used). Technē was the ability to follow reasoned procedures to procure intended results; it had nothing to do with personal inspiration. This made it plausible for Plato to insist that governance had to be a technē that a duly graduated élite alone was qualified to exercise. When working on the Parthenon frieze, Phidias received the same wages as other masons. This did not exempt him from another accusation: that he had "put men among the gods" in the sculptural procession on the frieze, of which part is now lodged in the British Museum. The Greek love of aesthetic pleasure did not extend to loving artists; nor was innovation regarded as a likely, still less as a necessary, improvement.[77]

---

77. See E. R. Dodds, *The Ancient Concept of Progress* (repr. 1973) and Armand D'Angour, *The Greeks and the New* (2011). In *The End of the Past* (2000), Aldo Schiavone claims that the notion of (scientific) progress was

Progress was neither celebrated nor expected in the ancient world. Greeks were more likely to refer back to their
Golden Age,[78] Jews to Eden (and later to lost Jerusalem); Romans
set great store by the *mos maiorum,* the routine of aristocratic
ancestors, who knew best. Annual festivals honored old habits
and, it was hoped, procured recurrent fruitful harvests and
happy omens; in Rome, if anyone faltered when recapitulating
a ritual formula, the principle of *instauratio* (known in the
theater and cinema as "going again from the top") required that
the ceremony be resumed from the beginning. Religion and
precise formulaic repetition went together. After Vatican II, a
number of Roman Catholics felt that something sacred had
been lost by rendering the Latin mass into the vernacular. Michel
Pic terms this sentiment "nostalgie de la rigueur."

Charged with impiety, Phidias absconded to Olympia,
where he was commissioned to create the enormous chrysele-
phantine image of Zeus, seated in majesty.[79] It was said that if
the king of the gods stood up, as he looked capable of doing,
he would put his head through his new temple's refulgent
marble roof. The divine image (regularly oiled to preserve its
uncreased complexion) came to be rated by Alexandrian

first formally propounded by Francis Bacon (1561–1626). The modern cult of
the new owes something to the rise of advertising, hence politicians' need to
make copywriters' promises of novelty (reform) to the people.

78. Today's extreme right-wing political party in Greece is known as
Chrysē Avgē, Golden Dawn.

79. In the next century, the great sculptor Praxiteles (whose career lasted
from around 375 until 330 B.C.E.) broke previous rules of decorum by depicting goddesses entirely naked. The story goes that his model and mistress
Phryne was accused of impiety but acquitted on account of her beauty, which
became standard for female divinities.

assessors as one of the Seven Marvels of the ancient world.[80] Phidias's workshop in the sacred grove at Olympia became another tourist attraction (a cup survives, marked "I am of [belong to] Phidias"), but rumor says that the sculptor was either done to death or had again to run for his life. It may well be that the Eleans, custodians of the site and collectors of revenues from services to tourists, feared that their Daedalian prize might excel himself elsewhere.

The privilege of oiling and cleaning the statue was bestowed, perhaps in apology for his maltreatment, on the sculptor's descendants. By the second century C.E., however, according to the satirical Syrian Lucian (who wrote better Attic prose than most Athenians of his time), Phidias's immortal Zeus was showing his age: "No one sacrifices to you now and no one crowns you. . . . They'll soon depose you, O noblest of gods, and cast you in the role of Kronos."[81] In the event, the statue was pillaged by the Byzantines, in the fifth century, and taken to Constantinople, where it was later destroyed in a fire.

The ambivalent chic of the adjective *daidaleos*—defined in Liddell and Scott's Greek lexicon as "cunningly or curiously wrought; dappled, spotted; shot with light; sheeny; cunning"— is a sweet fit for elusive artists. Craft and craftiness go together, as they did in lecherous Hephaestus, the divine handyman. After Hera literally threw her gauche son out of Olympus, "he fell from morn till dewy eve." His fall was arrested by the islanders of Lemnos, who spotted him coming (Robert Graves has it that his name means "shining by day"); but they must have

---

80. The first rankings were pronounced in the 2nd century B.C.E.
81. Zeus's father, whom he castrated with a sickle on his way to divine supremacy.

fumbled the catch: he broke his hip as he hit the ground. Having developed blacksmith's skills in exile, gimpy Hephaestus was conscripted to furnish a replacement shield and armor for Achilles.[82] He never hobbled to war himself.

Legend had it that the original female inhabitants of Lemnos were dumped by their Athenian husbands; they then murdered all the males on the island. When the Argonauts put in at Lemnos, they found the women unwelcoming and malodorous; suitable company only for the loutish, but randy Hephaestus. In hot and untimely pursuit of Athene, he had ejaculated on her thigh, whence his semen dripped onto Attic soil, giving rise to Athens's founder, Erechtheus. The spill also fathered the myth that Athenians were literally born out of their own soil. Like Agamemnon, Erechtheus was said to have sacrificed a daughter (Chthonia, the earthling) in order to procure success in war.

The recurrence of this bloody rite by archaic potentates argues for René Girard's notion that human sacrifice, later camouflaged by myth, preceded that of animal surrogates.[83] War, it seems, demanded some self-mutilating preliminary sacrifice. According to one mythical version, Erechtheus reigned

82. In book 16 of the *Iliad,* the sulking Achilles lends his fighting kit to his lover Patroclus, who is then killed and stripped of it by the Trojan prince Hector. Desire for revenge, rather than any vestige of team-spirit, impels Achilles to return to the war in Hephaestus's outfit. The "buddy" system in the US Army is in the Homeric tradition, as were the homosexual pairings in the élite military "Sacred Band" in 4th-century B.C.E. Thebes.

83. In the Bible, Judges 9, Jephtha, in order to achieve victory in battle, swears that he will sacrifice the first person to come out of his house on his return. It turns out to be his daughter. Girard (1923–2015) was an unorthodox anthropologist who argued for the universal use of the scapegoat in order to resolve communal tensions. See in particular his *Violence and the Sacred* (1972).

for 50 years and introduced the worship of Demeter (who lost her daughter, Persephone, to the king of the underworld) and attendant "mysteries" at Eleusis. Initiates were lowered into a cavern where indescribable rituals took place. On emerging, they were deemed to have been purified, as they have been in a suite of subsequent cults, including Scientology. Keeping a secret becomes, in itself, a form of superiority, if not of salvation.

The artist/artisan, rarely a warrior, never aristocratic, is the disreputable celebrity of Hellenism. Plutarch (50–ca. 120 C.E.) wrote that "no man of good birth and good sense, when admiring the Zeus of Olympia or the Hera of Argos, is thereby filled with the desire to be Phidias or Praxiteles."[84] Lordly bias against "banausic" occupations (*banausos* meant low-class craftsman) had a modern equivalent in contempt for people who made money in "trade" rather than in professions that did not soil the hands. In aristocratic eyes, "old money"— revenue from ancestral estates—was, for centuries, the only dignified form of income, apart from the spoils of war. Athenian gentlemen could not understand how inhabitants of the neighboring city of Megara managed to be so rich when their territory was so small. The undistinguished truth was, they were excellent and busy traders. In the fifth century, the Athenians banned Megarian ships from entering their own or their allies' harbors, an act of hubris (deliberate arrogance) that had limited effect, except to excite angry apprehension in other Greeks, not least the seagoing Corinthians.

84. In *The Imaginary Museum* (1952), however, André Malraux says that people do not become artists by looking at life but by looking at art.

Reluctance to concede merit to money gained by peaceful
actions has disposed scholars to bless conquering (and looting)
generals with greater virtues than enterprising civilians or cal-
culating investors. Formally barred from unworthy mercantile
enterprise, Roman senators used middle-class *equites* (knights)
as front men. Typical of the latter was Cicero's epistolary friend
Titus Pomponius, nicknamed Atticus because he had the cautious
wit to spend a good deal of his time, peacefully and profitably,
in Athens rather than stay in the turmoil of first-century B.C.E.
Rome. Senators funded their investments in trade by taking out
mortgages, at up to 15 percent interest, on their land. Gambling
has always been more aristocratic than going to the office.

10.

After Poseidon, earth-shaker and god of the sea (and, also, in
early versions, of horses) had dispatched a flawless white bull
to swim ashore on Crete, Minos conserved it to inseminate the
royal herd rather than sacrifice it to the donor, as piety advised.
Poseidon's pique led him to impel Minos's queen, Pasiphae
("the all-shining one"), to lust after the well-tasseled beast. In
her heat, she solicited Daedalus to contrive a way for her to be
pleasured without being crushed. The artist/panderer built a
rigid frame, covered it with cowhide, and rendered the appropriate aperture inviting with a dose of estrogen. The queen was
then able to cower inside and be mounted. The Minotaur was
the guilty and conspicuous consequence.[85] Despite Daedalus's

85. At once pathetic and predatory, the Minotaur's unique ambiguity
haunted modern artists such as Pablo Picasso, Michael Ayrton, and Maggie
Hambling. In 1968, Ayrton designed a brick maze on the Arkville property

complicity, Minos held him too valuable to be put to death. The artist had already furnished the king with a mechanical sentry. The robotic Talos (named, it seems, in shameless apology, after Daedalus's nephew, alias the precocious Perdix) patrolled the Cretan shore 24/7. Illegal immigrants were grilled against the furnace caged in his brazen chest.

Artful Daedalus had a historic double in Archimedes (ca. 287–212 B.C.E.). The great mathematician is said to have possessed a theoretical understanding, unique in antiquity, of the nature of a numerical system. Guru in residence at the court of Hieron II, tyrant of Syracuse, in Sicily, he is credited with inventing a lens so powerful that it concentrated sun rays on approaching Roman ships and set them on fire at a distance.[86] When, after a long siege, the Romans did eventually land, in irresistible numbers, a centurion found Archimedes on the beach, tracing figures in the sand. The geometrical genius called out, "Don't touch my triangles." He was then stabbed to death. In September 1945, the Austrian composer Anton Webern was shot by an American G.I. when he broke the curfew by stepping outside his Viennese home to smoke a cigar.

Archimedes had claimed that, given a suitable extraterrestrial platform from which to apply leverage, he could rival Poseidon and move the earth. His application of physics in order to kill at a distance would be transcended by Adolf Hitler's

---

of Armand G. Erpf in Delaware, NY. Ayrton's novel *The Maze Maker* is an elegant biographical impersonation.

86. The Byzantine invention "Greek fire," concocted in the late 7th century C.E., achieved a similar effect by floating "liquid fire" into the path of enemy fleets. Its precise formula remains uncertain, though naphtha was a key ingredient. The lake outside oil-rich Baku was famous for the flames that floated on its surface.

rocket scientist Werner von Braun. Archaic Greeks regarded archers and slingers as failing to "man up." In the seventh century B.C.E., Archilochus wrote about contending warriors of Chalkis and Eretria, on the island of Euboea (today's Evia, alongside Attica), who made a prebattle agreement not to use missiles. The sour poet commented: "But grim swordplay is even worse." The modern movement to "ban" nuclear weapons, quixotic in the light of the number and killing power of "conventional" weapons, has a tincture of the ancient notion that to kill with negligible risk of being killed smacks of murder. In the British army, gentlemen did not choose to serve in the Royal Artillery; the regiment's Latin motto "Ubique" (everywhere) promises its general utility. J. R. Oppenheimer, having supervised the creation of the first atomic bomb, "brighter than a thousand suns," likened himself, with conscience-ridden vanity, to the Hindu god of death.[87] No one in the ancient world let it be known that he was ashamed of how many people he had killed.[88]

87. Philosophers have long been torn between respect for science (Marx and Freud had in common the claim to be scientific) and suspicion, especially when it comes to physics, of symbolic systems without a literature. Heidegger put it plainly: "Science can't think." His own thoughts included the idea that Adolf Hitler was Germany's salvation. The Vienna Circle, in the 1920s, was of philosophers whose self-denying ordinance required what had been "the queen of sciences" to abjure its crown and become science's logical housekeeper. A. J. Ayer, in *Language, Truth and Logic* (1936), modernized Socrates' aggressive modesty. Unlike Socrates, he culled many honors and sat in enviable chairs in the sophistic course of disclaiming insight into sublime truths or Truth.

88. Jacqueline de Romilly's *La Grèce antique contre la violence* (2000) makes a brave attempt to argue for the pacific strain in Greek civilization. In the first book of Samuel, the Jews sing, "Saul has slain his thousands, and David his tens of thousands." In *The Second Sophistic* (2005), Tim Whitmarsh

After the German defeat, the character of Werner von Braun, the inventor of the V–2 rockets that had bombarded England toward the end of World War II, was blanched in a coat of the victors' whitewash and transferred to America, where he was reborn as a guilt-free, if carefully sequestered, pioneer of space exploration. The first man to claim to have been on the moon was Lucian. In *A True Story*, he describes the royal palace with a huge mirror at the bottom of a deep well in which it was possible to hear everything being said on earth and to see all the terrestrial cities. Lucian claims that he could see his family and homeland but couldn't swear that anyone had seen him. Anyone who didn't believe him was advised to go where he had been, and he would then see how true it was. A persistent urban legend has it that the first American landing on the moon was faked, for propaganda purposes, in a movie studio.

11.

Unsmiling Minos kept Daedalus under house arrest. The cribbed trickster found the wit to escape, with his adolescent son Icarus, by devising two pairs of wings, serried feathers stuck in a wax-coated armature. The boy's Cretan mother, Naukrate (ship mistress), was not considered airworthy. Before Flight 1 from Crete took off, Daedalus warned his son against soaring too close to the sun. Once aloft, however, the boy went up and up and up, until the sun melted the wax on his wings and he

---

notes that King David is said, by John of Antioch, in the 5th century C.E., as reported by John of Sicily, to have been requested to come to the aid of Troy. "The biblical tradition would simply not play ball with Greek epic because joining Troy would put David on the losing side." Hmm.

plunged, featherless, into the northern Aegean, off the island now named Ikaria.[89]

In the celestial sphere, Phaethon, son of the sun god Helios, was said to have been inversely reckless: craving a turn at the reins of the solar chariot, he could not control its plunging horses. They swooped so low that the earth would have been incinerated, had Zeus not canceled Phaethon's license with a thunderbolt. The errant jockey plunged into the river Eridanus (now the Po), in the far northwest of the Adriatic. His weeping sisters were transformed into poplar trees, their tears into the amber lozenges for which the river was famous. The versatility of myth served both to moralize (Plutarch contrasted the folly of Phaethon with the sanity of Socrates) and to account for natural phenomena. To disobey the gods was folly; but there was no promise of salvation in taking them at their word. Apollo's mouthpiece, the Delphic oracle, specialized in ambiguity. Life was characterized, memory ordered, time spaced,

---

89. The elder Breughel pictured the scene, prompting W. H. Auden's poetic ecphrasis:

> In Breughel's Icarus, for instance: how everything turns away
> Quite leisurely from the disaster; the ploughman may
> Have heard the splash, the forsaken cry,
> But for him it was not an important failure; the sun shone
> As it had to on the white legs disappearing into the green
> Water, and the expensive delicate ship that must have seen
> Something amazing, a boy falling out of the sky,
> Had somewhere to get to and sailed calmly on.

Mel Brooks supplied a briefer gloss: "If God had meant us to fly, he would have given us tickets."

There is an agency called Icarus Travel in the main street of the Cretan capital, Heraklion. Cadet pilots in the Greek air force are known as "Ikaroi."

creation displayed and colored by divine and heroic precedents, whether salutary or alarming.[90]

After Icarus had crashed and splashed, Daedalus flew on to land near Kamikos, in southern Sicily, where the local tyrant Cocalus gave him sanctuary, in return for useful services. From the earliest recorded times, Sicily and southern Italy were so widely scattered with Greek colonies (even landlocked, unadventurous Sparta had one at Tarentum on Italy's instep[91]) that the region became known as Magna Graecia. Mainland Greece was never big enough for all the Hellenes. The tightness of land (*stenochoria*) and internecine quarrels led its young, sometimes fugitive inhabitants to sail off, east and west, whether to the turbulent Black Sea—flattered as "Euxine" (welcoming) by nervous sailors—or as far, by way of Marseille, as mineral-rich Tartessus in southwestern Spain.[92]

In the eighth century B.C.E., Archias, from the family that ruled Corinth, left that city—probably in a hurry after murdering someone—and founded Ortygia, on a peninsula that became the bastion of Syracuse, the dominant city in Sicily.[93] The papyrus-fringed, fresh-water fountain of Arethusa, on the promontory of Ortygia in Theocritus's home city, was said to be the bubbling

90. See Paul Veyne, *Les Grecs, ont-ils cru à leurs mythes?* (1992). The preliterate world was itself a "memory theater" prompting the recall of common folkloric stories. See Frances Yates, *The Art of Memory* (1966).

91. In *La Grèce archaïque* (1984), Claude Mossé suggests that the colonists included bastards born of Spartan mothers and helot fathers. For what may be demographic reasons, Spartan women enjoyed rare freedom in the choice of sexual partners, especially among social peers; some, it seems, took this liberty too far. In general, what mattered was the production of male offspring.

92. Most commentaries claim that it occupied the site of modern Cadiz.

93. One of its best small restaurants (with excellent tiramisu) is named after Archimedes.

mouth of the river Alpheios, which had run under the salt sea
from Arcadia, in the western Peloponnese. Geographical fancy
supplied a submarine umbilical cord that tied Sicily to Greece.
Syracuse later spawned subsidiary settlements. Aerial archaeology shows colonial cities laid out with equal allocations of land
for all settlers. There is no record of fair shares being allotted to
indigenous inhabitants by any colonists other than Pythagoras
and his followers in Croton, on the heel of Italy.

To make sure of abiding asylum in Kamikos, Daedalus had
designed an unassailable citadel for his insecure patron: its
corkscrew, one-at-a-time entrance tower could be defended by
a single sentinel against any number of assailants. Conscious
that no petty potentate would willingly disclose that he was
harboring such a prize guest, Minos had sailed from one city
to the next offering a temptingly fat reward for whoever could
run a thread through a tight spiral shell. When the king's squad-
ron put in at Kamikos, Cocalus embraced the great Minos with
a proper show of philoxenia.[94] He had taken the precaution to
secrete Daedalus in a bunker, but he could not resist going to
set him the rewarding puzzle.

　　Minos knew very well that the devious rogue was the one
man who might have the answer; and so he did: Daedalus
dabbed a drop of honey at the deep end of the shell, tied a thread
around an ant, and inserted it to find its way to the lure. As soon
as Minos was shown the strung conch, he demanded that Daedalus be handed over. Cocalus induced his royal guest first to
take a predinner shower in his new bathroom. Since it had been

94. For the tradition of mutual, competitive hospitality in archaic Greece,
see Richard Seaford, *Reciprocity and Ritual* (1994).

designed by the duplicitous craftsman, Cocalus's daughters were able to use scalding water to kill the royal visitor.

According to Virgil's patriotic Roman version, Daedalus's first landfall had been at Cumae, a few miles north of Naples, where a numinous cave housed the oracular Sibyl.[95] The Sibylline Books of oracles were consulted in times of crisis in historical Rome; so too, later, were Virgil's works in the superstitious random selection known as taking the *sortes Virgilianae* (literally, Virgilian lots). Cumaean tradition had it that nearby Lake Avernus concealed the easy descent to the underworld. Minos was resuscitated to become Hades' deified, unsmiling monarch. It was his dutiful pleasure to make sure that no one found an exit.

12.

Assuming the skeptical style of Euhemeros,[96] some scholars have suggested that, since Daedalus cannot literally have soared up and away from Crete under his own power, he was "in fact" the inventor of sails. Minos is supposed to have read the fleeting whiteness on the horizon as flapping wings, since sails were unknown to him. This presumes that the wide-ranging Minoan fleet had, until then, been propelled only by oars. The back-story, however, requires that when Theseus first set out

95. Minoan contacts with Italy were enshrined in the ancestry of the Roman aristocratic family of the Sulpicii Galbae, who claimed descent from Minos and Pasiphae.

96. Euhemeros of Messene (ca. 300 B.C.E.) wrote a fantastic novel, *Sacred Scripture,* about a voyage on which he claimed to have found evidence that the gods of mythology were, in fact, great but mundane kings, exalted and deified by grateful subjects. Unitarians take a Euhemerist view of Jesus of Nazareth, whom they regard as an entirely human savior.

for Crete, with the Minotaur's annual installment of fourteen victims, his doleful ship carried black sails. In 1940, the Germans caught the British by surprise with a Daedalian ruse: their parachutists sailed down from the skies and captured Crete before an adequate defense could be rallied. Over 2,000 years before, Alexander the Great had mounted a similarly astonishing, if only seemingly airborne, coup at Aornos, in Bactria.[97]

Theseus had promised his father, King Aegeus, that if his mission had a happy outcome, he would sport white sails on his return journey. In hopeful vigil, the aged king installed himself above the cliffs at Cape Sounion, on the eastern corner of Attica, scanning the approach to the Saronic Gulf. Having dispatched the Minotaur, Theseus had taken the besotted Ariadne on board, to save her from her father's rage, before casting off with all speed. When he rested his crew at Naxos, his now superfluous foreign mistress fell deeply asleep (the local, somewhat heavy wine is still famous). Theseus whispered his men back on board and pushed off. The desolate Ariadne was discovered and consoled by the god Dionysos, which Euhemerists interpret as meaning that she took to drink.[98]

In ungallant scuttle from the Cyclades, Theseus neglected to hoist the white sails that would have advertised his success. Reading the black for bleak news, old King Aegeus threw himself off the tall cliff, on which a now-blanched temple of Poseidon

---

97. See section 62 below.

98. Ariadne has been kept alive in Richard Strauss's opera and by Giorgio de Chirico's paintings, in which her figure is usually lounging on a stone plinth in a depopulated, surreal urban setting. Henri Jeanmaire's *Histoire du culte de Bacchus* (1991) claims that Dionysos's association with wine comes late in his evolution; previously he was associated with the violence of festive mobs on the rampage. On this account, Ariadne embraces him because she is so full of rage.

still stands (Byron's name incised in its marble) and made the sea Aegean. Having mourned his father with brisk rites, Theseus assumed the throne and instituted the political centralism that rendered the Founder quasi-historic. Unlike Oedipus, who killed Laius in self-defense without knowing that he was his son, Theseus earned no entry in the psychoanalytic vocabulary by his inadvertent (but equally career-advancing) patricide.

Ariadne has a characteristic affinity with Medea, who also betrayed her father for love of a stranger. After helping Jason dope the dragon that guarded the Golden Fleece, Medea boarded the Argo with its heroic Greek crew and the loot. Pursued by her father, King Aētēs of Colchis, the witch/princess butchered her little brother Absyrtus and scattered the pieces on the water, so that her father would stop to collect and reassemble what was left of his heir. Settled in Corinth, Medea had two children by Jason, but was later dumped by him in favor of the nubile daughter of King Creon. In apparent forgiveness and resignation, Medea made an enchanting wedding dress as a present for the guileless bride. When she paraded in it, the material burst into inextinguishable flames. Medea then killed her two sons by Jason and literally took flight (in the winged chariot of her grandfather, the sun) to Athens, where King Aegeus had promised her sanctuary in return for a cure for his sterility. The two princesses' stories converged as Medea tried, but failed, to balk the young Theseus when he first came to Athens to claim his inheritance from King Aegeus.[99]

99. Euripides' *Medea* (the sole survivor from a tetralogy) was ranked third out of three entrants when first presented at the Great Dionysia, a theater festival in Athens, but has since been frequently performed, translated, and imitated, most memorably by Jean Anouilh's irreverent *Médée* (1953). Maria Callas played Medea in Luigi Cherubini's opera at La Scala in 1954. She

Theseus's heroic rite de passage, on his way from an alien
and obscure adolescence in Troezen to claim his birthright in
Attica, had led him to confront—among other challenging
tasks—the giant Procrustes, who commanded the (still) narrow
coastal road from Megara to Athens. In a savage parody of
philoxenia, Procrustes (the Stretcher) measured claimants to
hospitality against a bed of a certain length; too long, they lost
their legs; too short, they were stretched to conformity. Young
Theseus put the brute to sleep with a severe dose of his own
medicine, and went on to Athens with the sword[100] and sandals
that the transient Aegeus had left under a rock in Troezen in
case his temporary local (and royal) lover, Aethra, bore a son.
The most famous historic sandals in Greek history were the
lightweight models designed by the Athenian general Iphicrates
(415–353 B.C.E.). They liberated infantrymen (hoplites) from
stolid routine and allowed them to move swiftly (hop lighter,
some might say), especially on uneven ground, in order to
harass and evade cumbrously shod conventional soldiers.

13.

Despite Agamemnon's sacrifice of her sister Iphigenia in order to
procure a fair wind for the Achaean fleet to sail to Troy, Elektra
remained, like Athene, "strong for the father." Her long-preserved

---

reprised the performance for Pier Paolo Pasolini's film and in real life, when
she was deserted by her lover, the Greek shipping millionaire Aristotle Onassis,
who then married Jackie Kennedy. Ariadne had to wait for Richard Strauss.

100. According to Kenneth McLeish's *Myth* (1996), young King Arthur
extracted a sword from the rock in which Uther Pendragon had embedded it.
This sword was broken in a duel with a giant and replaced, thanks to Merlin,
by Excalibur, which was handed to him by the Lady of the Lake.

virginity was the proof. In Aeschylus's *Eumenides,* after he has avenged Agamemnon, her brother Orestes consigns Elektra, with diplomatic haste, to marry his taciturn friend Pylades, king of Phocis. She is not heard of again in any noble or outspoken context. The sacrifice of Iphigenia had an earlier mythical precedent: Athene's favorite, Erechtheus, was told by the Delphic oracle that he would be victorious over the invading Eleusinians only if he sacrificed one of his daughters. He did so, and he was; but soon afterward, according to a version of his myth which contradicts that of his long reign, Poseidon—who resented coming second to Athene as the patron deity of Athens—destroyed Erechtheus and his whole family. Oracles rarely delivered unambiguous good news. In historical times, Delphi's secretariat specialized in versified conundrums that lent themselves to ingenious interpretation. Hence the god was never wrong, only misunderstood.

The most typically Delphic advice—uttered as Xerxes' army was invading Greece in 480 B.C.E.—recommended that the Athenians trust to their "wooden wall." Athenian conservatives read this as meaning that they should barricade themselves in the Acropolis, which in the archaic period had had a timber palisade. Themistocles, who had persuaded his fellow citizens to invest all their treasure and hopes in the fleet, argued that Apollo was recommending that they set to sea and put all their faith in their wooden triremes (many-oared warships). Themistocles' interpretation of the Pythian text[101] was confirmed by a patriotic surge in which the able-bodied men of Athens, rich

101. It required reading the singular "wooden wall" as a synecdoche for Athens's wooden fleet. Tendentious explication of enigmatic pagan oracles has something in common with Jewish *Midrash* and the Christian sermon: officiating clergy could prove their wise ingenuity by divining whatever underlying meaning of scriptural rubrics seemed good to them.

and poor, warriors and horsemen, took their places alongside
each other on the oarsmen's benches.

After Troy was destroyed, the triumphant Agamemnon
came home, toting the Trojan princess Cassandra among his
prizes. Arrogance blinded him to the festering rage of Klytemnestra; she could not forgive the king for agreeing to the gagging
and ritual slaughter of their daughter. Homer has the queen's
lover Aegistheus chop Agamemnon to death, with a Mycenaean double axe, as he wallows in a celebratory bath. In
Aeschylus, Klytemnestra herself snags her husband in a net and
then plays the butcher. Cassandra, who had literally seen it all
coming, suffered the same fate. She had been alone among
mortals in successfully resisting the amorous advances of a god.
Apollo, the master of prescience, punished her by making her
a prophet whose forecasts would all come true, but never be
believed. In his *Agamemnon,* Aeschylus makes dramatic use of
Cassandra's futile accuracy by having her predict the king's fate,
and her own, with the ominous menace of a cinematic flash-
forward. The actual deaths take place offstage (only Agamemnon's last words are audible[102]), but the audience's horror is
redoubled because it seems already to have witnessed them.

Electra craved the return of her exiled brother Orestes to avenge
Agamemnon's murder. Was Electra's father-fixation overdeter-
mined? May she have been envious of Iphigenia's immolation?

102. "Oimoi peplēgmai kairian plēgēn eso": literally, "Ah me, I am struck
with a lethal blow in here." Although it is rarely remarked, the last word seems
what schoolboys, when writing verses, used to call a "filler." Aeschylus also
nods. Might not some New Critic have remarked that *kairian* (lethal) had
a punning affinity, ironically appropriate in Agamemnon's case, with *chair/
ian* (welcoming)?

Speculations about individual psychology have no place in ancient literature; custom demanded that those wrongly done to death be placated. Ancient motives were expressed by actions, however deviously contrived, warranted by familial loyalty or enjoined by pious precedent. Socrates' notion of the "examined life" was less a call to introspection than an incitement to dispassionate assessment. The Platonic *psyche* was a vestige of immortality, not an apartment for neuroses.

In Attic tragedy, the sacrifice of Iphigenia was treated literally by Aeschylus; Euripides preferred the novelettish version in which Artemis substituted a deer for the victim and spirited the innocent girl to the Crimea, where she became a priestess and, with convenient plotting, was able later to help her shipwrecked brother Orestes and his friend Pylades to elude the local priests' sacrificial knife. In Genesis, Abraham's substitution, on belated divine orders, of a ram for his son Isaac confirms René Girard's notion that human sacrifice was, at some primitive stage, a common recourse. To avoid *miasma* (blood guilt) the victims had always to be held not to have protested against, but rather acquiesced in, their treatment; hence Iphigenia's gag.[103]

---

103. In, in particular, *Des choses cachées depuis la fondation du monde* (1978; translated as *Things Hidden since the Foundation of the World,* 1987), René Girard's analysis of "the scapegoat mechanism" maintains that the sacrificial system was ruptured, once and for all, by the refusal of Jesus of Nazareth, and his followers, to demonstrate the guilty acquiescence on which ritual depended. Taking Girard's argument a little further, it could be said that the innocence of Jesus left "the people," specifically the Jerusalem Jews, with the guilt that his death was supposed to remove. In time, the Jews themselves became the victims whose "deserved" pariahdom held the Christian community together in the self-procured righteousness of those who had punished the deicides. Jewish guilt supplied a useful adhesive until the manifest scandal of the

In one of his dramatic monologues, Yannis Ritsos, among the greatest of modern Greek poets, and one of the most cruelly used by his countrymen, advanced Electra's unrebellious sister Chrysothemis to speak, with ironic Marxist undertones, of the consolations of bourgeois passivity.[104] The elasticity of certain myths, the ease with which they can be restyled,[105] secures their longevity, whether in narrative or in imagery. Perseus and Andromeda are often portrayed in European art; their story is, however, rarely revisited in literature. Sibling rivalries abound in mythology, notably in the mutual, simultaneous destruction of Oedipus's sons, Eteocles and Polyneices. That fraternal feud has been ignored in psychoanalytic jargon, but their sister Antigone gave rise to a copious literature.[106] In historic Macedonia,

---

Holocaust disrupted Christian conceit and rendered anti-Semitism disreputable, at least for a time. For an account of recent work on the Iphigenia *topos,* see Marina Warner's article in the *Times Literary Supplement* of Sept. 6, 2013.

104. Y. Ritsos, *The Fourth Dimension,* trans. Peter Green (1993). Ritsos (1909–1990) was nominated six times for the Nobel Prize but was deemed politically unsuitable. The scion of a rich Laconian family and a Communist militant, he was intermittently imprisoned by a succession of Greek regimes from 1936 into the 1970s.

105. The title of Jean Giraudoux's 1929 play *Amphitryon 38* incorporates the irony of how often that particular myth had been recycled. Amphitryon married Alcmene, who was visited by Zeus and later gave birth to Heracles. Amphitryon is said to mean "strong on both sides." Giraudoux was the first writer to be decorated for gallantry in the Great War. His 1935 play *La guerre de Troie n'aura pas lieu* was a rewrite, featuring Homer's characters, of the events leading up to the Trojan War. Giraudoux sought to warn the French against what he claimed was an avoidable war with Hitler's Germany. After that war was lost, he became a Pétainist minister and collaborator. He died in 1944.

106. Catalogued in George Steiner's *Antigones* (1984). Jean Anouilh's version of *Antigone,* written during the German occupation of France, has been accused of taking Cleon/Pétain's pragmatic part against the self-immolatory heroine who supposedly stood for de Gaulle's (futile) Resistance.

the death of the king was always likely to lead to a murderous knockout competition between his sons, only one of whom, by virtue of his ruthlessness, established his title to the succession.

Antigone's suicidal determination, when she says "no" to a life of compromise with the tyrannical Creon, is presented as heroic in Sophocles. Her defiance was echoed, on October 28, 1940, when the Italian dictator Benito Mussolini demanded that the Greeks allow his fascist forces to occupy their country and received the answer "Ochi!" This "No" in thunder was delivered by the Greek dictator Ioannis Metaxas, who in other respects was a twentieth-century equivalent of the playwright's Creon. "Ochi Day" is now celebrated annually as the Greek national day of pride. It asserts a brave unity ruptured, less than a decade later, by a savage civil war, its scars never quite healed, between left and right. In 2013, the left said "No" to the European Union, while the right said, "Why not?"

14.

In Euripides' *Hippolytus,* the mature Theseus is led to believe that his young son has forced himself on his stepmother Phaedra, the sister of her husband's earlier victim/lover, Ariadne. Affronted by the celibate Hippolytus's lack of veneration, the goddess Aphrodite has inflamed the virtuous queen with erotic desire. When Hippolytus rejects her, with disgust, Phaedra writes a suicide note accusing the young man of attempted rape and hangs herself.[107] Theseus returns home, reads and believes

---

107. See Nicole Loraux, *Tragic Ways of Killing a Woman* (1985). Mythical widows often kill themselves on the death of their husbands. Later they were

the note,[108] expels his son from the kingdom, and summons the sea god Poseidon, who owes him an answered prayer, to kill the boy. A serpentine monster surges out of the waves, terrifies Hippolytus's horses, and his chariot runs away with him. Tangled in the harness, he is battered against seaside rocks. As Hippolytus dies in his arms, the remorseful Theseus recognizes that his son was innocent. In the sixteenth century, St. Teresa of Avila warned against the risk of answered prayers.

Myth and Athenian propaganda credited the young Theseus with all sorts of exploits on the way to Athens to claim his birthright. He chose to go by land rather than sea; brigands made the road more dangerous and their defeat added to his luster. His literary image, however, does him small honor. Aeschylus's *The Cretans* might have enhanced Theseus's fame, but the trilogy survives only in tatters. Odysseus was, in many respects, a more perfidious scoundrel, but he had charm and nerve—and Homer to sing his praises. Odysseus/Ulysses comes to renewed life in a whole train of variations, from Encolpius, the impotent antihero of Petronius Arbiter's *Satyrica,* to James Joyce's Leopold Bloom in *Ulysses* and Derek Walcott's Caribbean *Omeros.*[109]

---

liable to remarry their brothers-in-law. This quasi-incest kept the inheritance within the male line.

108. Written evidence is not always valid, although severe French scholars often asked, "Vous avez un texte, monsieur?" as if it were. As a cautionary tale, the French classicist Jean-Pierre Vernant (1914–2007) recounts an incident in the wartime Resistance in which a forged letter, on "official" paper, was taken to prove that an escaper from the Nazis had not truly escaped. See his *La traversée des frontières* (2004). Vernant's nom de guerre while in the Resistance was Colonel Robert.

109. See W. B. Stanford, *The Ulysses Theme* (1993). Born in a generation previous to that of the heroes who went to Troy, Theseus must rely for modern literary sponsorship on Mary Renault's *The King Must Die.*

Crete never ceased to have ambivalent status in Athenian eyes: the island was held to be the repository of age-old wisdom (King Minos was famed, above all, as a law-giver); at the same time, its inhabitants were proverbial for mendacity. The pronouncement "All Cretans are liars" becomes the first leg of a philosophical crux when a Cretan is supposed to have said it. The paradoxical consequence is that if the speaker was a liar, the sentiment itself has to be false; but if he was not, then at least one Cretan was not a liar, which disproves the premiss.[110]

The Latin word *hariolari* took on a complementary double-meaning: both to prophesy, with oracular significance, and also to talk rubbish. Cicero was eager to be elected an augur, because of the social cachet the office always bore; he also admitted that when two augurs—who, according to ancient lore, had the power of divining the future from the innards of sacrificial fowl—passed each other in the street, they could not do so without a smirk of complicity. A double-strand of credulity and skepticism, conservatism and innovation, science and superstition, deceit and honor, cunning and candor runs through ancient Greece and Rome and drives on into Christendom.

In Greece and Rome, slaves were assumed to be liars unless their evidence was given under torture. They were expressly forbidden to testify otherwise. In Christian Europe, Jews were deemed incapable of giving trustworthy evidence in court.

---

110. During a talk on the Cycladic island of Ios, my friend, the late Uli Mittelmach, a mathematics professor, suggested that maybe the man was not a Cretan or that he did not know what he was talking about. In the evening, Uli sometimes wore a bowler hat; he did not care for the company of fellow Germans. No Germans wear bowler hats. Empirical possibilities crack old hard cases.

At the same time, their scriptures had to be accepted as the bedrock of monotheism. Hebrew has been held to be literally the language of God, hence the inconvenient priority conceded to Jewish scripture in most Christian eyes.[111] The birth of Jesus in Galilee confirms the sanctity of the Holy Land. That Zeus was cradled in Crete continued to enhance that island's mythical aura.

15.

The fierce old chthonic gods, penned beneath the ground, haunted the Greek imagination. Dread of repressed powers doubled with fear of the indignant dead. Heroes, regularly credited with a divine parent,[112] were lodged in diminutive palaces or put to rest in *koimeteria* (cemeteries are literally sleeping places) adjacent to their native city, which could be united in their proud, if apprehensive, worship. Solon decreed that the dead should not be lodged in the city itself. Heroes did, however, merit (and require) punctual honor and appeasement; their goodwill had to be procured with doses of sacrificial blood.[113]

111. The French philosopher Simone Weil (1909–1943) was of Jewish origin but became a nonbaptized near-Christian. Her zeal for Plato was such that she wanted to substitute his major works for the Old Testament.

112. Alexander the Great, whose mother, Olympias, claimed to have been visited by Zeus, was the last beneficiary, if Jesus of Nazareth is not included, of divine paternity.

113. Jane Harrison's *Prolegomena to the Study of Greek Religion* (1903) remains a dated, never dull treasury of literary archaeology. Inspired by James Frazer's *The Golden Bough*, Harrison unearthed the unadmitted dark forces, buried but never dead, that loitered behind the Olympians' arras. Minos is seen, in her book, as the bull-king; the bull itself as both Dionysos and the

After a bruising war with Kronos's generation of Titans and giants,[114] Zeus and his sibling team took up residence on the summit of Mount Olympus. The evicted Titans might be dispossessed of their powers, but they were not docked of their immortality. Buried under mountainous boulders, they and their earthy allies continued to grumble and, on occasion, erupt in flame and smoke. Old Kronos was both banished and placated: the sacred hill overlooking the site of the Olympic Games was named for him[115] and he was deputed to rule over the Isles of the Blessed, the home of heroic souls. The days before his eviction from power came to be known as the Golden Age, when the best of mankind sat down to dinner with the gods and enjoyed the unrecoverable *douceur de vivre* that Talleyrand, Napoleon's polymētis foreign minister and betrayer, remembered from the time before the French Revolution.

Mortals lost their right to entertain the gods when the Lydian king Tantalus, in the desire to give the gods something new for dinner, served his own son, Pelops, in a pot roast. Demeter was so distracted by the disappearance of her young daughter Persephone, who had been abducted (near steep Enna, in central Sicily) by the king of Hades, that she ate a chunk of Pelops's shoulder before the other gods gagged on the human flesh. Pelops was restored to life, his missing shoulder replaced with a prosthetic ivory plate. Tantalus was consigned to the underworld, where he was forever tantalized by proximity to a

---

victim torn to pieces in his worship. Harrison is the precursor of such female scholars as Mary Lefkowitz and Nicole Loraux. Her reputation is torn to clever pieces in Mary Beard's *The Invention of Jane Harrison* (2000).

114. Imagined by Robert Graves, in his poem "Ogres and Pygmies," as having "long yards and stinking armpits."

115. See *The Hill of Kronos* (1980) by Peter Levi.

bunch of delectable grapes that swung away from him whenever he reached for them; when he bent to quench his thirst,
the water, in its turn, receded. The story of the recipe from
which the Olympians flinched suggests that earlier gods may
not have been so fastidious when it came to human meat. Societies are regularly defined by what their members may or may
not eat and by rules of sexual propriety, especially with regard
to incest.[116]

Alerted by Gaea (Mother Earth) that if her daughter
Metis (Sly-boots) had a son, he would displace Zeus himself
(as Zeus had Kronos), the new master of Olympus married her
and, once she was pregnant (sex with gods inevitably entailed
conception), swallowed her alive, so that he could always know
where she was. Zeus was then literally unable to get the embryo
out of his head. Metis's unborn divine infant became a splitting
headache for the father of the gods. One of the Titans, the ingenious Prometheus, had had the foresight to go over to the
new gods, though he was never one of them. He was on hand
to brace Zeus's cranium while Hephaestus sectioned it with a
maieutic axe. Athene was said to have stepped out "fully armed"
with her helmet and her emblematic, intimidating *aegis*, or
breastplate (some pundits equate it with her virgin vulva).
Athene was both her father's favorite and, the subtext implies,
no candidate for trustworthy reproduction.[117]

To amuse the lonely young goddess, Prometheus made
toy figures out of clay and water. The clever virgin breathed life

---

116. See, for instance and pleasure, Lord Raglan's *Jocasta's Crime* (1933). For
a cinematic treatment of the story of Pelops, see my *Of Gods and Men* (1994).

117. See section 31 below for the Athenian tyrant Pisistratus's apprehensions in somewhat similar, if mundane, circumstances.

into them and they became the first human beings. Set down on the cold earth, they were denied fire by Zeus and seemed doomed to die of hunger or cold. Prometheus visited lame Hephaestus's forge on Lemnos and stole a brand of holy fire to warm his creatures and cook their food. Zeus was not amused by what even he could not reverse: his potency was hedged by Moira, the setter of limits.[118]

The great classicist Arnaldo Momigliano[119] said that, after studying the Greeks and their gods for 50 years, he was still uncertain what either party expected or hoped for from the other. The Olympians might be honored, for whatever fearful or social purpose, but—unlike the commanding and solitary Jewish god—they posted no official code of conduct apart from the moderation implied by Apollo's Delphic trademark "mēden agān": nothing in excess. As the fate of Hippolytus proved, to worship one god (Artemis) and exclude another (Aphrodite) could be a fatal indiscretion; it was nothing like a "sin."

The penalty for Prometheus's insubordination was to have Zeus's two strongmen, Kratos (brute force) and Bia (violence), chain him to a remote Caucasian rock. For 30,000 years, his renewable liver was repeatedly and agonizingly pecked by an

118. Homer gives the impression that Zeus would happily have seen the Trojan War abandoned as a draw, but the quasi-abstract force, sometimes known as *anangke* (force), sometimes as *moira* (fate, which in Hellenistic religion became *tyche,* chance or luck), had preemptive authority over even the king of the gods. In the Christian God, reason and good reason were combined in the notion of providence. The pagan *Tyche* and its Latin equivalent *Fortuna* could be, and were, worshipped but, in common with deference to logic, entailed no belief in their moral qualities or providential purposes.

119. His greatness was not in stature. Only five feet three inches tall, he inspired deference, so Joseph Epstein reports, even from the towering and never unduly modest Hugh Lloyd-Jones.

eagle. The eagle was then shot down by Heracles, another su-
perhuman with uncertain accommodation on Olympus. In
exchange for the disclosure by Prometheus (a byword for fore-
knowledge) of the intelligence that would arm Zeus against
being supplanted, as his father had been, by the next generation,
Zeus agreed to a political solution to his standoff with the
charismatic ex-Titan. In (pseudo-?) Aeschylus's play *Prometheus
Bound*,[120] Prometheus stands for intelligence against the thug-
gishness of Bia. The moral seems to be that regimes can stay
in power through brutality but are, in the end, stunted by lack
of inventive, sometimes adversarial, skills. Aeschylus's wary
endorsement of decision by jury, not by tyrannical fiat, is
elaborated in the *Oresteia*.[121] The irrepressible Prometheus
proceeded to teach human beings how to appease the gods with
burnt offerings that smelled delicious when wafted to Olympian nostrils, while secreting the best cuts for their own feasts.

Mētis was parsed as a feminine aptitude, hence of dubious
constancy. As Themistocles and Alcibiades were to prove, anyone clever for one side might, if crossed, turn out equally
clever for the other. Homer's polymētis Odysseus is the definitive Greek of whom other Greeks should beware. Combining
charm with ruthlessness, cunning with courage, mutability with

120. Some scholars suggest that *Prometheus Bound* may be the work of
Aeschylus's son.

121. See the translation (and introduction) by Frederic Raphael and Kenneth McLeish (1979). De Romilly's *La Grèce antique contre la violence* argues
for the Greek desire for a nonviolent way of resolving conflict. Under the
Promethean myth lies the message that gods require human modification.
Christians sometimes call Jesus a mediator; when he announces that "the
letter (of the divine law) kills," he plays the Promethean role.

persistence, he was the quintessential survivor.[122] Odysseus had the luck to have his subtle glamour and good name preserved by Homer's neglect of his venomous treatment of Palamedes, who either never appeared in the *Iliad* or was effaced from the authorized version.

In myth, Palamedes is said to be the inventor of four letters of the Greek alphabet (theta, xi, chi, and phi). He was also responsible for conscripting Odysseus to honor his oath to Tyndarus and to his overlord, Agamemnon, and fight in the Trojan War in order to redeem Menelaus's honor and recover his wife. An oracle had warned Odysseus that he would not return for twenty years and would be no richer for his service. When Palamedes came to Ithaca, Odysseus yoked a horse and an ox to his plow and, to avoid the draft, pretended to be crazy by sowing salt instead of barley. The clever visitor took the infant Telemachus and put him in line to be trampled. Obliged to halt his team and concede his sanity, Odysseus was outwitted and shamed into going to Troy. As the siege dragged on, his grudge against Palamedes was reinforced by the latter's regular dispatch of booty to his home on the convenient island of Euboea.

A credible Roman legend has it that, in 458 B.C.E., Lucius Quinctius Cincinnatus was plowing his fields when he was told that the Senate had appointed him dictator in order to save a Roman army that had been surrounded by the Aedui. Having accepted the commission, Cincinnatus took just over two weeks to lead a relieving force and save the day. He returned to Rome in triumph, resigned his office, and resumed his place at the

122. See Marcel Detienne and Jean-Pierre Vernant, *Cunning Intelligence* (1978).

plow within the month. Cincinnatus is said to have repeated
his military success and shown the same modesty when he was
eighty years old, though the second military operation, for
which he refused any reward, took him a week longer.

Odysseus went to Troy, but his grudge against Palamedes
was not canceled by panhellenic team spirit. According to non-
Homeric sources, he forged a letter from Palamedes to the
Trojan king Priam offering to betray the Achaeans. Odysseus
then dug a hole near Palamedes' tent and buried a stash of gold
to serve as evidence of his treachery. Arraigned for treason,
Palamedes sought help from his father Nauplius by writing
messages on oars that he tried, without avail, to float across the
sea controlled by his grandfather Poseidon. Palamedes—an
early instance of being too clever by half—was court-martialed
and stoned to death. Neither Odysseus nor that other hero of
the Trojan War, Diomedes, was ever criticized by gods or men
for bearing false witness.

16.

The fabrication of literary works and documents is a very old,
sometimes frivolous story. The *Diaries of the Trojan War,* allegedly written by Dictys of Crete, Idomeneus's supposed companion, were said to have been discovered, in the reign of Nero,
when an earthquake breached a Cretan cave.[123] Antonius Diogenes' *Wonders beyond Thule* were held to be modeled on a
manuscript discovered by Alexander's soldiers after the siege

---

123. In 1983 Hugh Trevor-Roper, a scholar of a rigorously skeptical nature and sardonic style, was deceived (by money and vanity) into the hasty
authentication of Adolf Hitler's palpably bogus diaries.

and capture of Tyre.[124] *The Donation of Constantine,* on the other hand, is a purposefully forged decree in which the emperor Constantine the Great (272–337) appears to deliver authority over Rome and the western Roman Empire to the pope of Rome. Composed probably in the eighth century, it was used, especially in the thirteenth century, to certify claims of political authority by the pope of Rome. It belongs in the category of forgeries too useful not to be validated. *The Protocols of the Elders of Zion* is a still-current instance, often cited as if, so to say, kosher by Muslim polemicists. Under Hosnai Mubarak's presidency, it was protracted into a 16-part series by Egyptian state television. Although revealed as a blatant forgery early in the 1920s, the *Protocols* continue to feature in the libraries of "faith schools" subsidized by British taxpayers.

What survives of ancient Mediterranean civilizations is a montage of historical events, original texts, sites, and artifacts set in what scholars have decided are accurate, or at least plausible, patches and confections. One specialist[125] in classical Greek fragments suspected that when ancient sources quoted "lost works" by earlier ones, as Diodorus Siculus does the "*Phrygia poiesis*" of Thyometes," there might well be an element of skittish parody or outright fakery. The play between credulity and credibility continues to be in flux: as Tim Whitmarsh

124. Whitmarsh, *The Second Sophistic.* The *Oxford Classical Dictionary* dates the Dictys fiction a century later.
125. Felix Jacoby (1876–1959), who described such bogus sources as "Schwindelliteratur." Cited by Lionel Pearson in *Early Ionian Historians* (1939). In the 1st century C.E., the Roman critic Quintilian ironized about those who invent authorities with confidence because "those who never existed cannot be discovered."

acknowledges,[126] authors who were, until recently, dismissed as second-rate or secondhand have received freshly clipped laurels from academics in search of a relatively neglected topic. The Greek past often lacks reliable agreed dates; until some time after the eighth century B.C.E., its writing had no common script. The first written notation, incised on clay tablets in Mesopotamia and in Minoan Crete, was for accountancy and tax collecting. It took patient (as it happened, amateur) intelligence to discover that the Minoan shards found on Crete were encoded in a primitive form of Greek.[127]

Theseus's galley, like his own character, supplied a metaphorical bridge between legendary past and practical present. In mythology, Theseus went down to Hades, accompanied by his reckless friend Pirithous, in order to kidnap its pretty queen, Persephone. After being invited to take a seat, the two bad boys began to be sealed into the stone of their thrones. A literal tearaway, Theseus ripped himself free, leaving strips of his thighs behind; the inextricable Pirithous was turned into a lapidary monument to his own insolence. In his historical role, a sensible Theseus was celebrated as the *oikistes* (founder) who mustered a sprawl of Attic villages into the walled city of Athens. Hero-worship and the construction of shrines and temples stood for social cohesion.[128] In the Mycenaean age, which

126. See his *The Second Sophistic,* in which Flavius Philostratus of Lemnos "once inadequate, even injudicious[, is] . . . now seen as the towering figure of Greek literary production under the Severans" (3rd century C.E.).

127. See *The Man Who Deciphered Linear B* by Andrew Robinson (2002).

128. See *Classics: A Very Short Introduction* (2000), by Mary Beard and John Henderson, where the placing of the Doric temple of Bassae (with three interior Corinthian columns) all by itself in the rugged middle of the Peloponnese is plausibly explained as a rallying point. Theseus was credited

ended in the eleventh century B.C.E., sanctuaries with famous tombs were adjacent to the kings' palaces. The most famous surviving instance is the walk-in *tholos* outside Agamemnon's Mycenae, excavated by the gold-digging Heinrich Schliemann in 1876.[129]

The skill of Phaleron's shipwrights rendered it difficult to detect where or when the antique vessel captained by Theseus had been caulked or patched. In maritime practice, the slug-like bivalve *mollusc teredo* and its larvae sapped the durability of Greek ships. Their inroads constantly required new pitch and the replacement of rotten planks. Linen mesh was used to bind ships' timbers, as it was for nets to catch tuna (or wild boars). It could be spun so fine that one pound of linen yielded several miles of thread. Not even the best-maintained trireme was likely to last more than 25 years.[130] Yet it continued to be claimed that the annual tribute that Athens paid to the sacred island of Delos was carried in the same ship, *Paralia* (the Coaster), that had brought Theseus home in triumph from Knossos. Its serial renovations furnished a philosophical puzzle: how many timbers had to be replaced before it could no longer be considered identical with the ship on which the hero sailed to Crete? The question suggests that, in daily life, definition is not a matter of discovering conclusive formulae, of the kind that

---

with enduring power to draw people together around his putative tomb when Cimon repatriated his supposed bones from Skyros in 475 B.C.E.

129. C. W. Ceram's *Gods, Graves and Scholars* (1954) is the classic, enjoyably anecdotal account of Schliemann and Co.'s entrepreneurial style of archaeology. For a more thorough study, see *Progress into the Past: Rediscovery of Mycenaean Civilization* by W. A. McDonald (1990).

130. John R. Hale, *Lords of the Sea* (2010).

Socrates sought to locate by quizzing his friends, but of pragmatic fixation.

The Greek word for truth, *aletheia,* is a negation, not an assertion: it means literally "not-forgotten-ness." The initial *a-,* known to grammarians as the "alpha privative," negates what follows. Plato's grand notion that human standards derive from a more or less vague memory of eternal and immutable Ideas issues from the belief, primed by etymology, that human beings' immortal souls have to cross the river of Lethe (forgetfulness) toward physical birth. The truth—*a/letheia*—was what stayed in the best minds while in transit. Although *psyche* is a feminine noun, the human soul, lacking physical qualities, was of its nature asexual. Logically, therefore, the souls of both men and women could have had a "sight" of the unchanging verities, before being consigned to a physical body. This may account for Plato's surprising decision to hold women eligible for "guardianship" in his ideal state and for the notion of asexual love/comradeship between clear-headed members of his ruling élite. The female sex had to be included, for reproductive purposes, in the republican top class, but the admission of females to administrative parity was a bold leap into equality of the sexes, impelled perhaps more by Platonic logic than by appetite.

The Christian doctrine of the immortality of the soul, primed by Platonism, derived its primordial "necessity" from play on the Greek *aletheia,* which, after translation as "truth," leaves no playful trace. The Christian notion of love, the asexual sentiment of *agapē,* resembles a generalized form of the philoxenia with which Homeric princes greeted each other. An early meaning of the verb *agapao* is to welcome or embrace. Jesus's recommendation that we should love our neighbors as ourselves can be seen as a sublime extension of the reciprocal genialities of Greek hospitality (a tradition which

is by no means dead, at least outside of Athens). It is also prefigured in the spiritual comradeship that allowed Plato's male
and female guardians to consort without the divisive complica-
tions and selectivity of sexual desire.

Fundamental truths are sometimes declared to make men
free: "In the beginning was the Word," says the authorized version of St. John's gospel, assuming equivalence between the
Greek *logos* and the English *word*. What is proclaimed as true
can be used, often, to lend authority to dogma. Logic may articulate alleged "truths" and tabulate their mutual compatibil-
ity; it does nothing to prove or disprove them. In the fifth
century B.C.E., *logos* was a suitable term both for counting
and for calculation; it could express esteem, worth, and significance. To "have *logos*" for something was to be inclined to
take it seriously; it never promised its validity. Heracleitus of
Ephesus, who delighted in being cryptic, said that one could
not "discover the boundaries of soul, even by traveling along
every path, so deep a *logos* does it have." St. John's pious trick
was to attach the certifying notion of *logos* to Christianity
alone.[131]

The paradigm of the use of the word *logos* in ancient Greek
is when Thucydides says of Periclean Athens that it was "logō
men" (in theory) democratic; "ergō de" (but in practice) what
mattered was the *arche* (command) of its "Olympian" first man.
The capacity, in theory at least, to rise above piety or partisan-
ship in order to assess human life is a uniquely Greek contribu-

---

131. In the 7th century C.E., Isidore of Seville compiled a voluminous
etymological study of classical literature that preserved numerous exemplary
passages which would otherwise have been lost. Informed rumor promises
that he is in line to be the patron saint of the internet.

tion to civilization. There is in the Old Testament a contrast between the conduct of kings and the chiding of prophets, but no radically new or contrary ideas emerge until after the destruction, in 70 C.E., of the Second Temple in Jerusalem, when the king and the prophet are said to become one in the incontrovertible person of Jesus Christ.

Polytheism seems to have encouraged early philosophers, especially those resident in the cities of Asia Minor, to generalizations which, having little to do with particular gods, transcended national boundaries. Perhaps because they were denied access to power in their native cities, individual thinkers sought to trump political realities by a kind of mental imperialism. Masters of truth, such as Parmenides, embraced creation in an overall logic to which their rare intelligence claimed privileged access. The notion of the golden mean (attributed by some authorities to Daedalus in his flight instructions to Icarus, not to fly too low or too high) was a philosophical revision of the Apolline slogan "nothing in excess." A man could rise above the temptations of power and self-indulgence by a measured response to life. This attitude was an ingredient of Socratic irony and, in due time, of Stoic aloofness. It implied that philosophers knew better than politicians how life should be lived. This has rarely disposed them to ignore opportunities for advancement when wealth, kudos, and power beckon.

17.

In Greek usage, *mythos* meant no more than "story," especially of the kind retailed by word of mouth. Hesiod's *Theogony*, composed sometime around 700 B.C.E., ranged a lively selection of stories about the Olympian gods into hexametrical order, but carried no scriptural warrant. Although it is now hard to see Hesiod as Homer's superior, in the early fourth century B.C.E. Alcidamas—a Sophist from Elea, in northwestern Asia Minor—depicts him defeating Homer in a poetic mano a mano, because he celebrates the uses of peace, not war.[132] Alcidamas stands as nice provincial evidence of the danger of taking Plato's scorn for "the Sophists" as necessarily righteous: siding with the Messenians, who were reduced to helotry by the Spartans, the Elean sage denied that slaves were naturally different or inferior, as Aristotle later claimed and Plato was too fine to question.

Myth's double role, fabulous and minatory, has been sustained by philosophers and divines, ancient and modern. The retreading of myth and scripture as "allegory" concedes that old stories may not be literally true, but insists that they retain moral validity.[133] Religion, it is argued, can be taken to embody eternal precepts, even if hellfire, or the resurrection of the body, is relegated by sophisticates to rhetorical fancy.[134] In science, the label of truth is now attached to whatever is true enough to be a viable working hypothesis until disproved or

132. The comedy of *odium academicum* is nicely illustrated by the fact that Nietzsche's attribution of this (fictional) encounter to Alcidamas was scorned by contemporary scholars, including Ulrich von Wilamowitz-Moellendorff (1848–1931). According to Arnaldo Momigliano (*Development of Biography*), a papyrus published in 1925 (Michigan 2754) confirmed Nietzsche's assertion, whatever his earlier source.

133. Philo Judaeus of Alexandria, in the 1st century C.E., interpreted the Old Testament as essentially allegorical.

134. The logical impossibility of proving a negative proposition renders atheism a gauche assertion of the order whereof, as Wittgenstein's translator put it, "one should not speak." This has not disposed Jean-Paul Sartre, Christopher Hitchens, or Richard Dawkins to remain silent.

rendered obsolete by more comprehensive theories.[135] Only tautologies are immune from disproof or improvement (they can still become trite). Outside of the field of ideology and creed, the view of Plato's old antagonist Protagoras[136] has prevailed: man is the measure (and measurer) of all things. Ancient scientists and medical writers[137] may prefer mundane explanations, but they are prone to pitch what are purported to be neutral ideas in terms with persuasive moral undertones. The claim that man is "rational" is a venerable instance: Aristotle's assertion that reason is the distinguishing characteristic of human beings all but underwrites Plato's claim that the philosopher should be king, because the most rational kings had to be philosophers whose *aretē* (special quality) is reasoning. Even if human beings, alone among animals, are capable of reason, that claim by no means entails that they are always, or even often, reliably rational.

135. In *Ethics and Language* (1944), C. L. Stevenson's notion of "persuasive definitions" analyzed how philosophers and ideologists "verify" their own propositions and theories by defining their terms in a tendentious way. What seems to follow is already implicit in the first steps of the argument. The ontological argument for the existence of God is a classic instance; by first claiming "existence" to be an attribute and then defining the deity as the possessor of all attributes, God is "proved" necessarily to exist. The late Richard Rorty was an extreme advocate of the volatility of what we choose to call "truth."

136. In Paul Cartledge's formula, Protagoras made man "the measure of things that are *that* they are, of things that are not, that they are not." In Laurent Binet's 2015 intellectual fantasy *La septième fonction du langage*, the title "Protagoras" is granted uniquely to the prevailing world champion philosopher.

137. Galen (129–199 C.E.), the most influential and prolific ancient writer on medical matters, was unusual in being both eclectic and undogmatic. He wrote at length on philosophy but also practiced empirical physiology. He undertook anatomical dissection on animals, "preferably apes," according to the *Oxford Companion to Classical Literature*.

Whether any ancient Greeks did "science" in anything approaching the modern sense is questionable; but their "philosophy"—a term first used by Plato—was distinct from anything propounded by anyone in either the Old or the New Testament. Strains of lyricism may have spread from Middle Eastern scriptures into Sappho and other poets, but the pursuit of "scientific" truth, beyond sacerdotal control, has no ancient source outside what Nietzsche called "those Greeks."

Aristotle's polyvalence set the style for centuries of academic activity. The appropriation of his metaphysical ideas by the Roman Catholic Church had dogmatic consequences. The Church also adopted the Stagirite philosopher's condemnation of lending money at interest. Since the whole of the Western economy came to depend on it, Christian hypocrisy made "the Jews"[138] emblematic of the wicked, indispensable practice of usury. Aristotle's magisterial status also allowed his declaration of the "naturalness" of slavery to serve, if incidentally, as a warrant in the post-classical world, at least until the end of the American Civil War. In a similar spirit, the scope of philosophy—regularly crowned "the queen of sciences"—was defined by the aristocratic assumption that serious intellectual ideas, being abstract, were incompatible with physical labor. In the first century B.C.E., Cicero summed it up with candid conceit: "The work of all hired men who sell their labor and not their talents is servile and contemptible." Such men belonged (like all "barbarians") to a different and lower echelon of mortal life.

This distinction chimed sweetly with the condescensions of imperialism. Christianity followed the flag. The "heathen"

---

138. When, strapped for cash, Byron, quite the philo-Semite, referred to going to "the Jews," he meant moneylenders in general.

were spiritual barbarians. Christian clergy and missionaries, of whatever competitive strains, administered their *logos* to congregations cowed by Toledo steel, gunpowder, and the Maxim gun.[139] Belief was a quicker route to salvation than knowledge, which—as Genesis promised—ripened on a doubtful tree. Creed trumped science and cramped thought as it never had in polytheistic Hellas. Even before the Renaissance, the art and literature of the ancient world supplied a two- and three-dimensional treasury that piqued officious Christendom with reminders of sexual, political, and intellectual liberty.

Karl Marx's early study of ancient philosophy left an imprint on him. Empedocles' *neikos* and *philia* (conflict and comradeship) were reconciled in communism's ambition to accelerate history through class warfare to a blissful final state. Marx's new social order proposed to redeem the despised laborer:[140] physical toil became the source of all wealth. The workers were postulated as the new élite; but that righteous class was soon to be capped, and captained, by the Communist Party, whose Central Committee creamed pontifical infallibility with the mandate of the people. Once in power, it incarnated the workers' interests, whether they liked it or not. Stalin was Epicurus with an efficient secret service. Yet Marx's

139. A machine gun of British manufacture which, according to Wikipedia, the missionary Henry Morton Stanley took with him to Africa. The Gatling gun, much used in British India, was of the same useful order.

140. When he inverted Hegel's notion of the dialectic, Marx announced that previous philosophies had described the world, but that it was now time to change it. He filched this dictum from Francis Bacon, who said, more than two centuries earlier, "the duty of philosophy is to transform, not to contemplate." The history of human thought is a game of tag. It is also not short of pickpockets.

underlying, neo-Epicurean fear was of the lumpenproletariat, the loutish barbarians beyond the garden gate whose riot might overrun civilization, derail the dialectic, and abort the coming of the Golden Age.[141]

18.

The cult of reason never abated the Greek dread, and experience, of violence and the irrational.[142] If Zeus was said to be just, he was not worshipped and appeased because he was good, but because—like his emblematic lightning—he was feared and unpredictable.[143] As for Ares, the god of war, no one questioned his divinity; few worshipped his bloody-mindedness. The *Iliad*'s Achilles accepts that success in battle is the sole worthy ambition for a hero: better to die young and glorious than to survive in

141. George Thomson (1903–1987) discovered the prototype of the classless state in the "primitive communism" of early Greek communities before the differentiation of labor. He also posited a connection between the invention of coinage and Western philosophy. See his *The First Philosophers* (1972).

142. E. R. Dodds's *The Greeks and the Irrational* (1951) broke the mold in which the image of the ancient Greek civilization had long been cast. It is tempting to see the sentimental reading of ancient Hellenes as a covert endorsement, not least by Percy Bysshe Shelley, of Athenian skepticism at the advent of Pauline Christianity. In Jewish philosophy, *segulah* is the characteristic quality of a substance which, nevertheless, does not figure in its formal classification. A familiar illustration is laughter: although humans may be the only creatures who laugh, the ability to laugh is not part of the definition of "human." In a medical context, segulah indicated a "faculty or power belonging to a drug, stone or plant that cannot be explained by the rational principles of Greco-Arabic medicine": Maud Kozodoy, *The Secret Faith of Maestre Honoratus* (2015).

143. For a now-classic account, see Hugh Lloyd-Jones, *The Justice of Zeus* (1983).

obscure, banal longevity. In the *Odyssey,* however, when Odysseus descends to Hades, on a visitor's pass, to see old friends (and his mother), the phantom of Achilles declares it better to be a simple peasant on earth than king of all the dead in the underworld.

Counterstrands thread through Greek literature from its earliest days. The emblematic antihero in the *Iliad* is the unsightly lowlife Thersites. A prototypical Spartacus,[144] he speaks out on behalf of the rank and file against the arrogance of the kings and their appropriation of what common soldiers have won. Class solidarity trumps Odysseus's personal aversion to Agamemnon: he whacks the insolent troublemaker with his staff. Thersites is reduced to the ranks and tearful silence; but he had an outspoken poetic counterpart in the works and person of Homer's near contemporary, the spiteful, antiheroic, lyrical Archilochus, whose stinging iambics have their rhythmic origin in Bronze Age entertainments in antique Mesopotamia.[145]

Unlike self-effacing Homer, Archilochus lodged splinters of his personal life in his serrated verses. If the *Iliad* and the *Odyssey* had a single author, little is known of him except that he is said to have been blind. Homer's in/sight resembled that

144. The charismatic Thracian gladiator who, in the 1st century B.C.E., led the widespread slave rebellion that threatened, for a long moment, to overthrow the Roman social order. It was repressed, with grim brutality, by Marcus Licinius Crassus, who lined the road from Capua, where the gladiators had been based, with thousands of crucified slaves. In Germany after World War I, Marxist revolutionaries called themselves Spartacists. Howard Fast's novel *Spartacus* was made into a film, directed by Stanley Kubrick, starring Kirk Douglas. Contrary to current Hollywood myth, Kubrick told me that Dalton Trumbo's scripted contributions were mostly worthless.

145. M. L. West, *The East Face of Helicon* (1997).

of the "blind seer" Tiresias, whose experience of sex as both a man and a woman inspired T. S. Eliot to call him "old man with wrinkled dugs." Asked in which incarnation he had more pleasure, Tiresias responded that the female orgasm was nine times more enjoyable. The silencing and seclusion of women never quite allay male fears that women have a secret superiority that the enigmatic Mona Lisa, for instance, appears to impersonate. In Greek vase paintings, the mirror and the spindle stand, with whatever ambiguity, for feminine self-satisfaction. Males are never portrayed looking in the mirror; Narcissus is the exception who underlines the rule.[146]

Homer's supposed tomb has been renovated on the bleak north side of the Cycladic island of Ios. His best monument is the preservation of so much of his work. Archilochus was a native of small, marble-rich Paros, a few miles from Ios, in the Cyclades. His poetry survives only in jagged fragments, like parting shots fired in posterity's face. Passersby were warned that his tomb was a sanctuary for wasps (Homer's, on Ios, is adjacent to the beehives where the island's famous honey is made). Hesiod anticipated the Parian in first-personal complaint, but his reproachful hexameters, in *Works and Days,* lack the velocity of Archilochus's iambic bullets. Hesiod depicted himself as a Boeotian rustic at odds with the "kings" who sided with his brother Perses ("the tricky one") to do the poet out of his share of the inheritance from their father, a disillusioned

---

146. See Françoise Frontisi-Ducroux and Jean-Pierre Vernant, *Dans l'oeil du miroir* (1997). According to Ovid, Roman women favored the sexual position in which they were on top. J. P. Sullivan said that this allowed them to "control the action." Richard Seaford notes that there is an Apulian (southern Italian) vase painting in which a man (said to be Pentheus) is looking in a mirror, but the reflection he sees is female.

Asiatic Greek immigrant from Cyme. Archilochus's prickliness
is encapsulated in a trademark couplet: "The fox knows many
tricks, the hedgehog only one; but it's a beauty!"[147] The polite,
prolific Plutarch, a family man of the first and second centuries
C.E., conceded that the Parian had genius, but he applauded
Hesiod (a fellow Boeotian) for reproaching his brother without
reviling him; he also rates him above Homer because he is more
useful to the community.

Archilochus (literally, "company sergeant") wrote about
his lusts, his battles, and his grievances. Soloist, hellraiser, and
the likeliest adaptor of iambic meter for Greek use, he was
praised in antiquity as Homer's equal, but never became canonical: his genius set deplorable examples. If Plato was a
censorious admirer of Homer[148] (he winced at the levity of the
Homeric gods), he could scarcely deny that the *Iliad* promoted
courage and comradeship. The character of Thrasymachus, in
The Republic,[149] is a prosaic revival of the polemic contrarian

147. Isaiah Berlin gave the title "The Hedgehog and the Fox" to a famous
1953 essay comparing the wide-ranging observations of Tolstoy with, for
instance, Dostoyevsky, who relied on a single defining vision of the world.
Berlin later affected to be embarrassed by the categorical solemnity with which
readers responded to his High Table allusion to Archilochus.

148. Homer did not lack defenders. Probably in the 1st century C.E.,
Heracleitus the so-called "Allegorist" (no relative of the Ephesian philosopher)
took lengthy and precise pains to show that Plato was wrong to take Homer
literally when he "honors all divine beings with exceptional expressions of
feeling, because he is divine himself . . . away with Plato, the flatterer, Homer's
dishonest accuser. . . ." See Donald A. Russell and David Konstan, *Heraclitus:
Homeric Problems* (2005). At much the same period, the Jewish savant Philo
of Alexandria was reading the Old Testament in an allegorical light.

149. It would be pompous to translate Plato's *Politeia* in any but the
traditional terms, but "government" is truer to the Greek. Plato did not
advocate republicanism, except in the sense that his proposed polity was not

from Paros. Archilochus, martial bastard, did nothing to endorse reticent rectitude; females were for fucking; rank stank. Odysseus's errant fidelity to patient Penelope had its come-off-it antithesis in Archilochus's obscene derision: Neobule, whom he claimed to love as a girl, is pilloried, after she has been denied him, as a fat old tart. In late republican Rome, clever Catullus would echo Archilochus when it came to vilifying his once beloved and idealized Lesbia. Archilochus's attitude to authority aped that of Thersites: "Now Leophilos is boss, / Leophilos is tops; / It all comes down to Leophilos; / Leophilos, you get me?" Six centuries later, Catullus again played tag with the Parian: "I'm not too interested, Caesar, whether I please you or no. / Who are you anyway? Mr. Black or Mr. White?" Caesar responded by inviting the poet to dinner.

The ancient world has almost always been construed with moralizing seriousness; laughter is assumed to be ephemeral and unworthy.[150] A Calvinist preacher once leaned over the pulpit to tell the giggling young Byron: "No hopes for them as laughs!" Ribaldry had an early source in Mesopotamia, where the *aluzinnu*—"the slanderer, the farter, the shitter"—played the gross fool and dared to make fun of priests.[151] A thousand

---

monarchical. Cicero's *De republica* was an homage to Plato, not a translation, but its title reflected back onto Plato's work.

150. In a largely laudatory review of Giulia Sissa's *Sex and Sensuality* (2008), Peter Green remarks that the author "is too earnest to see the funny side of much she describes." Since the teaching of classics was for centuries in the hands of Christian clerics, humor was close to godlessness, especially in regard to celebrations of sexual pleasure.

151. See West, *The East Face of Helicon*, p. 496. A scrapbook of Middle Eastern lore, much of which leaked into the Greek world, it might have been calculated, in a meticulous way, to take the conceit out of Hellenists. West is said to have been "reticent in seven languages." Martin Bernal's

years later, outrageousness becomes a staple element of the Greek theater's *alazon,* the boastful rascal whose antics Aristophanes underwrote when he mocked whatever Athenians were disposed to take seriously: war, the repression of females, the rights of the demos, and Socrates' affectations of rising above the common herd.

The unsmiling Spartans banned Archilochus's "shameful and indecent" poems from their state, "lest it harm their children's morals more than it benefited their talents."[152] The Spartan idea of a proper poet was Tyrtaeus, who—in the seventh century B.C.E.—wrote marching songs, even though, like Hephaestus, he was said to be lame. It was alleged, at one time, that Tyrtaeus was a renegade Athenian schoolmaster who lent his voice to the laconic Spartans, as Ezra Pound did to Mussolini, Pablo Neruda to Stalin.

 The complete works of Archilochus were still available in Alexandria in the second century B.C.E. Their irreverent rasp was, however, not popular enough to merit transcription onto parchment for mass circulation. After the invading Arabs destroyed the great ancient libraries, access to the poet's lines was limited to shreds cited by grammarians and critics. The few remaining copies of his work were incinerated in 1204 C.E., when the Crusaders pillaged the Byzantine city's Greek Orthodox treasures (including the four horses who now prance above

---

pugnacious *Black Athena* (1987) and its sometimes reckless sequels know no such caution.

 152. Valerius Maximus, *Memorabilia.* Archilochus is only the first of many poets—Catullus and Martial were others—who embarrassed pedagogues by the brazenness of their verses. Today, he would be liable to anathema as a homophobe, not that he showed any signs of fear of stoopers or stabbers.

the lintel of St. Mark's Cathedral in Venice) and burned the libraries for the greater glory of western Christendom and the enrichment of La Serenissima.[153]

In un-Homeric apocrypha, Thersites was said to be of noble stock, perhaps, like Archilochus, a resentful hybrid.[154] Robert Graves[155] tells an unsourced story that Thersites, having survived the Trojan War, gouged out the eyes of the Amazon queen Penthesilea, with whom Achilles had fallen in love even as he ran her through. When this deutero-Thersites accused the hero of "filthy and unnatural acts" as she lay dying, Achilles struck the impertinent lout "so hard that he broke every tooth in his head and sent his ghost scurrying down to Tartarus." Archilochus—his father Telesicles a Parian dignitary, his mother perhaps a slave—is Thersites' articulate double:[156] his verses have the same stroppy attitude to senior officers.

> I don't go for your popinjay general, the strut,
> The dinky hair-do, and the dandy facial.
> Give me a runt with a bow-legged look,
> An unbudging stance to rely on, heart to match.

153. The bitterness engendered by this treachery, like memories of the Roman conquest of ancient Hellas, may do something to explain the gleeful defiance of Greek politicians during the recent rupture between Greece and the memory-cleansed signatories of the Treaty of Rome.

154. Edmund, in *King Lear,* speaks for those disinherited by the bar sinister with his cry "Now, God, stand up for bastards!"

155. In his very popular *Greek Myths* (1955).

156. Almost 1,000 years later, the hobbling and scowling Thersites figures in Lucian's *Podagra* (Gout), written in elegiac couplets in which the pentameter is routinely mocked (notably by Ovid) for being a foot shorter than the preceding hexameter.

Archilochus's unabated grudge against nice society came of his broken engagement to the beautiful daughter of Lycambes, a rich Parian who promised his daughter Neobule to the poet over a ritual bonding dinner and then went back on his word. The poet's response is said to have been literally lethal: unable to bear his unremitting derision—"Daddy Lycambes, what's the big idea? / Who did your silly head in? / It worked all right before. Now the folks / Rate you good only for ha ha ha!"—Lycambes and his daughters hanged themselves in shame.[157]

Archilochus disdains modesty. His vision resembles that of the randy donkey (*myclos*) to which he compares the humped and hairy outline of the battleground island of Thasos, facing gold-rich Thrace,[158] where, in later centuries, both Thucydides (whose father Olorus owned mines in the region) and Alcibiades had profitable investments and found places of refuge remote from vindictive voters. The double uses of "fuck," literal and metaphorical, supply the fork on which, again and again, Archilochus prongs Neobule and her sister: "Like a Thracian or a Phrygian drinking beer through a tube / She sucked; doing hard labor at the stoop" (fragment 42). One of his longer

157. Perhaps they merely hung their heads in shame. Hyperbole is an antique Greek figure. A century after Archilochus, Hipponax of Ephesus also sported a lethal reputation: when the sculptor Bupalus and his brother Athēnis caricatured him, Hipponax lampooned them so viciously that they too are said to have hanged themselves. He was no kinder about females: "Woman is twice a pleasure to man, / The wedding night and her funeral."

158. Thrace was also famous for the quality of its timber, which was used for masts and oars. In his poem 4, on the skiff that carried him home to Sirmio, Catullus says that its timbers came from adjacent Cytorus.

fragments embodies the sweet and sour mixture that Catullus
came to echo, if never duplicate:

> I'm having nothing to do with it.
> I advise doing the same. . . .
> But if you're for it, desire stiffens you. . . .
> There's someone in our place
> Who's hotter than hot
> A beautiful, tender young piece. Ask me,
> There's nothing wrong with her at all;
> Make her your own.
>   . . .
> Under the lintel and through the gate,
> Don't "Don't" me, when I'm on course
> For the green, green pasture.
> Get one thing straight:
> Neobule? Anyone else can have her.
> Twice your age, her girlish charm
> Ain't girlish any more. . . .
>   . . .
> That's what I said. And laid the girl
> In blossoming flowers, soft cloak
> For a cover, her neck in the crook
> Of my arm . . . she held her breath
> Like a fawn . . . and with gentle hands
> Caressed breasts, the charm of her budding,
> Encircled her beautiful body. . . .
> Let her have it, my white manliness,
> Golden hair in my grasp.[159]

159. My translation.

Archilochus may have written unspeakable things for the first time in Greek, but clay plaques from Mesopotamia, in the Babylonian period, a millennium before the invention of iambics, show scenes of a man "entering a woman from behind while she bends over and drinks beer through a tube standing on the ground."[160] Martin West extracts a parallel to fragment 43 (". . . his prick / overflowed like a Prienian / stall-fed donkey's") from the prophet Ezekiel: "In the days of her youth, when she played the whore in the land of Egypt and was infatuated with her lovers there, whose members ('meat') were the members of asses and whose deluge (of semen) was the deluge of horses." The context is of two sisters (symbolizing Samaria and Jerusalem) who have abandoned themselves to lechery and grown old in it—"a parallel to the two daughters of Lycambes."

Literal and metaphorical bastard, Archilochus's martial image of himself comes early in what is left of his work. One version of fragment 2 has been translated as: "Spear in hand, I down my kneaded barley ration, / Spear in hand, Ismarian wine; I down it, / Spear in hand, when I pass out." Modern classical studies are likely to be based on the assumption that students will not know either Latin or Greek. Philology, with its dry, demanding curriculum, has little appeal in today's universities. The dependence of classical studies on translation seems inevitable. The question remains, *which* translation?

The cited lines of Archilochus, 15 words in the original, seem unambiguous. The late Geoffrey Kirk, Regius Professor of Greek at the University of Cambridge, rendered the first two

160. West, *The East Face of Helicon.*

words "en dori" as "in my spear" in one place and "on my spear"
in another. Both are consistent with the lexicon. Yet Douglas E.
Gerber, a scholar as highly rated as Kirk, has argued that "en
dori" is better rendered "on board ship"; if that is not right (as
he concedes is possible), he recommends "under arms," which
seems more plausible: the mercenary relies on self-help. Students who cannot check the original have to rely on the selective
intelligence of translators. Literal translation (which, in this
random case, favors "spear") does not always convey the specific sense; but improvements can be misleading. Even seemingly unambiguous transliterations (for instance, of *democratia*)
can dock words of part of their intended meaning. What is lost
in translation is, at times, less unfortunate than what is found
in it.[161]

In his advertisements for himself, Archilochus neither
solicited the gods nor praised them. Yet when he accuses Lycambes: "You turned your back on the great bond / Of salt and
table,"[162] the charge is of something close to sacrilege. Feasting

161. For a lively defense of "creative" translation against, for example,
Robert Graves's piety, see J. P. Sullivan, *The Poet as Translator: Ezra Pound
and Sextus Propertius* (1964). Peter Green has remarked that Graves's own
etymologies, in his classic *Greek Myths*, are open to question. Mary Beard
has bearded Graves on his failure to acknowledge the single main source of
his apparently very wide reading. Vladimir Nabokov favored the translations
which, in obsolete pedagogic terms, he called "ponies." After his own version
of *Eugene Onegin* was denounced by Edmund Wilson as "literal" to the point
of perversity, the two quondam friends never spoke again.

162. "Hebrew cereal offerings were seasoned with salt that was 'the salt of
the covenant before God.' In Arabic idiom 'salt' stands for the food shared,
even if it was only milk and had no salt in it. A man bound to another by this
bond would say 'There is salt between us'": West, *The East-Face of Helicon*.
West holds that the once presumed uniqueness of Greek culture has many
links, references, and similarities to earlier alien, not least Semitic, civilizations.

was a convivial ritual. Before the mythical Tantalus served up his own son Pelops as a specialty dish, men and gods could figure on something like an equal seating plan at top tables. The term "parasite," which now implies servile greed, is not disparaging in early Greek (as "sycophant" is).[163] Modern literal translation adds an anachronistic sneer. Ancient parasitism was simply "dining alongside" and implied communion.[164] When, in the *Iliad*, Priam comes to plead for the return of his son Hector's body, Achilles' arrogance softens into sympathy as they eat together.

Although Archilochus did participate in Paros's battles against its large neighbor Naxos (where he was eventually killed), he went to war for money, not for heroic *kleos* (fame). Poetry was his one priceless activity: "I serve the lord Enyalios,[165] but I

The quite modern social distinction between those seated "below the salt" and their betters indicates that inferiors should not have exorbitant expectations. "Parasite" has come to label one who lacks the means or status to render reciprocal hospitality. See Claude Lévi-Strauss, *The Raw and the Cooked* (1969).

163. The longest word in Liddell and Scott's Greek lexicon, *orthro-phoito-sykophanto-diko-talaiporoi,* was used just once by Aristophanes in *Wasps.* It is translated as "early-prowling-base-informing-sad-litigious."

164. The Bacchic procession, in which Dionysos leads his followers to tear animals apart and gobble them raw, preserved the tradition of gods and mortals eating together in a riotous parody of communal celebration. In Euripides' *Bacchae,* Dionysos literally disorganizes the city that fails to pay him respect. Its king, the prohibitionist Pentheus, is dismembered and chomped by his own mother. In Nietzsche's mold-breaking dichotomy, Dionysos and Apollo are the poles between which Greek shades of meaning are slung. Structuralism is a more sophisticated elaboration of Nietzsche's illuminating, if now questionable, scheme.

165. A.k.a. Ares, the god of war, whose "guest-gifts" are wounds and slaughter.

know / The Muses' lovely gift." He has no shame in announcing that on one occasion, in unseemly retreat, he dropped his round shield ("I can get another one just as good"), the better to live and fight another day. As an individual hit-man, Archilochus could get away with chucking it in occasionally. When infantry battles came to be fought by citizen-armies, a man's shield served to defend his neighbor's flank as well as his own. A mid-seventh-century Corinthian vase is the first surviving illustration of a regimented hoplite phalanx. Spartan mothers bade farewell to their warrior sons by saying, "Come back with your shield or on it" (the shield could serve as a stretcher or a bier). To return alive and shieldless was proof only of desertion.

For all his sweaty egotism, the randy Archilochus did not lack divine admirers. The Naxiot who killed him in battle, Callondas, nicknamed Corax (the Raven),[166] was denied access to Apollo's shrine at Delphi because he had caused the death of a man "sacred to the Muses." Corax protested that he was undeserving of *miasma* (the outcast's sacrilegious taint) since Archilochus had been killed in honest man-to-man close combat. He was then advised to propitiate the poet's soul by pouring libations in a place called Taenarum, in the far south of the Peloponnese, a destination likely to keep him out of sight for a tactful period. A fanciful elegist warned Cerberus, the three-headed watchdog of Hades, against the advent of Archilochus and "the mighty potency of his bile." Two centuries later, Aristophanes told a friend, with scathing flattery, "The longer you write, the better; like the poems of Archilochus." The Parian's

---

166. With seemingly premonitory wit, Archilochus wrote a poem in which a crow figured in a vulturous role. Ted Hughes published a volume entitled *Crow* in 1970, which has been widely glossed.

barbed brevity began a tradition that outlasted and outsmarted epic prolixity.

  A generation younger than Archilochus, Alcaeus of Mytilene, on Lesbos, assumed the same poetic license and confessed to throwing away his shield in battle. So did the Roman poet Horace (Quintus Horatius Flaccus);[167] after surviving the battle of Philippi, in 42 B.C.E., on the losing "republican" side, he relied on Greek poetic precedent to excuse his surrender to Octavian, later surnamed Augustus. Horace's generous imperial patron presumed on the "divine" descent of his adoptive father, Julius Caesar, to put his ascendancy beyond mundane criticism. Caesar had claimed the Trojan prince Aeneas, the son of Venus, as his ancestor. Once Augustus was the sole master of Rome, Virgil (another, if even less bellicose, youthful opponent of Octavian) was commissioned to lend poetic grace to his presumption of divine lineage. The Roman "New Testament" (to the *Iliad*'s "Old"), the *Aeneid* was a sublime instance of what came to be called "agitprop": literature designed to serve an ideology.

  As Christianity became the dominant Mediterranean religion, the ancient world was edited or interpreted to lend venerable luster to later doctrine. Virgil's Fourth Eclogue, written before 37 B.C.E., was labeled "messianic" because it celebrated the imminent arrival of an infant who would inaugurate

---

167. Horace's father, a freed slave, sent his clever son to be educated in Athens. There may well be a certain homage to Archilochus in Horace's satire in which he confesses to being overexcited when making love to a girl. A quite recently discovered Archilochan manuscript describes how, perhaps with prophylactic consideration (not that it sounds like him), he spills his white seed on a girl's pubis. Ian McEwan makes witless use of the same not unusual donnée in *On Chesil Beach* (2007).

a great New Age. Thanks to his prophetic réclame, Virgil would become Dante's guide in the underworld. By contrast, the emperor Caracalla, who may not have been an entirely nice man, was vilified because he persecuted Christians. It was not to his credit that, as a schoolboy, he rescued a Jewish pupil from a bullying mob. The notion that firsthand observers merit belief is rehearsed, to prize-winning effect, in *Jesus and the Eyewitnesses* (2006) by Richard Bauckham. Dates are corrected, with a due parade of scholarship, to ensure that the apostles' reports are seen to be as contemporary as they are held to be incorrigible. In practice, legal cross-examination often reveals that impartial witnesses are capable of seeing what they elect to believe is true.[168]

19.

Pindar, in the early fifth century B.C.E, vaunted himself on avoiding "the deep bite of malice." Archilochus might have responded that if his sword was for hire, at least his pen was not. He never sold his genius, as the elaborate Pindar did, to whoever would pay for elaborate eulogy as a champion at the games. Five hundred years later, Pindar's fellow Boeotian Plutarch also deprecated the venom with which Archilochus loaded his verses, but he did quote him with approval in his

168. Despite knowing that Solon's archonship in Athens preceded Croesus coming to the throne of Lydia by 35 years, Plutarch—in his biography of Solon—chooses to underwrite the story of their meeting because it is edifying and, although the chronology is unreliable, so many "witnesses" attest to it. The argument for the existence of God *e consensu gentium* (on account of the general agreement of so many people) is similarly appetizing.

essay *On Tranquillity of Mind,* which was rarely the poet's
condition:

It's nothing to me, Gyges' gold on gold,
Jealousy has no hooks in me, envy neither
Of the gods and what they do or did. Tyranny

A la big shot? I don't buy it personally![169]

Gyges straddles the line between fable and reality. He fails
to figure in the index of the fat *Oxford History of the Classical
World,* but he is said elsewhere to have been king of Lydia, in
the center of Asia Minor, between 685 and 657 B.C.E., which
coincides with Archilochus.[170] According to Herodotus, Gyges
was the captain of King Candaules' guard. The monarch was
so proud of his queen's beauty that he insisted that Gyges conceal himself where he could see her naked. The queen suspected his furtive presence (even Aristotle believed that looking
at something involved a sort of invisible, projected touching
through the eyes). She later summoned Gyges to choose between
instant execution and killing her unworthy husband and replac-
ing him on the throne and in her bed.

When Gyges had been crowned, he sent rich offerings
to Delphi in order to procure Apollo's endorsement. It seems

169. My translation. In *Iliad* 9, 378, Achilles claims that he cannot be
bought with all the money in Orchomenos or Egyptian Thebes, city of
100 gates. Independent pride trumps all riches. Sappho was more realistic:
"Wealth without quality is no harmless neighbor. / The two together hold
happiness's peak."

170. According to Paul Cartledge, Gyges features in Assyrian texts as
"Gugh."

that he succeeded: his dynasty, the Mermnadae, continued to rule. Anthropologists used to argue that the queen's invitation implied that power in Lydia passed automatically through the female line. On the same principle, it was supposed that, having solved the entrance test set by the Sphinx, Oedipus succeeded Laius as king of Thebes simply by virtue of marrying Jocasta.[171] Gyges' military backup (and his promise of suitable rewards) is a likelier explanation of his successful usurpation than any formal matriarchal scheme.[172] He became a byword both for slyness and as the inventor and distributor of coinage.

Scarcely the first cocky upstart to seize power, Gyges had need of rented muscle in order to retain it. Coinage was especially handy when hiring mercenaries. Their fate depended on the preservation of their paymaster's position in a country where they had no other stake. If he fell, however, they were glad to be able to take the money and run. Unlike land, coinage was portable; by its very currency (the "runniness" that Heracleitus noted), it dispersed economic power into the hands of people with low social standing. Wealth had previously been lodged in temples, or in the strong rooms of palaces (grimly fortified on the outside, gilded and bejeweled within), where it was often hoarded, unproductively, by priests and kings. Circulation generated prosperity and, especially among seagoing people, encouraged freedom of movement and enterprise.

171. Laius, Oedipus's natural father, is said to have been an early practitioner of homosexuality, which, in the mythic context in which he is to be found, was not creditable. *Sans complexes,* Oedipus did not, of course, have any idea that Jocasta was his mother. Ambition primed desire.

172. My novella *The Hidden Eye* (1990), illustrated by Sarah Raphael, is a gloss on Herodotus's account of Gyges.

The Greek word for law, *nomos*, derives from the verb *nemein*, to distribute: it was first applied to the allocation of food and drink after sacrificial ceremonies. In Mesopotamian epic, man was created to feed the gods. Priests, kings, and their acolytes grew fat on the accumulation of tithes and tribute. The invention of currency allowed transactions of many kinds to elude central control. Treasure was locked up and sterile; money promoted exchange without courtly ceremony. *Nomisma*, the usual Greek for coin, derives from *nomidzein*, generally translated as "to deem" or "to recognize" (hence, to believe to be true or valid). The word originally meant "to acknowledge as valid," first of a god and, later, of coinage. Nomisma can also be the "collective confidence, inspired by Athena, which rallies an army."[173]

Richard Seaford harps on the coincidental use of money and the rise of philosophy. Ideas too crossed frontiers, had no privileged owners, could be used anywhere, and applied to everything. Accountancy, like philosophy, simplifies and unifies: it both reduces and enlarges human calculation. Geoffrey Lloyd linked the growth of Greek scientific rationality with the "ideology" of democracy that encouraged "mass participation in political debate."[174] Is the connection beyond question? In practice, Athenian democracy was a means for making corporate decisions, not least about war and peace. The masses, who were going to do the fighting, participated by the weight of their votes rather than by any exercise of dialectical skill or dispassionate examination of cases. In fifth-century Athens, *parrhesia* (free speech) was most often, and most glibly, exercised by

173. Seaford, *Reciprocity and Ritual,* p. 143.
174. See G. E. R. Lloyd, *Early Greek Science* (1970) and the same author's other works.

aristocratic or wealthy leaders of political factions. It is pretty
to suppose that scientific "debate" was fertilized by democracy,
but how many "scientists" had their researches ratified by
popular vote or even discussed in public assemblies?[175] Ma-
jorities make decisions; they cannot determine or discover
truths. None of the first philosophers came from democracies.
No native Athenian before Socrates was famous (or infamous)
for his disputatious speculations.

If only as a result of its lack of full-time officious personnel,
polytheism's plurality of cults and rites fostered divergent
fancy. Ancient Greek religion had a range of practices; it was
short on formal doctrine. Despite their (and the common
people's) superstitious caution, pagan priests—never any part
of an established "church"—set no a priori limits on speculation, as the Holy Inquisition would later. In 1633, Galileo Gali-
lei was shown the instruments of torture as an argument against
persisting with the anti-Aristotelian notion of a heliocentric
universe. The idea that the earth went around the sun was first
proposed in the third century B.C.E. by Aristarchus of Samos,
a Greek philosopher not in fashion with the Holy Inquisition's
pot-bellied Cardinal Bellarmino.[176]

175. The quasi-Archimedean fate of the great scientist Antoine-Laurent
de Lavoisier (1743–1794) during the French Revolution hardly encourages
the notion of popular rule as a sponsor of original thinking. The chairman
of the tribunal that sentenced him to the guillotine, Jean-Baptiste Coffinhal,
was unimpressed by his genius: the Republic, he said, had need neither of
chemists nor of clever men.

176. A range of storage jars, now quite valuable antiques, were marketed
bearing his tubby image.

At the end of the sixth century B.C.E., Cleisthenes needed no theoretical prospectus or divine sanction for the constitutional changes by which the common people of Athens were allocated to ten new tribes, each named for a suitably iconic hero. Decimalization tidied the machinery of power but had no metaphysical overtones. Cleisthenes' reforms came well after the ideas propounded by the first Ionian philosophers, none of whom is known to have visited Athens and most of whose speculations had little overt relevance to practical politics. The reactionary Athenian pamphleteer who goes by the nickname the Old Oligarch said of the advent of popular government that, given that it was not virtuous (morally elevating) but economically energizing, it was "explicable, despicable and invincible."[177] Cleisthenes' remodeling of Athenian politics coincided closely with the traditional date on which the Roman people—led by its patrician élite—evicted the Tarquinian kings and instituted the annual election of two consuls in the place of hereditary monarchy. The common people (the plebs) were given some limited powers, but it took many years for the SPQR (Senate and Roman people) to achieve its abbreviated concord.

For Thucydides, a stable society did not require philosophical falsework: he favored moderation, honest government, and the avoidance of gratuitous suffering. If democracy had a

---

177. The converse is that when economies falter, democracy weakens. The economic model promises to reconcile contentious classes, creeds, and clans only as long as it is successful. Hence, for eminent instance, the European Union, being essentially an economic construct, cannot rely on any sentimental adhesive to keep it together. Its elaborately confected "democracy" has no tenacity. Having abated the 20th-century European fear of internecine war, it has small emotional claim on the populations it now affects to homogenize and from whose company Great Britain has recently voted to distance itself.

stimulating influence on thought, not the least of its effects was to provoke contrary ideas. Plato's *Republic* declares a magisterial cure for the disfiguring influence of rhetorical persuasion (peitho) on public opinion. Josiah Ober has it that in the " 'regime of truth' . . . one of the key 'truths' on which democratic Athenian society depended [was that] citizens were simultaneously equals and unequals." In one of Theophrastus's satirical archetypes, the Oligarchic man complains of having to sit next to inferiors in the Assembly.[178] Theophrastus (372–?287 B.C.E.), wit and philosopher, succeeded Aristotle as head of the Lyceum, the Athenian lycée, or secondary school.[179] "Theophrastus," divine talker, was a nickname bestowed on the prolific philosopher for his exquisite eloquence. Some say that he lived till he was one hundred and four. Legend also has it that he did not begin work on his famous *Characters* until he was ninety years old. He died regretting the brevity of human life.

In a democracy, political equality (one person, one vote) can coexist with economic differences, so long as the flux of money encourages common aspirations and makes gambling a hopeful pursuit. When things go well, social inequalities can be mollified by legislation or by the more or less willing generosity of successful citizens.[180] In societies articulated by popular

178. Josiah Ober in *Persuasion: Greek Rhetoric in Action,* ed. Ian Worthington (1994).

179. Like Aristotle, Theophrastus was not a native Athenian, although he was a master of Attic prose: he came originally from Eresos, in Lesbos. For all his many decades in the city, it is said that one day when he was buying herbs, the woman in the market could tell immediately, from his intonation and manner of speech, that he was not a born citizen.

180. See below for the "liturgies" exacted from ultra-rich Athenians. Charitable foundations are the modern equivalent in the US and elsewhere.

opinion, difficult subjects tend to be reserved for cloistered consideration. The truths of mathematics, for eminent Platonic instance, are held to be beyond dispute and likely to yield the abstruse key to universal, extraterritorial knowledge. Bertrand Russell spent years on the *Principia Mathematica*, which he believed could provide a basis for absolute certainty. After Wittgenstein proved to him that mathematical "knowledge" was of its nature tautologous, Russell lost faith in the supreme authority of abstract cerebration.[181]

Cleisthenes' contemporary Heracleitus of Ephesus constituted himself a deliberately enigmatic, oracular pundit. To parody his own style, he did and did not expect to be understood. He derided the eclectic garrulity of those—in particular the well-traveled Pythagoras—who affected omniscience. In their diversity, the so-called pre-Socratics had in common only the claim that all things are One: hence subject to a common logic. It was a homogenizing notion in a fractious world. Heracleitus declared fire to be the primary element, but its mystic power fused with the "all-transforming," impersonal nature of money. War was the father of all things, but its god, Ares, was known as "the gold-exchanger": glory became second to loot.[182] The word *ousia* embraced both wealth and, more significant, "being," a term that Martin Heidegger appropriated

181. Russell passed on the bad news to Gottlob Frege, whose work was founded on the same notion, on an Austrian station platform. Frege thanked him politely. It was, in effect, the end of the alchemical hope that mathematical certainties could entail some kind of "necessary" common logical and *ethical* scheme. Physics may be universal, but it has no morals.

182. Heracleitus set the fashion for enigmatic philosophy. Those with an appetite for arcane exegesis may care to consult Clémence Ramnoux's *Héraclite, ou l'homme entre les mots et les choses* (1968).

in the invention of twentieth-century "existentialism." As Seaford puts it, "If any single thing may be imagined as the *ousia*
of which all else consists, it is not land but money."[183] Money
was a thrilling and unnerving social solvent; it gave the hope
of parity even to slaves who had at least the possibility (more
frequent in Rome than in Greece) of buying their freedom.

Gentlemanly aversion to trading was habitual until the
middle of the twentieth century. Scholars—who often aped the
social attitudes of their betters—tended to concentrate on war,
literature, theology, and philosophy. In time, economists[184] came
to theorize about the inexorable machinery of what a medieval
pope called "the world's game." Greyness and eminence became
fused: economic advisers whisper in the ears of the powerful;
they are liable to find themselves wincing in the limelight only
if things go wrong. The mathematical model licensed impersonal analysis; statistics have no conscience.

Trade made the world go round, but tradesmen were associated with the furtive backdoor (so too were doctors, in
England, until 1901).[185] Never ceasing to tramp after conquerors,
historians remained stylishly disdainful of money-making. No
Roman has been more loudly written off than Marcus Licinius
Crassus (115–53 B.C.), who grew uncountably rich without having to leave Rome in order to pillage foreign lands, as Sulla,

183. See Richard Seaford, *Money and the Early Greek Mind* (2004), p. 256.
184. A sublime term derived from Xenophon's practical essay *Oikonomikos*,
on estate management. Economists have come to replace the oracular voices
of Delphi and Dodona in the formulation of predictive, often ambiguous,
utterances. That "economics" has a Nobel Prize testifies as much to the quasi-
prophetic, minatory role of its clerisy as to the utility of their prescriptions.
185. When Frederick Treves saved King Edward VII's life by a timely ap-
pendectomy. His knighthood dignified the medical profession.

Pompey, and Caesar had. Crassus—nicknamed "Dives" (Rich Guy)—died an unlamented death on an ill-conceived late-life expedition to conquer the Parthians, proving only that wealth could not purchase glory. Caesar, on the other hand, has unrivaled standing and lends his name to the noblest form of tyranny. Who cares to recall that he was impelled to military greatness not only by his envy of the great Alexander but also by his precarious finances and uneasy political prospects? By the deaths of at least a million Gauls, he added wide lands to Rome's *imperium* (empire) and secured an illustrious, if not quite unrivaled, place in the history he was sharp enough to compose for himself.[186]

20.

In *The Republic*, Plato appropriated and elaborated the myth of Gyges: in the version presented by Plato's brother Glaucon, Candaules' captain of the guard is changed into a shepherd who unearths an antique gold ring, which, when twisted, renders him invisible. Thus empowered, the twister is able to seduce Lydia's queen, murder the king, and assume the throne. The purpose of the Platonic recension is to ask whether anyone would elect to be virtuous if he could do anything he chose, without being detected. Glaucon wonders who would keep his hands off what was not his own, if he could lift what he liked out of the market or go into houses and lie with anyone at his

186. Winston Churchill took his cue from Caesar. As soon as Germany was defeated in 1945, he determined to get his own account of the victory into print before anyone else. In effect ostracized by the electorate, Britain's great wartime leader had time and motive to spread himself and his *kleos,* martial fame, with the aid of Clio, the muse of history.

pleasure, or kill enemies or release friends from prison. He would in all respects be like a temporary god. Socrates' response is more pious than plausible: anyone, he says, who abused the power of the ring of Gyges by committing crimes would have enslaved himself to his appetites; the man who chooses not to be self-indulgent remains in Apolline control of himself and is therefore happy.

Plato's rewrite is indebted to another Herodotean story. During his self-imposed rustication from Athens, Solon is said to have paid a visit to King Croesus, the last and richest of Gyges' royal line.

> On the third or fourth day after, he bade his servants conduct Solon over his treasuries, and show him all their greatness and magnificence. When the visitor had seen them all, Croesus addressed this question to him. "Stranger of Athens, we have heard much of thy wisdom and of thy travels through many lands, from love of knowledge and a wish to see the world. I am curious therefore to inquire of thee, whom, of all the men that thou hast seen, thou deemest the most happy?"
>
> This he asked because he thought himself the happiest of mortals: but Solon answered him without flattery, according to his true sentiments, "Tellus of Athens, sire." Astonished by what he heard, Croesus demanded, "And why do you consider Tellus happiest?" To which the other replied, "First, because his country was flourishing in his days, and he himself had sons both beautiful and good, and he lived to see children born to each of them, and these children all grew up; and further

because, after a life spent in what our people look upon as comfort, his end was surpassingly glorious. In a battle between the Athenians and their neighbours near Eleusis, he came to the assistance of his countrymen, routed the foe, and died upon the field most gallantly. The Athenians gave him a public funeral on the spot where he fell, and paid him the highest honours."[187]

Their ages make it unlikely that, in fact, Solon and Croesus exchanged two words together (no more did Queen Elizabeth I and Mary, Queen of Scots, whose only meeting takes place in Friedrich Schiller's play). Herodotus, however, cannot resist the story that when Croesus had been defeated by Cyrus the Great and was about to be burned alive, he remembered Solon's modest notion of happiness and conceded the point, in a loud voice. Moved by Croesus's heartfelt cry, Cyrus is said to have reprieved his captive and made him his friend.

For all Solon's fine sense of immaterial values, the transition from archaic to historical Hellas, under his aegis, is marked by the invention and circulation of money. Until recently, classical scholars mimicked the gentlemanly tradition of never talking about money. As Seaford shows in *Money and the Early Greek Mind,* the exchange of cash for goods and services subverted old hierarchies. If Gyges did not invent a way of distributing portable rewards to mercenary enforcers, he was prompt to make use of them. Coins both kept him in power and, because they had a general use, according to their value,

---

187. Herodotus's *Histories,* trans. John M. Marincola (Penguin Books, 1996), with my slight modifications.

they "dispersed unqualified economic power [in due course] into the pocket of the ordinary citizen."[188] Princely gifts and honors, with their specific, reciprocal magnificence, were depersonalized by the circulation of money. Coinage unhinged ancient connections and led "to the detachment of performance from specific function."[189]

One of the demystifying effects of cash may have been to detach hero cults and mystic initiation from the priesthood and promote their secular deconstruction in tragic theater. The amalgam of verse forms and the reworking of myth engendered both entertainment and social criticism. Plato and John Calvin deplored the loud laughter that can disorganize static solemnity; theatrical innovation and the stage's aptitude for surprise subverted immutable social and religious formalities.[190] Money, like clowning, was a solvent of unsmiling ceremonial. In *The Money God*, the Chinese philosopher Lu Bao, of the third century C.E., greets it as "a spiritual thing: it has no rank and yet is revered." Banks often resemble classical temples. In modern practice, mammon alone talks a universal language.

188. Some anthropologists claim that the first "pocket" in which small change was carried was the human mouth.

189. Seaford, *Money and the Early Greek Mind*. Leon Trotsky, following Karl Marx, imagined that in the classless society, following the revolution, man would revert to the polyvalent versatility of which capitalism (money) had deprived him and would "again" be a gardener in the morning, an artist in the afternoon, and what all else besides. There is no evidence that men were ever in such a paradisal condition.

190. T. S. Eliot's 1935 play *Murder in the Cathedral* is, albeit inadvertently, post-religious: it makes play with Christianity.

21.

The *Iliad*'s treatment of females is both courteous and cursory.
Sitting alongside old Priam, whose kingdom she is doomed to
ruin, the lovely Helen is a rueful spectator. She is the pretty pawn,
captured en passant by Paris as his reward for judging that Aphrodite was the most beautiful of the goddesses. His handsome
verdict made sure that Hera and Athene would be unforgiving
enemies of his native city. Paris's brother Hector's exemplary wife
Andromache serves the narrative principally to add pathos to her
husband's fate; her own is the consequence of events in which she
has no active part. Greeks paid lip-service to the justice of Zeus,
but Homer gave them little reason to trust in its fairness: after the
fall of Troy, the blameless Andromache was enslaved, her son
murdered. The Trojan women suffer all the horrors of rape, murder, and slavery; but when Menelaus again sees Helen, the cause
of all the trouble, and the cuckolded husband draws his dagger,
the mythical leading lady has the star quality to bare her unfallen
breasts and secure reprieve. In his antiheroic *Helen,* Euripides,
quick to bitch, had to remark that she had put on weight.

As the same playwright showed in *The Trojan Women,*
what Byron and his Regency friends called "the sex" might lament, but they had to endure. Vexatious and unstable, women
were of small account in public. Even Hector, who treats his
small son Astyanax with such tenderness when he takes fright
at his father's crested helmet, grows impatient with Andromache's apprehension: "Go home and think about housework,"
he tells her. "Leave fighting to men."[191] In 431 B.C.E., Pericles

---

191. *Iliad* 6, 490. In the *Odyssey,* when Odysseus's wife, the patient
Penelope, seems about to end her silence and take practical measures
against the parasitic suitors, her own son, Telemachus, tells her to stick to her

gave similar domestic advice to Athenian women whose husbands or sons fell in the war. They were expected to suffer the consequences of male virtue without complaint. After twenty years of war, Aristophanes' *Lysistrata* lent females the loud voice that common practice never allowed them. Dread of females getting together was exemplified in the myth of the warlike Amazons and in the uncivil practices of the bloody-minded bacchants.[192]

In his whole history, Thucydides names 431 individuals (not including those listed as endorsing a particular agreement); seven are female.[193] The failure of Greek women to feature among antiquity's leading killers may have more to do with want of opportunity than with feminine virtue. When 300 Thebans made an unprovoked and ill-prepared night raid on the small neighboring city of Plataea in 427 B.C.E., they were driven off by Plataean resistance. Its artillery was supplied by the female population, which pelted the intruders with tiles from the rooftops.

---

housework. The most famously outspoken woman in the late classical world was the mathematical prodigy Hypatia, who was lynched by a Christian mob in Alexandria in 415 C.E. because she dared to have her own ideas (and made no mystery of menstruation).

192. Lamentation at funerals is often Muslim women's only unstoppable way of expressing indignation at male violence. In mourning, Greek women habitually expressed grief by throwing themselves on the ground. Funerals can be dangerous occasions. Solon proposed that the parade of mourners be limited to avoid violence between hostile clans of citizens. The initial *A* in "Amazons" is another instance of alpha privative: Amazons were supposedly so called because they cut off one of their breasts (*mazoi*), in a singular mastectomy, in order to make it easier to draw a bow.

193. The figures are taken from Geoffrey Hawthorn's *Thucydides on Politics* (2014).

The Thebans returned, with Spartan support. In the negotiations that followed, the Plataeans reminded the Spartans that they had no quarrel with Sparta and had done nothing to provoke them. They also pointed out that, in 490 B.C.E., Plataean soldiers had been the only allies to fight alongside Athens against the Persians at Marathon.[194] The boast was justified and tactless: the Spartans had turned up at the battlefield of Marathon too late to do anything but congratulate the victors, tersely no doubt. As for the Thebans, when the Persians invaded Greece in 480 B.C.E., they had taken the advice of the Delphic oracle (which lay within their sphere of influence) and sided with the Medes. How could such trimmers now be allowed to decide the fate of the descendants of those who fought at Marathon? The Spartans did not deny Plataea's gallantry in the past; in defense of their present ruthlessness, they said only that, in effect, that was then and this was now. After this exchange of civilities, Plataea was razed to the ground, its male population slaughtered, and its women and children sold into slavery.

The Spartans' military reputation sustained their hegemony but never rendered it self-sufficient: their allies, Corinth and others, had only to threaten the withdrawal or redeployment of their favors to impel Sparta to revise its diplomatic purposes. Neither of the principal opponents in the Peloponnesian War had the autonomy that might have sanctioned profitable coalition: each had at once to placate and to dominate allies for whom a dyarchy of Sparta and Athens would have entailed unrelieved subjection.

194. Although duly honored, the Plataean dead, like the brave slaves, were buried separately from Athenian citizens.

Thucydides tells the story of Plataea's martyrdom in laconic prose. Had he dramatized it at the same length and with the same rhetorical verve with which he depicted the standoff between the Melians and the Athenians in 416, the rape of Plataea might have stood forever as a prime example of the heartlessness of oligarchic realpolitik. Was Sparta's conduct any less despicable than that of the Athenians in the Cyclades? While they had no direct quarrel with the Plataeans, the Spartans dared not offend the Thebans, traditional enemies of the Athenians, although never Sparta's active allies in the war. Thucydides, like many liberal historians (which is not to say that he was one), was keener to spell out the mistakes of his fellow countrymen than to blacken their enemies. Due to his artful skill, the Melian Dialogue became an emblematic, one-sided illustration of the horrors of civil war. Pablo Picasso's *Guernica* (a revision of Goya's *Desastres de la guerra* and *Fusiliamentos del 3 de mayo de 1808*) performed a similar service.

22.

The archaic use of the word *doulos,* slave, does not imply immutable or "natural" inferiority, as it did in the fourth century B.C.E., when Aristotle certified all barbarians as "natural" slaves, thus warranting their subjection by his pupil, the not-yet-great Alexander. To be a slave in Hellas was often the result of misfortune and entailed, not least, sexual submission: after Troy was taken, Andromache was compelled to be the concubine of Neoptolemos, who had slaughtered her son Astyanax to appease the ghost of his father, Achilles. In *Eumenides,* Aeschylus dares to state, to a male audience, that males are the true parents of a child, females no more than convenient furrows in which to set the seed.

When the first Ionian adventurers crossed the Aegean and
founded the eventually prosperous Greek city of Miletus, they
took no females with them. Once established, they enslaved the
women of Caria (further to the south of Asia Minor), having
killed all their previous male attachments. Their offspring furnished Miletus with a new generation of hybrid citizens. The
Roman "rape" of the Sabine women is in the same tradition,
with a charming coda: the pregnant females parade between
the Romans and the returning, vengeful Sabine warriors and
convince them to be reconciled.

In Homer, slavery was degrading (it took away "half of
the *aretē* [quality] of a man"), but not always ignominious. It
denied equality, not sociability. In the *Odyssey*, Odysseus's faithful old shepherd Eumaeus regrets his master's absence because
he would have rewarded him with a house and land and a classy
wife. When Odysseus does get back to Ithaca, he punishes the
goatherd Melanthius because he sat down to eat with Penelope's
suitors, which implies that they had invited him. In modern
Greek, *douleiá* means work in general; the repetition "douleiá,
douleiá" suggests, with a sigh, that someone is overdoing it.

Slaves might be well treated, and sometimes freed (frequently in Rome), but slavery as an institution was rarely
questioned. The existential difference between free men and
slaves was that the latter had no family connections: they were
property. Socrates' pupil, the cynic Antisthenes, was exceptional in adopting a minimalist lifestyle, as if to demonstrate
that ownership of slaves was a needless luxury.[195] In the early
fifth century, the Athenians agreed to help the Spartans put

195. An anonymous epigram in the Greek Anthology warns that to "own
many houses and many slaves" is the road to ruin.

down a revolt by the Messenians, although liberation of the helots would certainly have weakened Sparta.

Once at war, however, each side did offer asylum to the other's enslaved work force. Athens first established a fugitives' refuge at Pylos, on the west coast of the Peloponnese (in what had been garrulous old Nestor's kingdom); then, on the turncoat Alcibiades' advice, the Spartans provided a similar facility, at Decelea, in northwestern Attica, to escapees from the inhuman conditions of the silver mines at Laurium. Some 20,000 availed themselves of the opportunity, thus depriving the Athenians of valuable revenue. Their lease of freedom was short: the Spartans sold them on to the Thebans.

In Rome, an ancient law (confirmed, in the first century C.E., by the emperor Augustus) required that when a master was murdered, all the slaves in his household were to be tortured and then put to death. The rule had a terrible but plausible logic: it made it literally vital for slaves to police each other and to protect their masters. In 61 C.E., during the reign of Nero, the ex-consul Lucius Pedanius Secundus was killed in the middle of the night by a slave whom he had refused to free. All 400 of his urban slaves, including women and children, were immediately liable for execution. Tacitus reports that, as the case was being heard by the Senate, many of the common people, who never fraternized with slaves, were scandalized by the impending massacre.[196] Even some senators favored leniency.

---

196. Tacitus, *Annals* 14, chap. 42. Tacitus himself successfully pleaded the cause of a number of Africans who had been abused by the proconsul Marius Priscus, but he too made his peace with unjust emperors, not least Domitian, whom he outlived and could then depict in scathing terms.

So did Nero; he always doubted the loyalty of the senatorial class and was keen to stay popular with his allies, the plebs.

The conclusive case for upholding the law was made by Gaius Cassius Longinus, a proponent of the values of the old Republic (he later went into exile) and the greatest jurist of his day. His argument was coldly pragmatic:

> Grant impunity for such a crime and, if neither holding the highest office nor owning a large number of slaves gave Pedanius Secundus security, who will ever feel safe? Our fathers always distrusted the nature of slaves, even those who had been born in their own fields and in their houses and who, from infancy, had been raised in the affection of their masters. So now how can we, whose slaves come from a great diversity of peoples, practicing religions and following customs very far from our own (when they are not entirely heathen), keep them in check by any means but terror? It's true that innocent people will be sacrificed, but every exemplary punishment contains an element of injustice, visited on individuals for the well-being of people as a whole.[197]

197. See Tacitus, *Annals* 14, chaps. 42–45. Modern fear of alien immigrants was first declared in 1968 by Enoch Powell, a member of the British Parliament who had been a professor of Greek and a specialist in the New Testament. Citing Virgil's *Aeneid* (6, 37), "I seem to see the Tiber foaming with much blood," he predicted violent ructions if people of another culture (and color) poured into England. He was ostracized by his own Conservative Party, but his Delphic apprehensions have acquired a certain respectability in the face of the current flow of refugees and migrants into Europe from both Africa and the Middle East.

The "bond of terror" united the 900 senators who were "certainly not bloodthirsty . . . but prudent and realistic." While the executions took place, angry plebeian demonstrations were repressed by the Praetorian Guard, on whose hired loyalty every emperor, good or bad, depended.

Pedanius's murder occurred while Nero was still under the moderating, if waning, influence of his ex-tutor, the sententious Seneca, who asked leave to go into retirement a few months later. Having become enormously rich, Seneca offered, as a form of life insurance, to surrender a large part of his wealth to the emperor before excusing himself from privileged bondage. Nero never forgave him; but Seneca was granted a nervous lease of time, as a Stoic recluse, to devote himself to literary activities and affectations of happy modesty. In his forty-seventh letter to Lucilius, he recommended, if only in a wishful spirit, a more humane relationship between masters and the slaves who comprised over a third of the population of Italy, as they had of ancient Athens. Few histories mention the third-century C.E. neo-Platonist senator Rogatianus, who, less verbose than magnanimous, liberated his slaves, gave most of what he had to the poor, and stepped down just as he was about to take office as praetor, only one rung short of the supreme honor of the consulship. It is said that, when rich, he had gout and had to be carried in a litter. Poverty obliged him to take exercise and he was delivered from his affliction.

23.

The spiritual egalitarianism of Judaeo-Christianity was attractive to slaves (and to women such as Nero's wife, Poppaea Sabina), but neither St. Paul nor St. Augustine questioned the propriety of slavery. Jewish scriptures were alone in making open reference to the time when Jews themselves had been slaves in Egypt. This avowal, like their monotheism (and dietetic self-denial), was generally regarded with more contempt than respect. The Jews were alone in proclaiming that slaves who had escaped, and sought sanctuary with them, should not be returned to their owners, an attitude that was revived, north of the Mason-Dixon Line, in the years before the American Civil War. Until the defeat of the Confederacy, slavery itself was widely held to be warranted by virtue of its place in Greek and Roman civilization. Classically educated gentlemen were known to say that they would accept black men as equals when one of them proved proficient in ancient Greek. Phillis Wheatley (1753–1784), a black poet born in Senegal and transported as a slave to Boston, met the challenge, with small emancipatory consequence.

After the alarming experience of the long, almost successful revolt led by Spartacus, in 73 B.C.E., Roman society accommodated itself to the regular emancipation of, in particular, clever and useful slaves. Some became rich and independent, like Petronius Arbiter's fictional Trimalchio, the nouveau riche freedman whose caricatural vulgarity spices the surviving chapters of the *Satyrica*.[198] The freedmen of the emperor Claudius were the first, but never the last, to become decisive powers behind the throne.[199] Since their pampered lives depended

---

198. See, for instance, my 2001 translation and introduction. F. Scott Fitzgerald had the early idea of incorporating Trimalchio's Feast in the title of the novel that became *The Great Gatsby*.

199. In his forties, the ambitious Seneca was sentenced by the emperor Claudius to prolonged exile in Sardinia. He sought to ingratiate himself with Claudius's then all-powerful freedman Polybius by composing a long condolence letter of embarrassing effusiveness. When, thanks to his mother

wholly on the emperor's favors, they were more likely to be loyal than senators and knights (equites). The old Roman upper classes were often suspected, with justice, of more or less discreet nostalgia for the old Republic, in which their ancestors had taken timed turns to reap the dividends of the power now vested exclusively in the hands of the emperor and his entourage.

When Christianity became the imperial (and imperious) faith, the ancient dichotomy between masters and slaves was less abandoned than spiritualized: its refurbishment served to justify, if not demand, the coercion, torture, and killing of pagans, heretics, and unbelievers, especially "perfidious" Jews, whose evidence, in Christian courts, was deemed credible only when exacted by torture. The notion of the Hebrews' innate guilt and, during the Crusades, of the wickedness of the Saracen infidel reprised the "natural" inferiority previously ascribed to non-Greeks. The morality of the ancient world was transposed to make rejection of the Trinity, once its mystery had been officially defined, into a capital crime. Universal logic and unarguable doctrine converged in religious dogma; their union was then enforced, in philosophical and political ideologies, as the sole valid currency. The middle ground, central both to Greek democracy and to the Roman Forum, was foreclosed by church and state. The play of rhetoric that Plato found so loud and discordant was rendered formally illicit, except from the pulpit. The contrived spontaneity of Plato's Q-and-A-style dialogues prefigured the unquestionable answers of the catechism. Islam came to parody the same pitiless rectitude with regard to

---

Agrippina's machinations, Nero succeeded Claudius, the latter's freedmen were promptly dispatched. So too, not long after Seneca had been recalled to Rome, was Agrippina herself, by her son.

infidels, apostates, and fellow Muslims who, by self-righteous and demonstrative mutual carnage, honor what seem, to the outsider, to be trivial doctrinal variations.[200]

24.

The promotion of writers and poets as assessors of human (and divine) behavior tends to ignore their often obscure or marginal lineage. In Greece and in Rome, writing, like teaching, could lend dignity to articulate men of servile origin. Aesop, the great fabulist, was probably a slave in the seventh century B.C.E. on the intellectually fertile island of Samos. He was so successful an entertainer, and so spellbinding an orator, that he became the island's diplomatic envoy. In that role, he got so far above himself that he is said to have been pushed over a cliff in Delphi, after being accused of robbing the temple (temples doubled for safe deposits throughout antiquity).

Cicero's beloved secretary Tiro was an educated Greek on whose loyalty Marcus Tullius (surnamed "Chickpea," though few remark the fact) might have been wiser to rely than on that of his patrician friends. "Tiro" became a byword for a beginner, but he is more accurately remembered as a clever amanuensis who outlived his master (he died aged one hundred) and to whom posterity owes the assiduous collation of Cicero's papers. In the first century C.E., the Stoic evangelist Epictetus began life as a Phrygian slave of Nero's freedman Epaphroditus. Roman education was almost entirely in the hands of clever

---

200. Freud's observation of "the narcissism of small differences" has lost none of its savor.

Greek pedagogues like the one remembered as "plagosus," the whacker, by the poet Horace, himself the son of a freed slave. In the Greek and Roman theater, slaves are, like Beaumarchais' and Mozart's Figaro, less inhibited and more resourceful than their masters. While they might sometimes illustrate Auguste-Villiers de L'Isle Adam's mot "As for living, our servants can do that for us," the majority of ancient slaves lived in fear and were valued, if at all, as livestock (and its breeding ground). With heartless clarity, a slave was classed in Roman eyes as an "instrumentum vocale," a tool with a voice. In the age of Augustus, Publius Vedius Pollio fattened the lampreys in his private pool by throwing unduly talkative slaves into the water. Even the emperor, who had not scrupled to throw old friends, including Cicero, to the wolves, winced at the gourmet's callous extravagance.[201]

In the Roman world, both slaves and women were drawn in marked numbers to Jewish synagogues, where their curiosity must have been amiably received. Christianity—stigmatized as a "slave-religion," notably by Nietzsche—was at first not manifestly distinct from Judaism. It came to recruit adherents and martyrs from the same deprived classes. The Church was particularly virulent in denouncing Judaism, from which it sprang, as its diabolical rival. Once empowered, Christian clergy adopted, if they did not amplify, the hierarchical style of the pagan priests and rabbinic sages whom they had supplanted. The Trinity displaced, but never quite buried, Jahveh. The bishop of Rome took on the name of pontiff, which derived from the Roman office of pontifex maximus, a prestigious,

---

201. Joseph Epstein reminded me of this episode, reported by Ronald Syme, and also of the ascent of Epictetus.

part-time honor that Julius Caesar was pleased to procure. The Vatican Curia became the Roman Senate rehoused; many of its princely cardinals derived from patrician Italian families. Islam won converts by claiming to be a religion of social equals, although slavery, like the relegation of females, has been a persistent habit of its potentates.

25.

Sappho of Lesbos, an island famous for its beautiful females and for its poetic tradition, was Archilochus's junior by several years. Her Aeolian tenderness is complementary to his venomous quills: "I am not someone who likes to hit back," she wrote, "sooner a quiet spirit, mine." A great deal more has been written about Sappho than survives of her work; its shadow is heavier than the extant 5 percent of her seven books of poetry. Sexual politics have disposed activists to recruit Sappho to the lesbian cause, just as Constantine Cavafy has been recruited to theirs by purposeful male homosexuals.[202] Sappho certainly loved lovely girls: Peter Green cites Ovid's sly ambiguity, "Quid docuit Sappho nisi amare puellas?"[203] which means either "What did Sappho teach except to love girls?" or "What did Sappho teach girls except [how to] love?" or, of course, both.

In late republican Rome, Catullus took inspiration from both Archilochus and Sappho. He follows the former when vitriolic, in delicacy the latter, very closely in poem 51, "Et ille par esse deo videtur . . ." (That one seems to me as good as a god . . .

---

202. Notably Cavafy's not always masterful translator, Daniel Mendelsohn.
203. In the *London Review of Books,* November 2015.

who sits and watches you). On Martin West's reckoning, Sappho was influenced by the adjacent Semitic culture; he cites the Psalms: "I am poured out like water, and all my bones are dislocated; / My heart is like wax, it is melted within me." A Babylonian is reported to have said, "My eyes bulge, but see not, my ears are open but hear not." Amorous passion doubles with fear of demons. Sappho's fragment mentioning Adonis is the "earliest Greek evidence of cult for the West Semitic deity."[204]

It is modish to take the view that, in Sappho's time, "homoeroticism was by no means incompatible with heterosexual attraction." The more likely ancient distinction was between marital and passionate love, "the first associated with Hera, the second with Aphrodite."[205] Those who seek to recruit Sappho as a prototypical militant, sexually active feminist find little or no evidence in the work.[206] The Byzantine Suda (Lexicon) names her "shameful girl-friends" (Atthis, Telesippa, Megara), but it does so 1,500 years after the event.[207] Sappho not only wrote but

204. West, *The East Face of Helicon*, p. 52. Semitic seepage into Greek and Roman culture continued at least until the fall of Jerusalem in 70 C.E. Anti-Semitism was not a common sentiment until the triumph of Christianity made it an item of faith. Jews might excite derision (from Tacitus) or revulsion (from Juvenal), on account of their dietetic and other foibles, but there was no systematic persecution and a good measure of admiring curiosity.

205. See André Lardinois's introduction to Diane J. Rayor's translation of Sappho (2014). For a willfully reactionary, ultra-pedantic, richly informative treatment of Sappho and of modern translations in general, see Jeffrey M. Duban, *The Lesbian Lyre, Reclaiming Sappho for the Twenty-first Century* (2016).

206. In Monique Wittig's witty *Lesbian Peoples* (1979), "Sappho" commands a single blank page.

207. The modern, often lucrative, temptation is to find genital correlatives behind every literary mask. Colm Toibin's *The Master* (2005) does the business for Henry James, who is said by Hugh Walpole to have responded to the latter's practical overtures with "I can't, I can't."

also sang and played and, very likely, taught other girls to back her. The idea, propounded by the great Ulrich von Wilamowitz-Moellendorff, that she was some kind of finishing-school headmistress comes from overloading the word "teach," the common Greek term for rehearsing a chorus. In the ancient world, Sappho was eulogized for her verses (Solon determined to learn one of her pieces by heart before he died; Plato called her "the tenth Muse") and abused for her person: "contemptible and unprepossessing, swarthy of complexion and very short."[208]

In the first century C.E., the geographer Strabo said that "in all the centuries, no woman . . . could be said to rival her as a poet." Is his praise unduly partial? In the fragments of Sappho's work, even single words—"danger," "honey-voiced," "lyre, lyre, lyre"—retain the perfume carried on the pulse of her lines. It is possible that an early outbreak of *stasis* (Thucydides' term for civil conflict) forced her and some of her family to leave Mytilene, the principal city of Lesbos, and go into exile. One of her brothers, Charaxos, is said to have made a scandal by his expensive pursuit of an Egyptian courtesan called Rhodopis (Rosy Cheeks), the prototype of the *poule de luxe* who furnished Gustave Flaubert with indelible memories and syphilis.

Despite the pleasure she took in female company, Sappho is said to have committed suicide, by jumping from a cliff on the island of Leukas, off Epirus on the west coast of Hellas, after being jilted by her fiancé, Phaos. Whatever her actual tastes or practices, Sappho became an emblematic name. Lawrence

---

208. Today's Greece has a remarkable minimalist female poet in the (now elderly) form of Kiki Dimoula. Her *The Brazen Plagiarist* was published, in a Greek/English edition, by Yale University Press (2013). Like Sappho's, her themes are at once modest and universal.

Durrell, author of *The Alexandria Quartet*, wrote a verse play about her and named his daughter after her. Sappho Durrell became a lesbian and committed suicide. Her diaries claimed that she had an incestuous relationship with her father.

26.

Rebellion against fathers is recurrent in Greek religion:[209] no one can succeed, in divine or mortal circumstances, without violence. Before he could become king of the gods, Zeus had to supplant his father Kronos, who had previously castrated his father, Ouranos/Uranus (Sky), in order to take supreme power. Warned by an oracle that he too would be displaced by one of his own offspring, Kronos swallowed the first five infants as they were born. Then Rhea tricked her brother-husband, by wrapping a stone in swaddling clothes. While Kronos gulped the parceled dummy, she secreted the infant Zeus in a cave on Mount Ida in Crete. A party of rowdy young warriors, the Curetes, clashed spears against shields to drown the baby's bawling. Grown to potency, Zeus kicked Kronos so violently in the belly that he brought up his still undigested progeny. They were at once recruited as their youngest brother's adjutants. The regurgitated stone, previously mistaken for the infant Zeus, was installed in the sacred cave at Delphi and revered as the *omphalos*, "navel of the earth."

---

209. Jesus's cry on the Cross—"Father, Father, why hast thou forsaken me?"—has a faint Hellenic tinge. The Christian equation of Father and Son, mediated by the Holy Spirit, resolved conflict at the price of logic. Hence Tertullian's cry "Credo quia impossibile," the Latin, it might be said, for "It works for me." For a dissentient Jewish point of view, see Maud Kozodoy, *The Secret History of Maestre Honoratus* (2015).

Fierce old gods, displaced from power and penned beneath
the ground, haunted and fertilized the Greek imagination (even
in the twentieth century, George Seferis turned an antique
marble head in his hands with nervous awe). At the shrine of
the martyred patron saint of Naples, Januarius, miraculous
blood is said to appear three times a year in a glass reliquary.
Since Naples was originally a Greek city, tactful accommodation
arranged that Januarius, although Italian, should also be a saint
of the Greek Orthodox Church. René Girard argued that the
first sacrifices were of human beings: blood was a key component of the foundations of cities. Those who slay together stay
together. Girard claimed that many myths encoded bloody
formulae for placating dark forces. Their cryptic "words to the
wise" could be deciphered only by the initiated.

In Sparta and Athens, as in Judaea, kings were responsible,
above all, for observing sacrificial rites and the division of
victims between gods and men. Greed and duty were alike
monarchical; it was a pious obligation to finish every scrap of
the sacrificial beast; there was no ancient takeaway. The wine
and wafers used in Holy Communion are similarly reserved for
sacramental purposes.[210] Festivals, such as the Athenian Thargelia, at the beginning of summer, involved the expulsion of

---

210. In the Middle Ages, suspicious Christians accused neighboring Jews
of stealing the Host and maltreating it until it bled; this warranted righteous,
"reciprocal" bloodletting. Until well into the 18th century, the ancient martyrdom of Christians (in no very great numbers) was matched by the protracted
immolation of Jews by the Holy Inquisition, for the spiritual refreshment of
the faithful. This was secularized into the political anti-Semitism that made
the dispossession and murder of Jews into acts of civic virtue. See, for instance,
Hyam Maccoby's *A Pariah People: The Anthropology of Antisemitism* (1996),
and the same author's *The Sacred Executioner* (1983).

scapegoats, often condemned criminals, who took the evil out of the city on the day before the first fruits of the harvest were brought in from the countryside. Their elimination took place on the sixth day; on the seventh, offerings of ripening corn were paraded, along with the *eiresione,* a sort of Maypole, and new corn cakes baked. The well-being of the citizens depended on the harvest being received in the state of purity that Apollo impersonated. New fire was brought annually from Apollo's shrine at Delphi during the month of the Thargelia. The sixth day was particularly auspicious: it was credited with the birth of Socrates (and Artemis), and great victories of the Persian Wars—Artemisium, Mycale, and Plataea—were officially commemorated as taking place on it; so too, in due time, were the birth and the death of Alexander the Great.[211] This convergence synthesized the city's need regularly both to placate the mighty dead with blood and to purge itself of the taint of murdering the required victims. A sacrificial ox, once led to the altar, was induced to nod, by being offered food, and was then taken to have agreed to have its throat cut.[212] The blade that drew the blood was deemed guilty, not the man who wielded it.

211. See Robert Parker, *Miasma* (1983). The queen of England, actually born on April 21, 1926, has an "official" birthday in June, convenient for the ceremonial "trooping of the color" by her élite guards regiments.

212. See René Girard's *La violence et le sacré* (1972; translated as *Violence and the Sacred,* 1977) and *Des choses cachées depuis la fondation du monde* (1978). The opening scenes of Stanley Kubrick's *2001: A Space Odyssey* (1968) depict the first apes to turn murder into a binding ritual. A thigh bone flung triumphantly in the air mutates into a space capsule. In his *The Nature of Greek Myth* (1974), G. S. Kirk is unimpressed by the monotonous sprawl of much of Greek myth. Fighting in Greek waters during World War II may have taken the rosy tint out of Kirk's spectacles.

Wild animals could not be relied on to show the domesticated meekness needed for sacrificial charades. Only sheep, goats,
and oxen were regularly paraded to pious public execution. In
Greece and Rome, dogs might be sacrificed, mainly in covert
ceremonies[213] connected with childbirth and infant death. Macedonian armies marched out to war between the severed halves
of a dog. Under Xerxes' command, the Great King's armies proceeded to the presumed humiliation of the Greeks between the
two halves of the oldest son of a Lydian grandee, perhaps the
grandson of Croesus, who had requested his heir's exemption
from military service (three other sons had already enrolled).
Although neither Greeks nor Persians are conspicuous for their
tenderness toward animals, they are not on record as having been
entertained by deliberate cruelty. Any number of exotic wild
beasts, however, were dispatched to Italy with the sole purpose
of being, as Byron put it, "butchered to make a Roman holiday."

27.

The problem of how to contrive bloodless succession to power
in Greece, other than by royal inheritance, was not resolved
until lawgivers (often of alien provenance and hence, like eu-
nuchs, without family prospects in the city) were deputed to
devise codes of social regulation. In Sparta, the legendary Lycurgus ("wolf-worker") was revered as the initiator of *eunomia*
(law and order). His constitution was renowned for its durable
frame, but he was said to have forbidden any itemized register

---

213. Excavations in a cave near Pozzuoli, west of Naples, revealed the
remains of sacrificed dogs and the skeletons of dead, perhaps aborted or
miscarried, babies.

of his laws to be published. He postulated equality, but only among the top tier of warrior-citizens. The powers of Sparta's two kings, who came from different families often at odds, were subject to scrutiny by a council of five annually elected ephors. The Gerousia (a panel of men over sixty years old, of which the two kings, provided they were adult, were ex officio members) supervised the state's activities from an experienced angle. Solidarity and mutual suspicion (not least between the kings) held things together. Unlike Athenian wives, Spartan women could be independently rich and enjoyed a measure of sexual freedom; it seems to have mattered less whose child their sons were than that they replenished the ranks. Despite Sparta's social rigidity, Lycurgus allowed for a measure of mobility, up and down: both Gylippus and Lysander, two very successful generals, were mothakes, the sons of slave mothers and/or of impoverished or disgraced Spartiates.[214]

The Athenians' primordial lawgiver was Draco, at once dragon and guardian. His penalty for any serious crime was death.[215] In early sixth-century Athens, the aristocratic archon (annually selected chief magistrate) Solon was appointed arbiter, after rich landlords of his own class had forced many Attic smallholders off their land and sold them into slavery abroad. Solon's credentials had been validated by military success in a recent war with neighboring Megara. He canceled debts, by

214. Roman senators who lacked the means to maintain their dignity were liable to expulsion by the censors, whose office it was to preserve moral and social rectitude, of which solvency was practical evidence.

215. The Paraguayan dictator Dr. José Gaspar Rodríguez de Francia y Velasco (1766–1840) instituted a draconian regime in which the death penalty was the only sentence for any crime. It is still said that the Paraguay of "El Supremo" was crime-free.

removing the markers denoting mortgaged property.[216] He also made it illegal for free-born peasants to contract a loan on the security of their own person: no one could be sold into slavery for failing to repay a debt to an individual.[217] Previously, in the wake of fruitless harvests, men were left with nothing to sell but their persons, in order to pay off the 15 percent due to exigent landlords. Some of those already sold abroad were redeemed with the reformer's own money. Solon's measures, at once bold and conservative, alleviated the crisis and supplied a maquette for the formal constitutional mechanism operated, with sustained success, by Pisistratus and his sons.

Solon set a noble example by taking no steps to avoid heavy personal losses as a result of his own measures; some of his aristocratic friends were less gracious over not receiving advanced notice of them. Solon's final flourish was to extract vows from the citizens that they would abide by his memorable edicts, written in iambic verse.[218] These proclaimed the creation of a deliberative council and a public Assembly, in which all citizens—at least those within reach of Athens—could make their feelings known, although not advocate policy. The aristocratic archons continued to be the city's executive officers. To avoid recrimination, Solon then left Athens for ten years.[219]

216. The exercise of cancelation is known as *seisachtheia*.

217. There was, however, the equivalent of small print: an unpaid debt to the *state* could still entail being sold into slavery.

218. Iambics were the most prosaic form of poetic verse, and the punchiest: "iamb" implies force. The use of iambics in tragedy is always in dramatic exchanges, never in the choruses, which were musically and metrically ornate, verbally more lyrical.

219. There is no record of Attic prose composition in Solon's time. His program was made memorable by being spelled out in iambic verse. Some of his lackluster lines survived: for example, "If I have spared my country / By

The sage's decade of self-imposed exile supplied a sublime precedent for the procedure known as ostracism. Formalized by Cleisthenes, in 508 B.C.E., ostracism combined the scapegoat ritual with pragmatic politics. Once a year, a quorum of at least 6,000 citizens could vote one unpopular politician into a decade of enforced absence by inscribing his name on an *ostrakon* (clay potsherd). The exile's property remained immune to sanction. On his return (no woman was eligible for exemplary dismissal),[220] he enjoyed resumption of full rights. Cleisthenes was unique in the range of his innovations, but he built on antique foundations: even Lycurgus allowed exiles guilty of involuntary killing to return to Sparta after a purgative period of absence.

28.

Some Athenian legislation against antisocial individuals dated from before Solon. Anyone declared *atimos*—undeserving of honor or respect—was deprived of his citizenship and, as an outlaw, could be killed with impunity. Although it is rarely mentioned in genial histories, citizens convicted of *atimia* continued to be killed in democratic Athens at least until the end of the fourth century. After the Greek victory at Salamis, in 480 B.C.E., the councilor Lycides was stoned to death merely

---

not descending into tyranny and unrelenting violence . . . my policy won greater victories being commonplace." The earliest Ionian prose writer is said to have been either the philosopher Anaximander or his pupil Anaximenes of Miletus, who speculated, in the mid-6th century, that "air" was the unlimited, fundamental component of the universe.

220. Paul Cartledge reminds me that one extant ostrakon is inscribed "Let Cimon go, and take Elpinike [his sister] with him!"

because he had agreed to deliver the Persian general Mardonius's offer for a truce. According to Herodotus, "once Lycides
was dead, Athenian women went to his house and stoned his
wife and children to death." Atimia not infrequently entailed
the guilt, and killing, of a man's entire family.

The Athenians' principal and recurrent fear was that one
aristocrat would seize sole power. Since the machinery of justice
was at first in the hands of the upper-class conclave known as
the Areopagus, atimia must have originated as a means of making sure that power was balanced within the dominant class.
Timē (honor, respect) was a quality limited to citizens; it could
not, by definition, be withdrawn from *metics,* foreigners resident
in Athens. In time, however, a charge of atimia could be brought
against foreigners and have lethal consequences.[221]

Abiding dread of a tyrannical coup d'état, of the kind
instigated in 404 B.C.E. by Plato's uncle Critias, accounts for
the merciless attitude to citizens who failed to side with democracy. Even political neutrals who opted for discretion and absented themselves by taking refuge in Eleusis, several leagues
out of town, were denounced as complicitous with the oligarchs.
In a somewhat Hellenic spirit, St. Paul reproached the people
of Laodicaea because they blew neither hot nor cold. Dante
reserved a place in a low circle of hell for fellow Florentines who
sat on the fence while Guelphs and Ghibellines clashed.

After the killing of Critias and the restoration of democracy, in 403, the Athenians passed an unprecedented law, *mē
mnēsikakein,* forbidding citizens to recall the evil deeds of the

---

221. During the 470s, for example, when Arthmius of Zelea was accused of
bringing Persian gold into the Peloponnese, he and his family were designated
enemies of the Athenian people.

tyrants and their collaborators or to cite them, in order to blacken witnesses, during legal proceedings. Whatever ugly things had been said or done (except by a blacklisted very few) were not admissible as evidence. Magnanimity and the fear of renewed *stasis* led to a tactful sponging of the slate. General Charles de Gaulle's fabrication, in 1944, of the myth of all but universal French resistance to the Germans had a similar purposeful wish to efface fractious memories. Civil wars and divisions are shut away on the dark side of ceremonies of patriotic unity.[222]

In Athenian political debate, atimia continues to appear as a rhetorical charge, somewhat like that of being "un-American." In 399 B.C.E. the orator Andocides accused another politician, Epichares, of subverting the democracy: "So isn't it the case that anyone who kills you now will have unstained hands, according to the law of Solon?" While formally concerned with his impiety and alleged moral corruption of the young, the trial of Socrates in 399 B.C.E. came of the loud suspicion that he had collaborated with Critias and his friends. In fact, during the arbitrary rule of the Thirty Tyrants, he had, we are promised, refused to take part in the arrest of an innocent man.

Socrates' trial has served to indict Athenian democracy for the judicial "crucifixion" of a great and innocent man, but he had ample opportunity to defend himself with something more endearing than the flash of his famous irony. After being found guilty, the defendant was asked, as was customary, to

222. Memory can be silenced, but not obliterated. One line of a poem, "The Plural," by Kiki Dimoula, in *The Brazen Plagiarist*, consists of "E mnēmē, ē mnēmē, ē mnēmē" (Memory, memory, memory).

propose a suitable penalty. His habit of playing to the smart gallery impelled Socrates to propose that, like an Olympic hero, he should be given free meals for life. The people were not amused by his *eironeia*[223] and sentenced him to death. No "psychological" explanation is needed to account for Socrates' failure either to be more conciliatory or to go into exile, as could easily have been arranged. He elected to play the martyr. The publicity of his demise made sure that he crowned his life with the myth-generating panache that Empedocles had displayed by jumping into the crater of Mount Etna. If both philosophers lacked an appetite for gold, neither was indifferent to praise or glory. Socrates' personal appearance was notoriously and, to some at least, delightfully uncomely: thick lips, bulging eyes, and a belly like Silenus. Only his charm enhanced his person; later, however, his role as a martyr to democracy led artists to reduce his puckishness. Cosmetic sculptors came to grace him with the uncreased solemnity appropriate to an iconic luminary. The distinction most regularly discounted in studies of ancient philosophy is that between performers and pundits: holding an audience in public was a skill requiring mystique, wit, nerve, and charisma. Plato lacked them all, except on paper.

The speed with which heroes could become villains, especially when the city was humiliated by defeat, was a recurring feature of Athenian democracy. The lack of press or media did not prevent word of mouth from, as the moderns say, going viral. In both Homer and Hesiod, Pheme (Rumor), also known as Ossa, broadcasts bad news and malicious rumor. *Pheme* and

---

223. The common transliteration "irony" is a false cousin to what the word meant in Greek ears, which comprised a measure of sneering condescension.

the Latin *fama* lie at the root of "fame" and imply both its fragility and its dependence on word of mouth.

29.

In the second half of the fourth century B.C.E., the surge of Macedonian power, under King Philip II, reminded the city-states of their diminished power. At the battle of Chaeronea, in 338 B.C.E., the Macedonians crushed the Athenians and their allies. Philip then wrote to the Spartans, asking whether he should visit them as a friend or as an enemy. They had the brief temerity to respond, "Neither." Some years later, when Alexander was congratulating the Greek coalition (and himself, as the second Achilles) on victory over the Persians, he pointedly omitted the Spartans from the heroic roll.

The ostentatiously minimalist philosopher Diogenes, a native of the Black Sea port of Sinope, was alone in being almost as laconic as the Spartans. It is said that curiosity impelled the young Alexander the Great to pay a visit to the wooden barrel in which Diogenes lived in Corinth. He asked whether there was anything he could do for the mendicant Cynic (so called because he advocated a *bios cunikos*, a dog's minimalist life). Diogenes had the nerve (and vanity) to reply: "You could move out of my light."[224] Alexander is said to have been gracious enough to say, "If I were not Alexander, I should wish to be Diogenes." Perhaps his tutelage under Aristotle disposed the Macedonian king to be indulgent when it came to philosophers.

---

224. Diogenes foreshadowed Lenny Bruce's demonstrative scorn for humbug by making public masturbation into a kind of knowing accusation.

The battle of Chaeronea (where eighteen-year-old Alexander commanded the cavalry) proved to many Greeks that further resistance to Macedonian hegemony was likely to be fatal. Was Demosthenes perverse in failing to realize that the city-state was no longer a viable power-unit and that it was time to collaborate with Philip?[225] This view reckons without the education Athenians received from their brave past and the inspiration of the tragic theater.[226] If Demosthenes misjudged the odds, so—on the face of it—had Themistocles in defying Xerxes. Winston Churchill played the Demosthenic role in England in 1940. Had the duke of Marlborough not been among his ancestors, he might have gone along with Lord Halifax and asked for terms from Adolf Hitler. If the British had lost the war, post facto historians would be observing how misguided Churchill was.

The distinguished, gallant, and 45-times-reelected Athenian general Phocion, renowned for both probity and poverty, is said to have urged Philip's eighteen-year-old son Alexander to leave the defeated Greeks in peace; better sate his desire for Achillean greatness by attacking Persia.[227] After taking the Athenian's lucrative advice, Alexander sent him 100 talents of Persian

225. See George Cawkwell, *Philip of Macedon* (1978).
226. In *Thucydides Mythistoricus* (1907), F. M. Cornford argues for the tragic maquette in Thucydides' vision of events. Oratory and theatrical performance have always had much in common. Cicero learned how to "project" from his friend Roscius, a famous actor of his time. Ronald Reagan's presidency led politics and folksy soap opera onto the same track.
227. In this he endorsed the Athenian orator/politician Demades, who had secured what were generally agreed to be honorable terms from Philip.

treasure. Phocion demonstrated his virtue by declining to accept them.

Following the death of Alexander in 323, the Athenians attempted to retrieve their independence. The Macedonian general Antipater marched on the city and besieged Piraeus. He dangled fat bribes, which were refused. Nevertheless, when Phocion failed to hold Piraeus against overwhelming odds, the great man was accused of treason. He sought asylum with Antipater's legate, Polyperchon. For whatever sorry motive, Polyperchon delivered his suppliant to the Athenians. On a show of hands, Phocion was condemned to death. Before drinking the decreed poison, without flinching and, surely, with Socrates in mind, he remarked to a friend, "This is no more than what I expected, the same treatment the most illustrious citizens have received before me."

A year later, Demosthenes (not on record as having spoken for, or against, Phocion) himself took poison to avoid capture, after his old opponent Demades had moved for his and his friends' execution. Two years later, Demades fell foul of the Macedonian general Cassander and was executed. Greek history has few grace notes and even fewer happy endings. Five hundred years later, the peripatetic Pausanias observed, "A man who devotes himself unsparingly to his country's affairs and trusts his people never comes to a good end."[228] In 1936, the only somewhat self-mocking George Seferis wrote, "Wherever I travel, Greece wounds me."

228. This observation was echoed, without attribution, by the English politician and Hellenist Enoch Powell at the end of his uneven, if not notorious, political career.

30.

Convictions, formal or spontaneous, for *atimia*, with its unforgiving penalties, ran alongside the more humane, hence well-
publicized, sentence of ostracism. That device was used for the
last time in 417 or 416 B.C.E., when the unimportant Hyperbolus
(the Overreacher) was voted into exile by a very temporary
consortium of the supporters of Alcibiades and Nicias.[229] Had
one or other of the last two been expelled, as the triage of ostracism was meant to procure, Athens might have adopted a coher-
ent policy for the pursuit of the war.

If Nicias had been left in control, the Sicilian expedition
would have been scaled down or abandoned; if Alcibiades, it
might have been waged with enough verve for the gamble to
pay off. At the best of times, ostracism allowed a leading figure,
Pericles in particular, to enjoy what amounted to unopposed
hegemony, although the choice lay between him and Thucydides, the son of Melesias, as to who should go into exile in
443 B.C.E. When things went wrong on what was undoubt-
edly his watch, even "the Olympian" could be sanctioned, if
only by measures voted against members of his entourage, such
as Anaxagoras, or his "foreign" partner, Aspasia, who was in fact
of aristocratic Hellenic stock.

In rare instances, ostracism was abridged by the same
popular demand that instigated it. In 480 B.C.E., with the Persian menace bearing heavily on the city, Aristeides was recalled

---

229. Hyperbolus's bad luck lasted till literally the end of his life. He was
killed on the island of Samos in 411 B.C.E., probably at the instigation of
Alcibiades, whose return to favor among Athenian democrats he had good
reason to oppose. As a result of its cynical use in 417, ostracism was, it seems,
never used again as a means of averting domestic political schism.

after less than three years and, when Xerxes invaded Greece, drafted as a general. At the battle of Salamis, where Themistocles' investment in sea power was vindicated by the annihilation of the Persian armada, Aristeides—who had favored land forces—had an honorable but subsidiary role. His hour of glory came as chief of staff, under the Spartan Pausanias, at the conclusive land battle of Plataea. Xerxes' still formidable army was routed and its commander Mardonius killed. An enormous haul of booty, left behind in the Great King's mansion-sized tent, was divided among the victors.

A facetious, not necessarily false account claims that Aristeides' ostracism was provoked by his supporters repeatedly calling him "Aristeides the Just." This was taken to imply that the mass of people lacked his rectitude. Themistocles' determination, in the 480s, to put all of Athens's wealth into shipbuilding had been a gamble at odds with tradition. Aristocratic chivalry and martial dignity were typified by Miltiades, who had defeated Darius, Xerxes' father, at the battle of Marathon in 490. Ten years later, when the second Persian invasion began, Miltiades' son, the very tall and stolid Cimon, rode down to the Piraeus, tied up his horse, and set an example to his class by taking his place with the fleet.

Cimon's qualities and stature procured him prompt command. He showed outstanding bravery at Salamis and proved so successful an admiral that, after the war, he incurred the emulous hostility of Pericles. Cimon was ostracized in 461, on account more of his merits than of his faults. The notion of loyal opposition, like that of political parties, had no reliable place in Athenian democracy. Themistocles, who had been cheered all day at the Olympic Games in 480, was ostracized less than ten years later. He chose, with versatile insolence, to go and serve the new Persian king, Artaxerxes, as a provincial governor. After his death in 459, his bones were repatriated to Athens and interred with forgiving ceremony, outside the walls he had built.

Modern Greek history has similar reversals of fortune. Constantine Karamanlis, made prime minister in 1955, retreated into exile in 1963, after being accused (with some cause) of complicity in the death of Grigoris Lambrakis, a left-wing politician.[230] He lived in Paris until 1974, when the seven-year tyranny of the "Colonels" came to an ignominious end after Turkey invaded and, without military opposition, annexed a large part of the north of the island of Cyprus. Lacking a plausible figurehead, the politicians in Athens called on Karamanlis to come home. The exile's first question was, "What kept you so long?"

Karamanlis returned as a hero, his dubious history expunged in the mē mnēsikakein tradition. He led a renovated conservative party, Nea Demokratia, which soon became indistinguishable from the old. He later became president of Greece and its grandest old man since Eleftherios Venizelos. In the early 1920s, the latter had had a spell out of office during which the revanchist policies he had been among the first to sponsor led Greece into its greatest modern humiliation. More than a million Hellenes were expelled from Asia Minor, where many of their ancestors had lived for thousands of years.

Ernest Hemingway's *In Our Time* has vivid "eyewitness" accounts both of the Greek flight from Smyrna in 1922 (fugitives are depicted breaking their donkeys' legs with sledgehammers

230. The Lambrakis case was the subject of Costa-Gavras's *Z*, which won the Oscar for Best Foreign Film in 1969. Known in Europe, outside Greece, as *Zed*, the title, if said aloud in Greek, is a pun on the word *zee*, which means "he lives."

in order to deprive the Turks of their use) and of the execution by firing squad of six of the Greek cabinet ministers who were the scapegoats for the failure of the Big Idea of a new Greco-Byzantine empire.[231] Hemingway actually witnessed no more of the Ionian catastrophe than Herodotus did of the victory of Salamis. History and fiction have ancient affinities. Venizelos returned to prime ministerial office in 1928. First as a local political militant in Crete and then as the postwar diplomat who successfully expanded Greece's borders, despite the catastrophe of 1922, Venizelos had the charm, the guile, and the luck of Odysseus.

31.

If Homer is evidence, public meetings took place even in archaic times, for the announcement of royal decisions.[232] It seems that the common people had a right to be informed and express their views, if only by barracking. Again in the *Odyssey,* the wise Mentor is depicted speaking against the suitors in the Ithacan *agora* (marketplace), which argues for the early influence of public opinion. When script becomes generally legible, laws were spelled out in the agora. The finest extant instance is posted, on vertical slabs, in the once-powerful inland city of Gortyn in Crete. Codification of the laws allowed the citizens

231. In 406 B.C.E., the Athenians had elected to execute the same number of admirals after their victory at Arginusae was soured by their alleged failure, after the battle, to save shipwrecked Athenian sailors struggling in the water. Two other admirals were wise enough never to return to Athens. In July 2016, after a failed coup, eight Turkish military personnel sought asylum by landing their helicopter in the northern Greek city of Alexandroupolis.
232. For instance, see *Odyssey* 2, 27.

to challenge arbitrary decisions by their rulers by pointing to the published text, literally set in stone.

The struggles for power in sixth-century Athens led to what has been called the "invention" of democracy, although the principal players had no doctrinal blueprint. After Solon's measures had failed to procure stability, another local aristocrat, Pisistratus, came to power. He too first distinguished himself in a successful campaign against Megara, after that small, enterprising city had recovered from its defeat by Solon. Pisistratus was Solon's second cousin and claimed descent from Codrus, the last king of Athens. Codrus died in the eleventh century B.C.E., after an oracle had forecast that the Dorian invaders would conquer Attica if its king was not killed. He went into the enemy camp in disguise, provoked a quarrel, and was done to death, upon which the intruders withdrew, presumably having had notice of the same oracle. Solon was apprehensive of the charm of his young cousin and later warned the Athenians against "treading in the footsteps of the fox," whose trickiness had been made memorable by Archilochus.

The foxy Pisistratus could affect to represent honest folk, since his family fiefdom was in the hills of rural eastern Attica, but his methods were Odyssean: in 561 B.C.E., he made a dramatic entry, wrapped in bloody bandages, into the Athenian Assembly.[233] Claiming to have been assaulted by unscrupulous

233. In 1954, François Mitterrand staged his own kidnapping in order to enhance his fame and lend a heroic aspect to a personal history blemished by decorated service to Philippe Pétain's wartime regime. The revelation that the episode was faked did little or nothing to impede Mitterrand's eventual accession to the autocratic presidency of the Fifth Republic, an office that he had previously labeled as the fruit of a *"coup d'état permanent."*

enemies, he asked the people to vote him a bodyguard. As soon as it was granted, he used it to garrison the Acropolis and declare himself the master of the city. The coup failed when the other aristocratic leaders, whose interests were in farming and maritime activities, united against him.

Forced into exile, Pisistratus retained commanding influence over his constituency of "hill people" (Herodotus calls them *hyperakrioi*, "over-the-hill people," that is, rough rustics out of the eyeline of metropolitan Athenians). In the mid-550s, their leader combined another coup d'état with a coup de théâtre: he rode into Athens in a chariot that he shared with a statuesque country girl called Phyē, whom his supporters were primed to salute as the goddess Athene herself. Athene's sponsorship may have had some validity among the credulous, since she doubled as the patron goddess both of the mythical revenant Orestes (whose name means, literally, "mountain man") and of Homer's crafty Odysseus.

Pisistratus's impudence was now seconded by one of his previous enemies, the coastal leader Megacles (the Big Shot), from the powerful Alcmaeonid clan, whose daughter he agreed to marry. This diplomatic union collapsed after the bride reported that her husband refused to consummate the marriage through the usual channel. The likely explanation is that Pisistratus already had two sons, Hippias and Hipparchus, by a previous marriage. If Megacles' daughter conceived a male child, the Alcmaeonids would have a palpable lien on the succession to power.

Pisistratus's announced reason for renouncing her was that his new wife's family were stained by *miasma*, ritual pollution. This had been incurred when, in 632 B.C.E., an aristocratic clique, led by Cylon, seized the Acropolis and tried to take control of the city. The contemporary Megacles, head of the Alcmaeonid family, and his supporters surrounded the putschists. Cylon and his brother got away to Megara. Their less resourceful allies sought asylum at the altar of Athene, but were dragged away and killed. Because of this sacrilege, Megacles and his clan were deemed to be damned in perpetuity. They seem not to have endured any practical loss of face or power. Like atimia, *miasma* gave a man's enemies opportunities for rhetorical denunciation, but—as the ascent of Pericles would prove—ancestral sins had none of the disqualifying or potentially deadly consequences of atimia. In the case of the Alcmaeonids, the supposed taint may have served to remind political adversaries of their unforgiving pedigree.

The second exile of Pisistratus lasted for another decade. He used it to consolidate his power base in his family's traditional fiefdom in the uplands of eastern Attica. His charm and wealth (from mining interests and the collection of harbor dues in the region under his control) lubricated his diplomatic contacts in the Aegean. In 546, he and his mercenary army landed in his coastal fiefdom of Marathon. They were joined by enough discontented Athenians to achieve mastery of the city. He was backed by ancestral credentials as well as by physical force. The circuitous course toward democracy was thronged with aristocratic runners.

It was often easier to seize power in Greece than to retain it. In the seventh century B.C.E., the tyrant Periander of Corinth sent a herald to Thrasybulus, tyrant of Miletus, to ask for a reliable recipe for remaining unchallenged. Thrasybulus took the herald into a wheat field. As he walked through the wheat, he slashed off all the tallest ears (he had been ruthless in curtailing the power of the established Milesian aristocracy). When Periander's herald returned, he reported that Thrasybulus was a silent madman who destroyed his own best crops. Periander had the wit to understand that he was being advised to stay on top by cutting down his outstanding fellow citizens, which he accomplished with the help of 300 mercenary spearmen. The tyrannical habit of eliminating the old aristocracy was an involuntary prelude to democracy: to remain on top, a tyrant's subsequent policies had to appeal to popular opinion, above all by fostering economic success. "Tyrant" now has pejorative connotations alien to the early use of the Greek term *tyrannos.*

Once on top, Pisistratus traded more on his charm than his muscle. His very name suggested that he was persuasive (its root, *peitho,* was the power to convince).[234] His inclination to win or buy friends secured amiable diplomatic relations both with Sparta and with that city's traditional enemy, Argos, as well as with Macedon, in the far North. While unashamedly autocratic—he never relinquished his bodyguard and took hostages from, in particular, the Alcmaeonids—Pisistratus preserved and amplified Solon's reform. By undemanding taxes on peasants, and perhaps by timely subsidies, he ensured that they were too contented, and too busy, to excite trouble in the city. Overseas, he secured access to the Black Sea by reinforcing Sigeum, on the Hellespont, and encouraged Athenian naval expansion, without alarming the Persians, unlike his contemporary, Polycrates of Samos. Thucydides speaks of him with nostalgic approval: "He held virtue and wisdom to great account for a long time, taking from the Athenians but a twentieth part

234. Names (often based on nicknames that became emblematic in some families) were important in the ancient world. The Romans were disposed to appoint generals called Felix, the lucky one. Napoleon preferred lucky to merely efficient or obedient commanders.

of their revenues, adorned the city, managed their wars, and administered their religion worthily."

32.

The island of Samos, neatly sited, for trading purposes, under the lee of Asia Minor, flourished for some years, during the second half of the sixth century B.C.E., under Polycrates' ostentatious direction. Having chained the island of Rhenaia to Delos to advertise his command of the sea, he enhanced his regime's glamour by recruiting poets, philosophers, and artists to his court. Philosophers have a long history of ambitious courtesy to autocrats. Artists, academics, and poets rarely take exception to generous funding. In the second half of the sixth century, however, the local boy-wonder Pythagoras fell out with Polycrates and quit the island. Eventually, he landed in Italy, where he and his followers assumed intellectual and social authority in the city of Croton (modern Crotone, on the Ionian Sea coast).

Polycrates became so flagrantly successful that Amasis, the king of Egypt, advised him to avoid the envy of the gods by jettisoning a possession he particularly valued. Polycrates threw his favorite and valuable seal-ring into the sea. The ring had been designed by the daedalean Theodoros, a Samian artist who invented the set square, the lathe, and—while working on the ground plan for the temple of Artemis at Ephesus—the architect's level.[235] A few days later, the ring was returned to Polycrates by a fisherman who had found it in the belly of one of his catch.

---

235. Perhaps because of deference to Egyptian geometry and temple builders, Greek architects ignored the structural possibilities of the arch, which was widely used by Roman engineers.

Convinced that the gods had refused to be appeased and that that tyrant was doomed, the Egyptian king abandoned contact with him.

In around 522 B.C.E., Polycrates was gulled by the flattery of the Persian satrap Oroetes and went, without escort, to the mainland, imagining that he was being solicited to play a key role in a plot against the Great King, Darius. He was captured and crucified. His adjutant, Maiandrios, called a meeting of the Samians and announced the end of the tyranny and proposed a state of equality under the law (*isonomia*). In the event, the island soon fell under the power of Darius. It was not delivered from Persian control until after the Greek triumphs at Salamis and Plataea in 480–479 B.C.

In the post-war alliance of Aegean cities and islands, the men of Chios and the Samians, always enterprising sailors, elected to maintain their own ships rather than make docile insurance payments to the Athenians. Greek islanders are nothing if not insular. Demodocus of Leros[236] (which, in 1967, became a grim prison island under the Colonels) wrote: "The Chians are bad, not one bad and another not, but all bad / Except Procles and Procles is a Chian." The Cambridge classical scholar Richard Bentley (1662–1742) parodied this: "The Germans in Greek are sadly to seek, / Except only Hermann, and Hermann's a German." The 1918 Loeb Classical Library edition of the Greek Anthology declares that this squib is "well known." Those were the days.

236. In modern Greek, *leros* means "dirty."

33.

Pythagoras was Plato's predecessor not only in maintaining the primacy of number; he was also the pioneer in the creation of a blueprint (based on the golden section) for a model society. If the sources are to be believed, the elements of his philosophy, at once original and eclectic, were culled as the result of incessant travel. Pythagoras's father Neanthes is said to have been Phoenician, unless he was Tyrrhenian (from the west coast of Italy). The caustic Heracleitus said that Pythagoras "forged for himself a wisdom, a polymathy, a quackery"; but Empedocles—Pythagoras's pupil, as Pythagoras was said to be of Thales and Anaximander— claimed that his master had "the learning of ten or twenty lives." Thales is said to have advised Pythagoras to head for Egypt, where he is reported to have spent ten diligent years, even though that country's priests were forbidding and its inhabitants lacked philoxenia. The notion that Greek culture derived, more or less entirely, from Egypt (otherwise known as "Africa") has been re- newed by Martin Bernal's followers. One zealot has gone so far as to suggest that Aristotle filched his ideas after frequenting the stacks of the great Ptolemaic library at Alexandria, which was built a good many years after the philosopher's death.[237]

Pythagoras anticipated Plato in the notion of *anamnesis,* whereby the soul was blessed with the power to remember the eternal truths it witnessed when on leave from the body. This was

237. See Mary Lefkowitz's *Not Out of Africa: How Afrocentrism Became an Excuse to Teach Myth as History* (1996). Lefkowitz's husband, the ex-Regius Professor of Greek at Oxford, says only one word in her book. When a revi- sionist "historian" claims, in a lecture, that Aristotle plundered the library at Alexandria (which was not built by the time Aristotle died), Hugh Lloyd-Jones cries out, "Rubbish."

said to prove the immortality of the soul, although the psyche was sentenced first to circulate from body to body for 3,000 years. The notion of the "music of the spheres," elaborated in Plato's *Timaeus*, derived from Pythagoras, who asserted that the earth was spherical (rather than cylindrical, as Anaximander had said or floating on water, as Thales had). Cultivating his eccentricity, Pythagoras let his hair grow long, in the Doric style, and also wore trousers, like the effeminate Persians. After solitary travels in Egypt and Babylon (where the theorem associated with his name may have been known for several centuries), he solicited and gathered disciples. When he played the cithara (a primitive lyre), men and animals were said to be mesmerized, as if by Orpheus. In this, he had attributes in common with his near-contemporary, Buddha: the parade of modesty, a break with idolatrous orthodoxy, the capacity to recruit and hold followers by some kind of mystic power, and the substitution of his ascetic person for the deities whose superstitious worship he deplored.

Pythagoras's eccentricity was enhanced by his "golden thigh," a flashy mark that he shared with Apollo, whose favorite (if not reincarnation) he was happy to appear. His religious slogan was a confection of Hellenic, oriental, and Egyptian elements: "what had neither beginning nor end was the divine."[238]

---

238. See *Pythagoras* by Peter Gorman (1979), passim. Gorman has in common with his subject an enthusiasm that disposes him to encomiastic recklessness. Not well regarded by, for sour example, the reviewer in the *Classical Quarterly*, his mixture of fancy and intelligence, legend and practical possibility is probably no more false to the shaman's life than the accounts of other miraculous saviors, such as Apollonius of Tyana, who trod consciously in Pythagoras's footsteps. Edward Gibbon's footnote on Apollonius merits repetition: "Apollonius of Tyana was born about the same time as Jesus Christ. His life (that of the former) is related in so fabulous a manner by his disciples that we are at a loss to discover whether he was a sage, an impostor, or a

Hence number was divine; matter was not. Pythagorean numerology subtended a certain morality: 1 and 2 were not numbers but the bases on which numbers were conceived. Odd numbers were good and masculine; even, bad and feminine. The world was articulated by ten opposing principles, "the paradigm of the cosmic music"; 10 was the perfect number: it "represented the limit of the cosmos."

Pythagoreanism leaked into medieval philosophy, notably that of Maimonides of Cordoba in Al-Andalus. The Great Rambam, as he is known in Hebrew studies, attempted to reconcile Aristotle with Judaism; he was also attracted by the Pythagorean notion that the creation had a numerical scheme. The number 7 was ubiquitous in temple ritual and in the scriptures: "composed of the first of the evens and the second of the odds and of the first of the odds and the second of the evens, it is called by the early sages a *mispar kolek* (a 'complete' or 'inclusive' number), and it hints at one of the mysteries of creation." It was also said that "all astrologers agree that after 49,000 years (seven times seven times 1,000), the heavens will have gone through all possible configurations." Trinitarian Christianity appropriated the number 3: it was significant that Christ rose on the Third Day.

Belief in reincarnation—central to Pythagoras's system— is said (to lend it dignified antiquity, but with no reliable evidence) to have originated in Egypt. Anaximander's claim that man had once been a fish may have impelled Pythagoras to

---

fanatic." See *The Decline and Fall of the Roman Empire*, vol. 1. L. Ron Hubbard, the founder of Scientology, was another such guru; so was the "Reverend" Jim Jones, who inspired 900 of his followers to assemble in Jonestown, Guyana, and kill themselves with poisoned nonalcoholic drinks.

denounce the eating of all animals (human souls in transit might be lodged in any living creature) and also of beans. One reason for this aversion is said to have been the resemblance of broad beans to human embryos; but beans were also an early, sacred sign of life in the mud of the Nile delta when the waters began to rise. According to another account, the Master detested beans because they were "used to count votes in oligarchic societies"; this sounds cranky enough to be credible, not least for a Samian. In the early 1960s, my family and I spent spring on Ios, in the Cyclades, where the only available vegetable was broad beans.

Pythagoras made few converts in mainland Greece, though he gained some publicity, not least by saying that the spectators at the Olympic Games were more important than the competitors whose sporting feats were so elaborately celebrated, for a suitable fee, by Pindar.[239] It is not clear why Pythagoras elected to go to southern Italy, nor why he made landfall in the ill-regarded city of Croton. Like that other mendicant preacher, St. Paul, he was an immediate success in the sticks. He attracted an audience of 2,000, 600 of whom became his "akousmatists," listeners who stayed tuned. He is said to have required initiates to observe a five-year period of silence, perhaps absolute, more probably during the time that he was

---

239. But not by the 2nd-century B.C.E. Latin satirist Lucilius: "After 20 years, Ulysses returned safe and sound, / His features recognized by his faithful hound. / But you, you boxed for just four hours / And not your dog but we can't count you ours. / Look in the mirror and you'll agree: / That Stratophon just isn't me." According to the apocryphal *Telegoneia,* Odysseus was to meet his death at the hands of his own son, Telegonos, by the witch Circe, who had turned his men into pigs and from whose island and desires he had escaped with his usual cunning. Telegonos was conducting a piratical raid on Ithaca and killed his father without knowing who he was. Matthew Arnold's mini-epic *Sohrab and Rustum* reverses the sorry tale.

addressing them.[240] The stringency of their discipline often attracts converts to charismatic leaders.

Pythagoras was said to have walked on water since, despite the long distance by road between them, he was seen in both Croton and Metapontum on the same day. He was also said to have died at the age of ninety-nine and to have ascended into heaven from the temple of the Muses in the latter city, as Elijah and the prophet Muhammad did from the temple in Jerusalem. Pythagoras's control of his followers was stringent and unforgiving, but he disapproved of slavery: he freed his slave Zalmoxis, a Thracian, who set up a minicult of his own. Pythagoras made friends with Croton's Italian neighbors and welcomed women into his fraternity (logic entailed that the human soul, the immaterial ruling faculty, had no distinct sex). Like many charismatic teachers, he both advocated egalitarianism and exercised tyrannical authority over his adherents.

Empedocles' idea of the world being governed by the waxing and waning of *neikos* (strife) and *philia* (love/friendship) derived from Pythagoras. So did his notion of man having fallen from the golden age of vegetarianism. "The greatest pollution among men," he said, "is to wrench out an animal's life and eat its strong limbs."[241] Because of the transmigration of

---

240. After World War II, Martin Heidegger deigned to visit French admirers only on condition that all their questions be put in writing before he arrived and that he not be quizzed afterwards. Isaiah Berlin tells of a meeting of the Cambridge University Moral Sciences Club at which Berlin had been invited to read an essay. After it, Wittgenstein delivered a sustained, critical monologue, shook the visitor's hand before he could reply, thanked him for a "good discussion," and left the room. Berlin abandoned the practice of philosophy and became a sage historian of ideas.

241. Parker, *Miasma*.

the soul, eating meat was akin to murder and cannibalism. Unlike his master, Empedocles (a Sicilian from Acragas, modern Agrigento) was a champion of liberty and the simple life. According to the early fifth-century proto-historian Xanthos[242] of Lydia, when offered regal honors, he refused them.

34.

Pythagoras's geometry supplied Plato with a matrix for immutable truths and may account for his prescription of prolonged mathematical studies for trainee philosopher-kings. Plato put his long and unamusing mathematical curriculum into practice, around 387 B.C.E., after being invited to tutor Dion to be the next and ideal ruler of Syracuse. His high-mindedness aroused the paranoid suspicions of Dion's brother-in-law, the pragmatic tyrant Dionysius, who is said to have sold the philosopher into slavery. If so, his servitude was brief and conveniently located, on the island of Aegina, opposite Attica, whence his friends were soon able to ransom him. In Plato's Seventh Letter, now generally considered a fabrication, the suggestion is that the philosopher had a closer relationship with Dionysius than with Dion. At Olympia in 360, he confessed that he found it difficult to defend Dion against the tyrant.[243] Power trumped propriety.

After his one-man Sicilian expedition, Plato became decidedly impractical. He retreated upward to install himself as the head of

242. Xanthos is said to have known about or seen (the words are akin in Greek) "in many places far from the sea . . . stones in the shape of a bivalve . . . scallop shells and a salt-marsh," and concluded that the plains were once sea.
243. Arnaldo Momigliano (*Development of Biography*) would have it that this shows how honestly Plato faced his own shortcomings.

his own Academy. In *The Republic,* he took revenge on the world of practical politics by proposing, in book 7, to "send out into the countryside" everyone in the city over the age of ten, thus isolating the youngest children for intensive indoctrination. The desired result would be the evolution of an informed democracy of "equals" of the valiant Spartan order. It is civil to suppose that the straightfaced Plato may have been aware that he was reducing his whole project to something close to absurdity.[244]

By Plato's time, Athens was a fulcrum for the Sophists, whom he satirized as venal opinion-peddlers. They had been preceded, in the fifth century, by Anaxagoras of Clazomenae, in Asia Minor, who became the rather too public éminence grise of Pericles. When voters grew disillusioned with the Olympian's policies, his pet philosopher was accused of impiety (Anaxagoras had said that the sun was a lump of rock larger than the Peloponnese) and of sympathizing with the Persians, a routine—seldom implausible—charge against those of foreign origin. An anecdote has it that the philosopher took to his bed and covered his head. Pericles came and said how he would regret the loss of such a valued adviser. Anaxagoras then supposedly uncovered his head and said, "Pericles, people who need a lamp put oil in it."[245] Condemned to death, he was reprieved,

244. The irony was lost on French-educated Pol Pot, the Cambodian dictator. In the interests of a cleansed new Marxist society, his Khmer Rouge evicted hundreds of thousands of people from Phnom Penh and forced them into the countryside, where most of them starved. The only historical regimes (the USSR and Mao's China) to have planned the starvation, or murder, of millions of their own citizens have been guided by a "philosophy." Nazi philosophers (working in the footsteps of "respectable" German theorists) also delivered warrants for mass murder, but only of "racial" inferiors and aliens.

245. Vincent Azoulay, *Les tyrannicides d'Athènes* (2014), p. 109.

thanks to Pericles' suave oratory, and returned to his home city, Lampsacos, on the Asian side of the Hellespont, where he opened a prestigious academy.

Another *peri*-Periclean, Damon from the Attic deme (township) of Oē, was ostracized in around 430 B.C.E. He was an expert musicologist, adept in the playing of music to moderate the moods of the citizens. An Olympic victor, he also advocated less tuneful forms of discipline, which may have contributed, along with his Periclean connection, to his unpopularity. He recurs as a musical expert in Plato's *Laches* and in *The Republic*. Like many humorless and didactic persons, Plato wanted to impose an immutable political ethic. He scowled at pleasure, whether private—in family life—or public, when procured by a certain kind of music and by the theater. Virtue had to derive from adherence to a priori principles, never be incidental to the flux of mundane life. The notion of mortal existence as a preparatory school for immortality, rather than valuable in itself, is implicit in the Platonism coopted into Christian theology, although secondary to its Aristotelian element.[246]

The neo-Hellenist Martin Heidegger also made a sortie into practical politics. In 1933, as the newly installed rector of Freiburg University, he saluted Hitler as a world-historical figure (Hegel did something similar, first when he witnessed Napoleon Bonaparte riding through Jena; after Waterloo,

---

246. For a sophisticated elaboration of Catholic neo-Aristotelianism, see Alasdair MacIntyre's *After Virtue* (1981/2007). MacIntyre's appetite for the conservative form of Catholic doctrine is another instance of Michel Pic's "nostalgie de la rigueur."

however, he tailored his philosophy to suit Prussian hegemony). In 1934, Heidegger saw the folly, if never the wickedness, of putting his tick in the margin of National Socialism. He returned, scarcely chastened, to the lecture room. His Aryan colleagues welcomed him with "Back from Syracuse?" No doubt he took the Platonic reference; there is no evidence that he smiled at it. Nor did he ever resign from the Nazi party or apologize, after the war, for his membership.[247]

Heidegger was an evangelical proponent of a selective vision of pre-Socratic philosophy: in his view, the Germans, alone of Europeans, had a privileged affinity with ancient Greece. He insisted that his notion of Being was rooted in the teachings of the pre-Socratics. He was only the most self-conscious and long-winded—he wrote a how-to-do-it essay in praise of boredom—of a series of German, often anti-Semitic, philosophers who claimed license (and priority) from "the Greeks," and selected whatever readings suited their books. German historians, headed by Theodor Mommsen, tended to reject a schematic "logic" common to Kant, Hegel, and Heidegger, and set to music by Richard Wagner. As an admiring biographer of Julius Caesar, however, Mommsen was, if inadvertently, a precursor of what became the "*Führerprinzip*" (the idealization of a single, unquestionable leader).

Pythagoras's followers in Croton instituted a prototypical one-party state. In the fifth century, they expelled the brilliant Hippasos, originally from Metapontum,[248] and may have driven him to his death, supposedly for "revealing the secrets of the dodecahedron." Hippasos's discovery of irrational numbers clashed with the party line. Hippasos did indeed trump the Leader with a valid theory; he also spent an irrational amount of time in the futile attempt to square the circle (Isaac Newton devoted himself, at length, to alchemy). After their leader's death, the Pythagoreans dominated Croton for some years. During their supremacy they incited the citizens to attack the adjacent and rival city of Sybaris. The hedonism of the Sybarites excited as much envy as their affluence. Late sleepers, they barred early-rising cocks from roosting within their walls.[249]

The Crotoniate army was led by Milon, a six-time winner of the Olympic wrestling title. He might have won a seventh time, but it is said that, after observing him working out, no one dared to go to the mat with him. Milon's reign as champion in a violent sport was unequaled, even by Muhammad Ali. It did not dispose either of them to modesty. After one Olympic victory, Milon raised a heifer above his head and toted it around the arena before killing and making a meal of it. When Sybaris was defeated, its population slaughtered or enslaved,

248. In the bay of Tarentum in southern Italy. Pythagoras himself is said to have died there in a political fracas. His followers set the style for pantisocracies of the likeminded. Sixties-style "communes" supply recent, often fractious, instances.

249. In *The Colossus of Maroussi* (1941), Henry Miller, once loud in reviling classicists, confessed that he had fallen in love with modern Greece. His narrative stars George Katsimbalis, a larger-than-life poet who, in a memorable nocturnal scene, crows the cocks of Athens awake, until the whole city is roused.

the victors diverted a local river to drown all trace of their easy going neighbors.

In the mid-fifth century, Croton's Pythagorean élite became intolerant and intolerable, and were killed or expelled by the unphilosophical native citizens.[250] The sect degenerated into a wandering band of proto-hippies. As for Milon, hubris finally did for him. In defiance of his aging strength, he set himself to uproot a tree by splitting it in half in order to get a firm hold on it. In the process of an exhausting extraction, the two halves of the trunk snapped back together, clenching the champion in an inescapable bracket. He was eaten by wolves. He might have learned from the story of Theseus's early opponent Sinis that it was unwise to wrestle with trees.

35.

In the Athens of Pisistratus, appearances furnished the new reality: prosperity muted opposition. The exclusion of the unforgiving and unforgiven Alcmaeonids was justified by renewed reference to their ancestral *miasma*. The top man's aptitude for dramatic display was seconded by the promotion of his Marathonian constituents' cult of Dionysos: the divine outsider became the acclaimed patron of the new festival of the Great Dionysia. The first tragedies had been staged, it is said, by Thespis, peripatetic founder of the acting profession, whose

---

250. Among the great library of lost books is the 3rd-century B.C.E. biographical compendium by Callimachus's pupil Hermippus of Smyrna, in which were included lives of those who "passed from philosophy to tyranny and despotism." Who, we wonder, was on the charge sheet? The link between philosophy and presumption to power is spelled out, with names, by Karl Popper in *The Open Society and Its Enemies*.

one-man traveling shows (his original stage was the back of a wagon) were backed by an unmasked dithyrambic chorus chanting in honor of Dionysos. A second and then a third major actor—always male—were added as the drama developed into a full-scale, operatic spectacle.

Aristotle's retrospective history of tragedy, in his *Poetics,* graces its development[251] with a schematic form. He credits it with cathartic intentions somewhat like group therapy: the consummation of tragedy was, in the timeworn phrase, "to purge the audience through pity and terror" (in the British style, Samuel Butler deprecated them as "these two maggots").[252] In fact a composite of elements, Greek theater evolved through trial and error, not least in playing on the mood and appetite of the audience. Solon's use of iambics in propounding his ideas became habitual in dialogue, though the choral passages were in a variety of meters. The grand solemnity of Aeschylus's *Oresteia* trilogy was relieved, at the end of the day, by a long-lost satyr play, a skit on earlier gravity, in which the author lightened the mood with risqué ribaldry and—he hoped—left his audience laughing. Only one such satyr play, Euripides' *Cyclops,* survived the purge of time and censorious Christianity.

The tragic theater was an education as well as an entertainment for its audience. Before performances took place on the Athenian stage, actors paraded before the audience without

251. Aristotle asserted, in particular, that it originated in "the dithyramb," the choral lyric associated with Dionysos. Tragic choruses were composed in Doric dialect, the narrative/dramatic dialogue in iambics, perhaps under the influence of Solon, who spelled out his reforms in didactic iambic verses.

252. Describing it as "nonsense upon stilts," Jeremy Bentham took a similar view of talk about "human rights."

their buskins (elevating footgear) and without dignifying masks and costumes. In time of war, the names of those who had died for the city were read out in solemn obituary. Were the Athenians being warned against taking too seriously the stylized, almost always mythical, if frequently morbid events that they were about to witness and, some scholars believe, commit to memory after a single session? However fine the verbal upholstery, the show was, they were reminded, no more than a show.[253]

Pisistratus paid three-dimensional tribute to Athenian primacy with a new temple to Athene on the Acropolis. By also supplying fresh, distinct accommodation for Hermes, Apollo, and Zeus, he spread his bets on divine favor. Differentiation of the powers of the Olympian pantheon was quite a late development of Greek religion, as was Catholicism's distribution of saintly duties (St. Jude, for instance, came to specialize in lost causes). The divine statuary that lent majesty to classical Athens froze the feuds of gods, monsters, and men into occasions for aesthetic complacency. Thanks to Pisistratan prosperity and policing, the tranquil city was, it seemed, no longer liable to civic disturbance.[254]

By purifying the island of Delos, sacred to Ionian Greeks, Pisistratus asserted Athenian hegemony in the Aegean Sea

253. Cf. Alfred Hitchcock's "It's only a movie" and Marcello Mastroianni's "Cinema non è gran cosa" (Cinema is no big deal).

254. After the bloody Civil War of 1936–1939, the smug Francisco Franco "sold" his own vindictive, fascistic dictatorship to the exhausted and cowed Spanish population under the slogan "tranquilidad." Medical practitioners believed for many years that patients could be calmed by bleeding. In Missolonghi, in 1824, Byron greeted the ministrations that did for him with "Come on then, you butchers."

without threatening his island allies or alarming the Persians. His geniality allowed him to extend Athenian power without exciting envy or apprehension. Nothing was less admirable, in Plato's eyes, than the power to persuade (peitho) that Pisistratus had so ably impersonated and that Sophists promised to teach, regardless of the merits of a particular case. In Hesiod's *Theogony*, Peitho was one of the bastard children of Aphrodite and the war god Ares; Eros, desire or lust, was the other.

36.

For two decades (half an average Greek lifetime), Pisistratus gambled, successfully, on his wit and his luck. When Thucydides looked back, in the glum years of the Peloponnesian War, he could scarcely conceal nostalgia for the enlightened tyranny that preceded the democracy on which the Greek reputation for political genius often seems to depend. Pisistratus's long and virtually uncontested tenure of power has been an embarrassment to liberal ideologists. Literally and metaphorically a showman, he covered his back with a hired, probably foreign bodyguard (like the Vatican's Swiss halberdiers), who would have no future in the city if they allowed him to be overthrown. His autocracy enjoyed such popular support that there was no audible opposition when, on his death in 527, he was succeeded by his older son Hippias, who retained power for another 17 years. Hippias's younger brother Hipparchus held no official position, but power without responsibility licensed his self-indulgence.

Thucydides delivers a dispassionate account of the events that brought about the end of Pisistratid rule and the elevation of the two "tyrannicides," Harmodius and Aristogeiton, to the status of social saviors: "Harmodius was then in the superb flower of his adolescence; Aristogeiton, a middle-ranking citizen, became his *erastes* [lover] and lived with him. When Harmodius became the object of advances from Hipparchus, he refused to be seduced and denounced Hipparchus to his lover. Fearing that Hippias, being all-powerful, would enable his brother to get his way by violent means, Aristogeiton immediately plotted to use his own honest reputation to overthrow the tyranny."

Hipparchus had not taken rejection well. He is accused of having humiliated Harmodius's sister by inviting her to carry a basket in a religious procession and then deleting her from the cast as unworthy. This hardly sounds like an insufferable slight, but it underlined the arbitrary nature of tyranny. It certainly stiffened the lovers' resolve to be avenged: during the celebration of the Panathenaia of 514, they stabbed Hipparchus to death, but either failed to touch Hippias or never intended to do so. Harmodius was killed instantly by a bodyguard, Aristogeiton taken alive. His courage under savage torture and his denunciation of arbitrary power lent idealistic luster to a crime of passion. No tyrant, however, had died at his hand.

The incident primed a reaction, fanned by the sidelined Alcmaeonids, against Hippias and the "un-Greek" opportunism that had led him to give his daughter in marriage to the Persian tyrant of Lampsacus, on the Asian bank of the Hellespont. Hippias was diplomatic enough to stay on the right side of the Persians. His policy kept the route open to Greek trade, through the Hellespont into the Black Sea. The Athenians may have resented dependence on barbarian favors, but "Medism," in one form or another (usually mercenary), was too regularly denounced not to have been a rewarding temptation. The Ottoman Empire would have similar attractions for many Greeks, not least in the nineteenth century. Byron's tripper's dream, in *Childe Harold*, that "Greece might yet be free" inspired European philhellenes, but emigration from Greece to Constantinople was more common than any patriotic flow in the opposite direction. Ahmed Vefik Pasha, a sophisticated Ottoman official, observed in the 1850s, "There is no Greece, there are only Greeks."

Looking back, Thucydides declined to subscribe to the quasi-deification of the tyrannicides. Depicting Harmodius and Aristogeiton as killers without any noble political motive, he emphasized the public service of the Pisistratids to both men and gods. They encouraged external trade, protected the peasants from exploitation, and improved the roads.[255] If the exercise of supreme power was capricious, local justice was administered more promptly, and more fairly, than before by local assizes. The arrival of magistrates on circuit allowed rural residents to plead their cases without having to abandon their fields and walk to the city.

In Thucydides' view, the murder of Hipparchus during a religious festival tarnished the virtue of the assassins. Embittered, if not unnerved, by his brother's death, Hippias became

255. For military rather than commercial purposes, the Spartans anticipated the Romans in energetic road building: their city was at the hub of eight ways to march quickly to the scene of any trouble. For similar reasons, Napoleon, Mussolini, and Hitler improved the network of roads in the states they dominated. The American interstate highway network was promoted by the notorious Teamsters' Union to enhance its own political clout. This enabled it to lobby against federal investment in a comprehensive railroad system as a viable competitor for carrying manufactured goods and oil. Due to the ruggedness of the Greek terrain, commercial land-carriage was hazardous and expensive. For this reason, seagoing powers (not only Athens, but also Corinth and Megara) had a mercantile advantage.

increasingly dictatorial. In 510, a donation from the Alcmaeonids procured the Delphic oracle's endorsement of a righteous invasion of Attica by their friends the Spartans. Hippias was deserted by the people and forced into exile in Sigeum, near Lampsacus, which his father had redeemed as an Ionian bastion. It was a convenient location from which to enlist Persian support for his restoration in Athens. There were no good losers in Greek politics. Patriotic allegiance was not likely to inhibit ousted Greek rulers (the exiled Spartan king Damaratus would be another) from repairing to the Persians in the hope of subsidized restitution and revenge.

Once dead, Harmodius and Aristogeiton became apt for mythical reconstitution as iconic liberators (a term applied, by themselves, to Marcus Brutus and his friends after the assassination of Julius Caesar). The poet Simonides, who—with other cultural ornaments—had been glad to come to Athens under Pisistratid patronage, accepted a commission to versify the inscription on Antenor's statue of the tyrannicides. It was set up, against pious precedent, in the agora, not far from the Enneakrounos, a nine-jetted fountain of diverted water installed by the Pisistratids to ensure ample water for the city. Simonides lived to write a victory ode after the Persians were conclusively defeated at Plataea in 479 B.C.E.

Solon had had the poise to create a precedent for reform without attributing blame to any particular section of society.[256]

256. Totalitarian ideologists, on the other hand, require the machinations of some scapegoat group to account for their own inability to deliver the promised utopia: Hitler vilified "the Jews" and licensed first their dispossession, then their murder en masse; Stalin improved on Marx's denunciation of "capitalism" by postulating the existence of a class of rich peasants, the so-called kulaks, who were said to be conspiring against the creation of a

It was left to Cleisthenes, a century later, to devise the first constitution in any state that conceded no a priori entitlement to aristocratic or royal blood. By dexterous reshuffling of the electoral pack, so that everyone seemed to have a better hand than before, he was able to vest power in a majority of the citizens as a whole. After his introduction of isonomia—the rule of the same law for everyone, as against the capricious decisions of tyrants—the statue of the two lovers stood for an impersonal ideal that they had shown no appetite to honor. Their erotic aspect was reduced by representing the mature Aristogeiton as an ephebe of much the same age as his fellow assassin. The Nobel Prize winner George Seferis sustained their parity, in the twentieth century, in his letter to Mathios Paskale: *"Kai phevgame m'ena lepidi crymmeno mesa mas ki' / Eleges 'ho Harmodios k'ho Aristogeiton"* (And we made off with one blade hidden between us and / You said, "Harmodios and Aristogeiton!").

The cult of the tyrannicides was evidence as much of the resurgent power of the Alcmaeonids as of democratic idealism. Harmodius and Aristogeiton became a mythical patriotic duo, even though, according to Herodotus, they were probably Boeotians of Phoenician origin. Their image became a motif on winners' vases at the Panathenaia when up to 140 40-liter amphorae were awarded to winning athletes and equestrians. On Cup Day, a herald signaled for contestants to

---

rural paradise. As a result of Stalin's a priori faith in communal farms, some five million Ukrainians died of starvation. Orlando Figes supplies undeniable details in *The Whisperers* (2007).

down a three-liter pot of wine as fast as possible. Freedom and indulgence were celebrated in one draught.[257]

The common Roman desire to emulate Greek models led to the claim that the last Tarquin king was expelled in the same year as Hipparchus was killed, and that the creation of the Republic coincided with Cleisthenes' renovation of Athens. When, in 52 B.C.E., Cicero was defending the thuggish Titus Annius Milo after his murder of Publius Clodius, he could expect the jury to take the reference when he reminded them that "the Greeks decree divine [sic] honors for the killers of tyrants . . . what songs, what poems!"[258] Clodius, a populist patrician and notorious playboy, had been persistently and vindictively hostile to Cicero. In 56 B.C.E., he was elected curule aedile, a minor but prestigious municipal office on the lower rungs of the ladder to higher things. Although a troublemaking man about Rome, Clodius never threatened to be any sort of a tyrant. One of his persistent charges against Cicero was that, in putting down the Catilinarian conspiracy, the vainglorious consul had taken advantage of martial law to execute Roman citizens without due process of law. Lucius Sergius Catilina himself, an aristocratic revolutionary, was killed in battle in 62 B.C.E., along with some thousands of his renegade army, all of whom are said to have died with wounds in their front, proving that they never turned their backs. Julius Caesar deplored

257. For a lively and thorough account of Harmodius and Aristogeiton and their iconic role, see Azoulay, *Les tyrannicides d'Athènes.*
258. In fact, Cicero was intimidated by a posse of Pompey's henchmen and dared not deliver the speech in the bold form that he later published. Milo was convicted and went into exile. He and Caelius Rufus, Cicero's protégé, later combined in a futile conspiracy against Caesar and were ingloriously killed.

Cicero's execution of Catiline's civilian friends in Rome. Thirteen years later, when Caesar crossed the Rubicon and marched on the city with an army of seasoned veterans from his Gallic wars, he knew very well that it was all or nothing.

37.

When Hippias was courteously received by the Persians, the fear of his vengeful return to Athens doubled with louder hostility toward the barbarians than the clever Pisistratus had cared to excite. In 499, the great Ionian city of Miletus in Asia Minor planned to rebel against the Great King. A deputation went to Sparta in search of allies. Their leader Aristagoras showed King Cleomenes a map on which Susa, the Persian capital, was highlighted as a rich source of booty. Three days later, Cleomenes asked how many days' march it was from the Ionian coast to the royal treasury. Aristagoras said, "Three months." "Stranger," Cleomenes said, "get out of Sparta before sunset. You're saying nothing that will ring sweet in Spartan ears, if it takes that long to get it." When the same deputation presented its case to the Athenians, the Assembly en masse made a sentimental and untenable promise of aid. A token force of 20 ships failed to remain on station once the Persians approached in large numbers.

In 494, after a disastrous naval defeat at Lade, Miletus was captured and burned, its inhabitants deported. Two years later, the playwright Phrynichus, sponsored by the ambitious and aggressive Themistocles, broke with traditional themes and wrote a drama-documentary on the fall of the city that Athens had pledged to help. It reminded the audience, too vividly for comfort or applause, of their abandonment of their fellow Ionians. The unduly clever author was heavily fined for his tactless innovation. This may have inclined later tragedians to refer to day-to-day politics and personalities only by recourse to more or less allusive mythological données. Aristotle took the studious view that what he termed *katharsis* was effective only when "audiences find themselves in circumstances that they have not lived through." Common sense suggests that the Athenians flinched at the reenactment of their own chagrin.[259] To witness the destruction of a Greek city was intolerable; it was never depicted in any other Greek tragedy, although Euripides represented the agony of Troy with unnerving relevance to what might happen to Athens.

In 490, when Darius the Great's forces invaded Greece, Hippias piloted the Persians, under Datis and Artaphernes, to a landing place in his family stronghold of Marathon. He clearly expected to be restored to his lost supremacy. In the battle that followed, Miltiades and his well-drilled Athenian infantry put an end to Pisistratid hopes; but it was claimed that signals had been exchanged between the Medizing Hippias and his partisans in Athens by the coded flashing of their shields. Victory would have indicated that the gods favored Hippias's cause; defeat confirmed his eclipse. He repaired to the island of Lemnos, a favorite refuge for the dejected,[260] and did not live to

259. There have been several American films about the disaster of Pearl Harbor in December 1941. None was a hit. *From Here to Eternity,* with Burt Lancaster, Montgomery Clift, and Frank Sinatra, was a success because it concentrated on the hard daily life of ordinary soldiers on the base.

260. In 1749 C.E., Constantine Mavrocordato, a polymath Phanariot Greek who was prince of Wallachia under the Ottomans, was imprisoned—literally dejected—down a well on Lemnos until he paid a fat ransom. Mansel's *Constantinople* includes a sustained account of Greek life under the dangerous aegis of the Sublime Porte. Byron's Greek friend when he was in Missolonghi was another Prince Mavrocordato. See my *Byron* (1982).

see the next, much more elaborate invasion of Greece, by Xerxes, ten years later.

Once Xerxes had been defeated, Phrynichus had a theatrical comeback, in 476, with his *Phoenissae,* which celebrated the Athenian victory over the Persian fleet and its Phoenician crews at Salamis. In 473, Aeschylus wrote his *Persae,* on the same topic, and Phrynichus's innovative work slipped from the canon. *Persae* flattered Athenian vanity; it also displayed gloating magnanimity in imagining the aftermath of the war from the point of view of the defeated Persians. Aeschylus's treatment of a contemporary topic was not repeated; but there was never another Athenian victory quite like Salamis.

38.

The posthumous prestige of the three great Attic tragedians has obscured the fact that, like Phidias, they were not regarded with unmitigated awe by their fellow citizens. Like many writers, Aeschylus moralized at a higher level than he lived. Although he fought at the battle of Marathon (where his brother bled to death, his hand severed by a fleeing Persian, whose boat he tried to capture), the playwright was said to be a rowdy drinker and, despite his many victories, a bad loser when defeated by Sophocles in 468. The *Oresteia* furnished Athens with a modernized dignity not matched by any other Greek city. In another now lost work, its author's depiction of the gods led to a charge of sacrilege. Athens's greatest poetic encomiast decamped to Sicily, where he died, some say at the age of ninety, supposedly after an eagle dropped a tortoise on his bald head, which it had mistaken for a suitable boulder on which to crack the shell.

Aeschylus's sonorous verses were mocked respectfully by Aristophanes, who reserved his unguarded scorn for Euripides. Aeschylus is said, in the *Oxford Companion to Classical Literature*, to have "accepted the presuppositions of his time: guilt is inherited; the guilty man . . . shall suffer but it may be in the person of his son . . . prosperity deludes men into . . . acts of insolence that lead to destruction." The suggestion is that, for all his genius, he lacked the wit to question the prevailing morality. Does the richness of his language not display and distress his society's contradictions? His characters' apparent lack of individual consciousness is of a piece with the values of a city in which, as Pericles would say in his Funeral Oration, a man who pursued solely private satisfactions and avoided public political involvements was a literal "idiot" (*idiotēs* implies a man who thinks only of himself). Is the modern conviction that an individual's motives are determined by "psychological" factors any less arbitrary?[261] Terminology procures its own conclusions.

If Aeschylus lived within the logic of his language, he also explored its limits: in *Suppliants,* he postulates—for the first time in any known text—a society in which even the ruler has to defer to the opinions of the majority.[262] The mutual destruction of the brothers Eteocles and Polynices, in his prize-winning

261. Gilbert Ryle's *The Concept of Mind* (1949) can be seen as a straight-faced satire on the idea of mental interiority. William Lyons tells me that Ryle's essay on Rodin's *Thinker* suggests that the statue's solemn pose is that of a man without anything going on "in his head." Might it be that Ryle, a noted wit, was "smiling inside"?

262. Noted by Pierre Lévêque and Pierre Vidal-Naquet in *Clisthène l'athénien* (1964). An enlarged English edition was published in 1996, edited by D. A. Curtis.

Seven against Thebes, can be read as a warning against bloody internal divisions in the city. Lacking the music integral to tragic performance, we have little certainty how audiences reacted. Extant tragedy has few evident laughs in it, but the Greeks have now, and may well have had in the past, a sense of humor that can be as heartless as it is often ribald. The scene with Orestes' old nurse, in the *Libation Bearers,* must surely have been greeted as light relief.

The public life of Sophocles, priest and general, gives the impression that, like his refined verses, he was a model of measured dignity. Among his obiter dicta was his reply, in old age, to the question what it was like no longer to experience sexual desire: it was, he said, "like escaping from a dangerous beast." In truth, even in mature days, Sophocles was much excited by young men. While on active service, as an elected general, he was reproached by Pericles for allowing sexual pursuit to interfere with the singlemindedness expected of a responsible commander.[263] Unlike many writers, Sophocles—who won more prizes than all his rivals put together—was quick to salute the talents of others. Hearing that Euripides had died, in Macedon, he came to the theater dressed in black and led a tribute to the exiled and embittered genius.

Euripides' later plays, written when Athens was on the verge of losing its struggle with Sparta, made overt allusions

---

263. The poet Pier Paolo Pasolini (1922–1975) directed films based on Sophocles' *Oedipus tyrannus* and Euripides' *Medea.* While having lunch with Orianna Falacci, an outspoken journalist, he left the table in pursuit of a handsome waiter. When he came back after a short time, he boasted that he had "made love" with the young man. Falacci said that he could call it whatever he chose, but not love.

to contemporary events. If he was the least sumptuously poetic of the great Attic tragedians, his influence outlasted them. Even during his lifetime he was widely quoted. When the Athenian army was captured by the vengeful Syracusans, some were spared execution, though not slavery in the *latomia* (stone mines), if they could recite a Euripidean chorus. It would be nice to presume that this entailed a common culture;[264] it is just as likely that the abject recitation was extracted to remind the captives of their lost supremacy. Aeschylus's *Persae,* celebrating the victory at Salamis, where its author had been present, as he had at Marathon,[265] was given one of its earliest performances in the theater overlooking the great harbor in which the Athenian fleet was cornered and destroyed by the Syracusans in 413 B.C.E.

Nineteen of Euripides' plays survive, more than those of the other two great (and prolific) tragedians put together. Tradition claims that he was born in 480 B.C.E., the year of Salamis. His rich family had property on the island where he is said to have composed his 92 plays in an isolated cave. Unlike the

---

264. There is a vestige of the old role of Latin as a civilized lingua franca in the often-told tale of the German general Kreipe, after being kidnapped on Crete by Patrick Leigh Fermor, reciting some verses from Horace and, when he "dried," being prompted by his captor. His response—"Ach so, Herr Major!"—was courteous, but the Germans later executed hundreds of Cretan hostages. With sour, self-serving *Kultur,* the Germans spared some Jewish musicians to form camp orchestras, to whose sad airs thousands of others were murdered. Leigh Fermor stayed in Greece after the war. His travel books—*Roumeli, Mani*—catch the scent and flavor of ancient'n'modern Hellas, before the advent of mass tourism.

265. In the obituary that, supposedly, he composed for himself, Aeschylus drew attention, with ostentatious modesty, only to his military service.

allegedly bibulous Aeschylus[266] and the sexually versatile Sophocles, Euripides had little disposition to make himself agreeable to his fellow-citizens. He won few prizes in the city's annual drama competition. Euripides may wheel out the deus ex machina to provide surprise endings, but his gods neither provide salvation nor deliver any happy form of justice. He has been labeled a rationalist and associated with the Sophists,[267] but his last extant play, *Bacchae*, is a reminder of the place of unreason in human society. When the young King Pentheus of Thebes refuses, against the advice of sage old Tiresias, to admit the worship of Dionysos to his city, its foundations are literally shaken by the androgynous god. The voyeuristic Pentheus, grotesquely dressed in drag, is revealed to the rampaging ravers and becomes the sacrificial victim of the disruptive deity whose immortal credentials he has denied.[268]

Euripides' reputation for misanthropy reflects his indifference to popular success (or his inability to command it). If he lacked faith in either gods or men, he had the confidence of his uncertainties: riven by the stress of human existence, his

266. Richard Seaford insists that Aeschylus's devotion to Dionysos, the god of the theater, has been exaggerated to suggest, without warrant, that the playwright was a wine-bibber. "Most of what we are told about ancient poets is fictional."

267. See (if only for curiosity's sake) the Victorian scholar A. W. Verrall's *Euripides the Rationalist* (1895) and D. J. Conacher's level-headed *Euripides and the Sophists* (1998).

268. According to Pausanias (2.2.7), Pentheus was associated with a tree cult in his native city of Thebes. René Girard might argue that, because the young king's sacrifice revived the city, Dionysos's victim becomes its posthumous savior.

characters express no consistent morality; they echo the quickness of Athenian parrhesia, free speech and debate. Despite his supposed lack of affection for his fellow citizens and distaste for women, Euripides was inclined to side with the defeated and the humiliated, especially females: he seems to find it easy, perhaps liberating, to imagine himself a woman and an outcast.

Like Aeschylus, Euripides had been arraigned for impiety (but not convicted); hence his eventual retreat to Macedon. *Bacchae* was written where the worship of Dionysos was given free rein. It warns of what Freud would call "the return of the repressed." Euripides' Dionysos somewhat resembles the "gentle" Jesus of Nazareth, whose divinity is denied and whose enemies in Jerusalem were punished, in the Christian reading, by the destruction of their temple and the doom of whoever failed to recognize the pale Galilean as their savior. Euripides, however, offered no gospel. As Athens tilted toward defeat in the long war with Sparta, plays such as *Phoenissae* (409) suggested no salvation for the vanquished in this world or in any other. If he took morbid pleasure in the crack of doom, he seemed to agree with Sophocles: the best thing for human beings was not to be born at all.

The Athenian demos were schooled to delight in coups de théâtre. In 427 B.C.E., they voted, on Cleon's advice, that the whole population of Mytilene, the principal city of Lesbos, should be put to death for rebelling against their hegemony. On the following day, on the motion of Diodotus (a speaker mentioned just once by Thucydides), the Assembly was moved, as much by pragmatic as by humane considerations, to send a fast trireme to pursue the one that had already left with the death warrant. The rowers bearing the reprieve arrived just in time.

39.

Aristotle, the first and most influential analyst of Athenian tragedy, was the son of the court physician of the Macedonian king
Amyntas III, grandfather of Alexander the Great. The notion that
"creative writing" can be taught derives from his *Poetics*. After
careful reading of some 300 scripts (ten times more than are
available to modern scholars), he proposed a maquette for the
well-made play that instructed many later playwrights and infu-
riated others. In his philosophy, everything had a natural form.
Its growth was determined by an innate impulse to reach its full-
est expression. Unlike Plato, he did not expect poets to serve some
general or abstract truth: "Homer," he observed in *Poetics*, "has
above all taught the rest how to speak fictions as a poet ought."
Plato offered no place in his ideal city for such amiable license.

Although he taught in the city, Aristotle was not mortified by
the local difficulty of what had gone wrong with wayward, imperial Athens. Intellectually assimilated, but in appearance an
oddity, he never pretended to be other than a visiting professor
from a part of Greece where beauty and brutality lived together
(he was born in Stageiros, in the Thracian Chalcidice). In Peter
Green's description, he was "foppish, not to say eccentric ... bald,
spindle-shanked and had small eyes ... he wore dandified
clothes, cut and curled his hair in an affected manner, and spoke
with a lisp ... rings sparkled on his fingers: the overall effect
must have been like the young Disraeli at his worst."[269]
    When King Amyntas III of Macedon died, his son Philip
first secured the throne by having all his brothers killed. He

269. Peter Green, *Alexander the Great* (1992).

then turned his marginal monarchy into the most powerful state in Hellas. Means and ends grew on the same royal stem. No theory warranted Macedonian practice; no morality inhibited it. Aristotle was recruited as tutor to Philip's son, Alexander. He may have taught him to appreciate Homer (and emulate Achilles), but he was wise enough not to try to improve the young prince, as Plato had Dion of Syracuse, with the sustained study of mathematics. Aristotle was, in essence, a biologist: he looked closely at physical things and catalogued their variety; metaphysics came, literally, later. Plato, the pundit, had subordinated everything to a seemly, seamless Whole. He would have it that art should not be privileged above the official version of divine order. If poets would not honor that line, they could have no place in his society. Aristotle, whose own dialogues are lost, was straight-faced enough to anticipate Nietzsche and classify Plato's own Socratic dialogues under poetry.

Aristotle's *Poetics* had enduring didactic effects. In Renaissance England, Sir Philip Sidney and John Dennis (who called the Stagirite "the legislator of Parnassus") were keen to rig themselves in his colors. A century later, John Dryden was saying, " 'Tis not enough that Aristotle has said so; for Aristotle drew his models . . . from Sophocles and Euripides; and, if he had seen ours, might have changed his mind." Dryden deplored the promotion of tragedy over epic "because it turns in a shorter compass, the whole action being circumscribed within the space of four-and-twenty hours. He might prove as well that a mushroom is to be preferred before a peach because it shoots up in the compass of a night."

The long debate over what Aristotle really meant, not least by katharsis, and whether he was right was described by one of the first professors of English literature, Henry Morley (1822–1894), as "a grotesque monument to sterility."[270] Aristotle confined his study of plays to the library. Wincing at the vulgarity of *opsis* (spectacle), he subsumed poetry under rhetoric. He scarcely noticed how deeply theatrical gesture had affected— Plato might have said *in*fected—Athenian life. It was common for the accused, in capital cases, to parade their weeping wives and children before juries who, they could hope, had been schooled in pity by plays such as Euripides' *Trojan Women*. Wisdom, Aeschylus said, came through suffering; and, presumably, by drawing the right conclusions from its reenactment.[271]

Thomas Gray (1716–1771) spoke for many when he said, "Aristotle is the hardest author by far I ever meddled with; then he has a dry conciseness that makes one imagine one is perusing a Table of Contents rather than a book." The received wisdom is that the philosopher unpacked his ideas more explicitly and attractively in seminars. The sediment of his lectures suggests that Aristotle relished piquing Athenian conceits: he points out that the word *drama* (from *drān*, to do or to act) is of Dorian origin; Athenians more regularly used the synonymous *prattein;* not even comedy, Aristotle prattled, was an original Attic mode: sixth-century Megarians were the first to stage it.

Aristotle's condensed obscurity (which, according to Roger Bacon, the thirteenth century's *mirabilis doctor,* lends

270. Cited by Stephen Halliwell in his 1998 edition of the *Poetics*.
271. The technique of editing, especially of pictorial images of carnage and cruelty, can serve as well to "vaccinate" its audience (which smells nothing and hears only what is deemed suitable) against unhappy reactions to the painless horrors served up to it by the media. A plethora of information can be the prelude to indifference.

itself to tendentious translation[272]) is a function of how much he has to say. As Alexander Pope put it, "Poets . . . / Receiv'd his laws, and stood convinc'd 't was fit / Who conquered nature should preside o'er wit." The solemn observation that a composition must have "a beginning, a middle, and an end" elicited Jean-Luc Godard's qualified endorsement: he said that, as far as films are concerned, they did not have to come in that order.[273]

The notion that tragic heroes generally meet their fate because of a single characteristic flaw, which Aristotle termed *hamartia,* was elaborated by Christian exegetes so that it could seem to prefigure the un-Greek notion of sin (and the possibility of redemption). Hamartia meant the "mistake" or "error" of transgressing established limits; it carried no sinful connotation: it implied something like, in the modern cant, "my bad." Kenneth McLeish compares it to a dropped stitch that wrecks the pattern of stability until repaired, by whatever abrupt means. In the same sense, hubris was whatever did violence to due process; it could involve, but did not *mean,* arrogance.[274] Halliwell suggests that Aristotle's notion of katharsis is analogous to the "cleansing" of pilgrims when they underwent "the curative purge of the Eleusinian mysteries," an experience akin to the rebirth that Christian sects affect to deliver by immersive baptism. In *Samson Agonistes*—the most Greek play in English—Milton

---

272. Especially from Arab versions of the text, which was the common case in Bacon's time.

273. Jean-Luc Godard (b. 1930) was a leading critic and then director during the radical Nouvelle Vague of the 1960s. Modern university courses on film theory tend, however, to be in the Aristotelian, quasi-essentialist tradition. Skepticism is recommended when it comes to their practical relevance to making movies.

274. Kenneth McLeish, trans., Aristotle, *Poetics* (1999).

signals the moment of cathartic quietus as one in which all passion is spent. Aristotle may have been capable of more levity than his Christian appropriators thought proper. The donnée of Umberto Eco's *The Name of the Rose* depends on the plausibility of a monk, during the Middle Ages, piously destroying the last copy of Aristotle's essay on comedy because it failed to chime with the philosopher's solemn place in Christian doxology.

There is a cleavage between Aristotle's biological and his metaphysical styles. His fieldwork set an example for attention to the specific and respect for variety; in teleology and divinity, he ceased to be an observer and became the proponent of a priori theories later modified and incorporated into official theology by the Vatican. Aristotle's contempt for the banausic chimes with Seaford's linkage of philosophy and money. Desire for a universal currency is matched, in a sublime register, by the application of an imperious logic. Pythagoras's mathematical scheme also affected to warrant a social project along previously ruled lines. His frequently adopted notion of the golden mean suggests the existence of a proper meta-economic balance.

Aristotle's central place in the theological bracing of Catholic doctrine closed Western minds to freethinking science until Copernicus's and Galileo's ideas could no longer be interdicted. The Stagirite's notion of the sequence of four causes why plants and animals grow as they do has lost its categorical status, but it was not without some observed sense. The same cannot be said about his theory of vision,[275] especially when it came to mirrors and the effect menstruating females were said to have on them:

275. In his essay on *Dreams* 459b, cited by Françoise Frontisi-Ducroux and Jean-Pierre Vernant in *Dans l'oeil du miroir* (1997), from which the quoted passage is loosely translated.

it produces a sort of bloody cloud on the surface. If
the mirror is new, it is not easy to remove the stain
by rubbing it. If old, it's easier. The cause is . . . that
our vision is not only affected by the air. . . . Sight is
one of the things that shine and which have color.
When a woman is menstruating, her eyes are affected along with the rest of her body, since they
too have veins in them. . . . the eyes, as a result, are
invisibly inflamed with blood (sperm and menses
have an identical nature), and the air is put in
movement and has an effect on what it strikes,
hence on the appearance of the mirror. . . . Bronze,
because it is smooth, is particularly susceptible to
such contact. . . . In new mirrors . . . the stain pen-
etrates deeply and in all directions because of the
smoothness of the surface. In old mirrors, the effect
is more superficial. In view of these facts, it is clear
that small differences produce the movement, that
the sensation is rapid, and . . . the perceiving organ-
ism is not only affected but itself has an effect.

Aristotle's credulity may have been enhanced by the fact
that mirrors were associated with female self-regard. Narcissus
was the exception that underlines the rule. On vases and wall
paintings, women are frequently depicted looking at themselves.
Perhaps the tactful philosopher took some female's word for it
that her mirror blushed when she was menstruating.[276]

276. Aristotle's "conceit" has a figurative echo in the ideas of Jean-Paul
Sartre's friend and rival Maurice Merleau-Ponty (1908–1961), as unpacked by
Michel de Certeau (*Esprit*, 1982): "seeing is already a language-act. This act

40.

Macedonian queens presided over rites in honor of the Muses' local birthplace, Pieria, in southern Macedon. Women were crowned with snakes, live animals torn to greedy pieces. In the early Iron Age (1000–700 B.C.E.), rich aristocratic women in the region are said to have held greater power than their husbands and to have "communicated with the supernatural for the benefit of their people." The mother of Alexander the Great, the Epeirote witch-queen Olympias, inherited the aura of her female ancestors. She claimed that her son was conceived after Zeus had paid her a nocturnal visit, a form of conception that blessed the infant Alexander with accelerated legitimacy.[277]

At the beginning of the fifth century, Macedonians were regarded as semibarbarian (they sported tattoos); only the reigning king was admitted, reluctantly, to the Hellenes-only Olympic Games. Macedon was snubbed not least because its rulers had had little choice but to yield to the invading Persians in 490 and 480. Since, at that time, their military power was limited and their tenure uncertain, the country's kings, several of whom were called Perdiccas, had to be like that clever bird (one was nicknamed Aeropos, the walker on air). During the Peloponnesian War, Perdiccas II was an

---

makes things seen an expression of the invisible texture which holds them together." Bloody-mindedness, on this reckoning, colors what we *think* we are seeing.

277. *The Myth of the Goddess* by Anne Baring and Jules Cashford (1991) is a magnificently thorough account of the mutation of feminine power in prehistory and, incidentally, of the priority of the moon goddess, whose regular appearances might be said, however fancifully (and not by the authors) to have given rise to the use of the future tense.

unreliable, because nervous, ally of the Athenians. In 413 B.C.E., as Athens was losing its hegemony, Euripides' ambitious future patron Archelaos came to the Macedonian throne. Euripides' lost play *Archelaos* dignified the mythical king with divine instructions from Delphi to follow a goat to the site of Aegae (Goatsberg). The state's ancient capital was similar to Sparta in being a collection of villages, although the royal compound was imposingly fortified.

A bastard prince, the historical Archelaos murdered his legitimate rivals (noblesse obliged: to have killed someone was a certificate of manhood in Macedon) and confirmed his authority both by his ruthlessness—Plato winces at his name in *Gorgias*—and by the splendor of his plans for the new capital at Pella. Like earlier tyrants, he dressed his court with artistic company. The great painter Zeuxis, nearing the end of his life, decorated his palace; the Athenian actor/playwright Agathon and the poet Timotheos lent his capital a civilized ambience. Archelaos was murdered in 399 by a courtier, perhaps his lover, after he had gone back on a promise to have him marry his daughter. He had laid the foundations both for the recently excavated splendor of Pella and for the ascent of Macedon, which was confirmed by the nerve and cunning of Philip II, the father of Alexander the Great.

In the same period, the Gauls invaded Italy, routed the Romans at the battle of the Allia in 390 B.C.E., and sacked their city.[278] That humiliation was the low point from which Rome

278. A century later, tribesmen also known generically as "Gauls" invaded and pillaged Hellas. Some continued into Asia Minor and became the "Galatians" in central Anatolia to whom St. Paul addressed one of his epistles.

was to rise and rise until, just over two centuries later, Lucius Aemilius Paullus defeated Perseus, the king of Macedon, at Pydna. His victory was so lucrative (more than 150,000 prisoners were sold into slavery) that it encouraged wholesale Roman domination of the sprawling, disparate empire that Alexander the Great had converted to Hellenism in a blend of what Empedocles called *philia* and *neikos*. Love/hatred came to bind and divide Greeks and Romans, Jews and barbarians in the web of cordial animosities known as the Pax Romana.

41.

Cleisthenes personified the Greek genius for calculated innovation. What other ancient culture engendered such a congeries of schemes for the conduct of public and private life? Since men such as Pythagoras were of hybrid origin, it is as if the articulation of the Greek language itself spawned dialectal variety and metrical ingenuities. Unlike Hebrew—the language of a single god who brooked neither dissent nor division[279]—Greek was detached from sacerdotal and doctrinal constriction. Plato is notorious for banning poets from his ideal republic, but he was hardly less apprehensive of the generative power of what was written in prose. In the *Phaedrus,* he says that script allows words to take on a life of their own, distinct if not divorced from the intentions of their original authors.[280]

279. This did not, of course, prevent His people, the Jews, being notorious on both deplorable, stimulating counts.

280. The so-called intentional fallacy was a term devised to make literary critics the best judges of what an author really meant to say: the fallacy was to privilege what a writer claimed to have intended. Cleverly modified, this disqualification of the writer issued in the idea, propagated by Roland

By Cleisthenes' time, legislators and town planners had proposed various schemes for social regulation; none matched his combination of principle with self-effacing opportunism. The son of Megacles devised the complex democratic constitution on which the success and renown of ancient Athens was founded. Never before had the votes of all male citizens carried, in theory at least, the same weight. Yet his person was little celebrated. He won no famous victories; he neither said nor did anything that men cared to remember. No statues or illustrations idealized his person as they did that of the two accidentally heroic tyrannicides.

Although his initial motives may have been as partisan as his Alcmaeonid lineage promised, Cleisthenes' redesign of the civic calendar and division of power among all of the citizens of Attica marked an abrupt distinction between how things had been and how they turned out. The motive for the new measures was of far less significance than their consequences. Herodotus says that when the city was governed by tyrants, the Athenians were not superior in war to their neighbors; but once given the

Barthes and others, that authors have no proprietorial rights over their texts and can be said, with a straight face, to have done nothing more than prepare a ground on which those who deconstruct them can compose cleverer, more nuanced analyses. Inadvertently, this has also encouraged the demanding assertiveness of publishers, editors, and academics, whom it licenses to have quasi-sacerdotal authority to revise or deplore what deferential scribes have been commissioned to compose. The disparagement of the canon of Great Writers leads to new rankings in which the best authors are those around whom academics can make clever rings. In *The Second Sophistic,* Tim Whitmarsh is candid in his determination to "do away entirely with the idea of the culturally central, the paradigmatic . . . hierarchies of cultural value." His principal target is Werner Jaeger's once standard notion of *paideia.* Elaborate locutions are, however, commonly deployed by the newest critics to intimidate the layman.

vote and an equal voice (*isēgoria*), they were by far the best. When, at a meeting of the Peloponnesian League, late in the sixth century B.C.E., the Spartan king Cleomenes proposed to march on Athens in support of the deposed Hippias, he was challenged, eloquently, by the Corinthian Socles: "In truth, the sky is going to disappear under the earth, and the earth fly above the sky, men are going to live in the sea and fish where men used to be, since you Spartans, by ruining egalitarian regimes [*isokratias*], are preparing to reestablish tyrannies."

Cleomenes' support of Cleisthenes' oligarchic opponent Isagoras did more to confirm than to threaten the democratic leader. Previously, Athens had been divided between rival clans, but Cleisthenes' unobtrusively calculated plan to enfranchise the demos procured him an irreversible majority. He took his name and his radical methods from his maternal grandfather Cleisthenes, the sixth-century tyrant of Sicyon, on the north coast of the Peloponnese, west of Corinth. The older Cleisthenes anticipated—perhaps inspired—Plato by banning Homer from his city, because the *Iliad* heroized Argives, whose Dorian descendants in contemporary Argos threatened Sicyon. He also gave derisory names (Piglets, Asses, and Porkers) to the three Dorian tribes whose members his city had in common with the rival city. His own tribe was entitled "Heads of the People."

The younger Cleisthenes went further: he revised the structure and renamed the Attic tribes in order to integrate the demos into the new social system. If his motives were self-interested (he needed supporters to head off the anti-Alcmaeonid Isagoras), his remodeling of the political topography of the city liberated energies that led to its ascendancy in the fifth century. However radical, he was more reformer than revolutionary: while everyone's prospects were enhanced, and a pivotal role assigned to the demos, the office of archon (chief magistrate) was still reserved for the wealthiest citizens; the old aristocracy continued to monopolize the priesthood, a symbolic eminence without pastoral duties or affectations of privileged access to the gods.

That the Athenians accepted Cleisthenes' reforms, when no blatant force was used to impose them, suggests that the eviction of the Pisistratids had left a confusion in need of resolute treatment. Enrolling all male citizens in the electoral register won support without the need to sweeten any particular constituency with palliative privileges. His grandfather's example inspired the reformer to create ten new tribes whose composition owed nothing to tradition. Each was to consist of elements drawn from the three previously antagonistic segments of Attica: city, coast, and rural hinterland. As if by chance, the menacing solidarity of the mountain fiefdom of the Pisistratids was dismantled. Its members were flattered by what seemed like increased influence, but in fact dispersed and diluted local solidarity. In the same spirit, poorer citizens had to pool their enhanced powers with colleagues from two other districts. No one territorial caucus, however vociferous, could assert itself without the support of those from elsewhere. Compromise and balance were of the essence of a system without an ideologically loaded logos.

Cleisthenes' electoral map replaced old local cult centers, dominated by aristocratic hierarchies, with new premises for common worship. The ten new tribes were named from a list of 100 possibilities submitted to the judgment of the Delphic oracle. This decimal resection eliminated the priestly unction of the old families as if by divine ordinance. The majesty of the old gods was not in question; but the landed gentry could no longer rely on inherited priesthoods to fortify its dignity.

Even Theseus, who had been favored by the Pisistratids, was deleted from the eponymous team sheet.[281] Aias (Ajax) was annexed to it, in order to graft his birthplace, the island of Salamis, recently furnished with Athenian settlers, into the body politic. Theseus's father Aegeus was also evicted. His cult had been too enthusiastically honored in Marathon, a power base of Pisistratus.

Although the radical democrat Ephialtes reduced the judicial powers of the Areopagus (as part of a campaign to damage the aristocratic Cimon), Cleisthenes' reforms endured for a century without substantial change.[282] Rhetoric, with its appeal to immediate action, determined policy, rather than piety, with its penchant toward cautious immobility: the Spartans had arrived too late for the battle of Marathon because, so they said, probably truly, ancestral lore required them to conclude a three-day festival in honor of Apollo. Thucydides reports with muted scorn how, at a crucial moment in the Sicilian expedition, after the defeat of the Athenian fleet in the Great Harbor, Nicias delayed the retreat of his remaining troops for

281. Sentiment soon restored Theseus to the iconographic register in which he was portrayed as the unifier of Attica and even as the creator of democracy. On some vases, he is depicted in a posture like that of the later tyrannicide bronzes by Critias and Nesiotes (see Lévêque and Vidal-Naquet, *Clisthène l'athénien*).

282. Plato took sly aristocratic revenge on Cleisthenes by giving his fictional Atlantis ten tribes and making *orichalcum* (literally, "mountain copper") its most precious metal, the equivalent of the silver from the Attic mines at Laurium that funded Themistocles' development of the Athenian fleet. The fictional defeat of Atlantis was Plato's way of wishing away his own city's pursuit of maritime glory. Philosophers have often sought to impose some desired pattern on an irregular world. See Ronald Hayman's 1986 critical biography of Jean-Paul Sartre, *Writing Against*, and Karl Popper's *The Poverty of Historicism* (1957).

three times three times three days because of his superstitious
inertia in the face of an eclipse of the moon, on August 28, 413.
The victorious Syracusans were given time to rally the rest of
the Sicilians to their side. As a result, the Athenians were harried
and encircled as they set off, belatedly, to retreat across the island
on foot. Not one escaped. Disaster became catastrophe.[283]

42.

Antique rituals and annual festivals in the social calendar were
banded around Phidias's colorful Parthenon frieze. Yet the
political institutions of fifth-century Athens were at odds with
the power structure of the Olympians. While the furniture of
the city paid gilded tribute to the autocratic Zeus and his
family, its institutions were designed to balk autocracy and
check presumption. There were contrary consequences: freedom of speech licensed theatrical impertinence; it also primed
Plato's rejection of the shocking morals of the Homeric gods.[284]
His disparagement of "poets" was of a piece with nostalgia
for a world that never was, but—as his own Atlantis myth
suggested—might better have been, in his view at least.

Innovation, like "revolution" in the modern world, was
seen by some as a promise, by others as a threat. Democracy

283. Bad news traveled slowly. The disaster was not known at Athens
until a Phoenician sailor went into a barbershop in Piraeus and mentioned
it, in casual conversation, assuming that it was common knowledge. He was
chased down the street and, the story goes, murdered. Messengers in tragedy
never suffered the same fate.

284. While on rather lazy war service in Yugoslavia in 1943, Randolph
Churchill was incited by Evelyn Waugh to read the Bible for the first time. He
was heard to exclaim, on several occasions, "What a shit God is!"

civilized divisions and also, by the annual rotation of its officers, civil and military, implied in the form of its own institutions that a self-critical society could never take conclusive form. Adversarial rhetoric and theatrical comedy were the strident criers of freedom. Contradictions were of the essence of a constitution in which the majority was empowered to make decisions but could never determine truths.

Socrates was buoyed on the cross-currents of the old and the new: his notion of conscience, in the form of his personal *daimon,* was deemed heretical by a popular jury that, in his case at least, opted for traditional values. The angriest charge against him, in 399 B.C.E., was of disloyalty to the democracy that Plato deplored and to which his paragon claimed—with only some justice—to have remained faithful. Socrates had, in truth, been enrolled, perhaps involuntarily, by the Thirty Tyrants, in 404–403, as one of the 3,000 trustworthy citizens. By accepting the sentence of its democratic court rather than go into resigned exile, Socrates conceded that life would be without savor anywhere but in the same city on which he had sprinkled his Attic salt. The "examined life" for which he argued was less introspective than self-regarding. His pettish modesty had a measure of preening. He asked many questions, but showed small practical curiosity. The world beyond the city limits had no appeal for him.[285]

285. After a tracheotomy for cancer in Athens, in 1932, Constantine Cavafy convalesced in a clinic in Kifissia, from which he had a panoramic view of Mt. Pentelikon and other marbled mountains. "They bore me," he said. Before returning to Alexandria to die, he was happier in a hotel whence he could enjoy the "evening bustle" of downtown Athens: *Cavafy* by Robert Liddell (1976).

43.

Commanding the isthmus between the Saronic Gulf and the Ionian Sea and the Peloponnese from northern Greece, Corinth was geographically placed to be a major power. In the eighth century B.C.E., the Corinthians were quick off the mark in creating overseas colonies, but they proved to have enterprise without self-assurance or diplomatic charm. Their city had a luxurious, unheroic history. Its black-figure pottery, the first and finest on the export market in the sixth century,[286] was outproduced and outsold, a century later, by Athenian red-figure, which could be manufactured more quickly, marketed more cheaply. The dimensions of the Athenian ceramics industry remained no more than artisanal: even at its peak, the Keramikos quarter employed scarcely more than some 400 potters and painters. Militarily, Corinth was overshadowed by Athens on sea and by its nominal ally, Sparta, on land. The first recorded sea battle, in 734 B.C.E., was between the Corinthians and their colonists on Corcyra, Calypso's island, and was won by the latter. Colonists rarely remained deferential to their mother cultures.[287] While preserving some ancestral

---

286. Instances have been found at Megara Hyblaia in Sicily and in Romania. Pottery was a common form of payment in kind (especially for metal) when money was not available, as far away as Spain, Gaul, Egypt, and the Black Sea.

287. The British have suffered repeatedly from emulous ingratitude. New England was first populated by refugees from old England, whose religion and culture they imported and whose aristocratic social institutions they abandoned. Like many Greek settlers, the colonists attempted both to absorb and, eventually, extirpate indigenous people. The English used Australia as a dumping ground for convicts whose descendants developed the country, and showed small mercy for the "aborigines" whom they displaced and

traditions, they often made social experiments in defiance of the old country. Corcyra became as prosperous and at least as powerful as Corinth itself, from which its founding fathers had sailed.[288]

The outbreak of the Peloponnesian War in 431 B.C.E. was due to a marked degree to Corinth's ostentatious inferiority complex.[289] The city's bad luck would reach its nadir in 146 B.C.E., when it was part of the rebellious Achaean League's opposition to the Romans. Lucius Mummius put its inhabitants to the sword and, historians say, razed it to the ground. James R. Wiseman, an archaeologist who did extensive work there, claims that reports of the severity of the destruction were greatly exaggerated. Classicists used to rely almost entirely on canonical texts. Philology did not encourage travel, nor piety skepticism. As late as 1970, Thucydidean scholars gave the impression that "Epipolae," the district through which, in 415 B.C.E., the Athenians mounted an almost successful surprise night attack on Syracuse, was some sort of suburban

---

often maltreated. The natives of Tasmania had already been systematically massacred by the British. Australians have long had a love-hate relationship with the motherland and an ambivalent admiration for its culture, the game of cricket not least. In 1933–1934, there was a cricket "war" between the Australians and the English during a tour led by the supercilious Douglas Jardine, the very type of aristocrat who had transported the first Australians to their penitential paradise. Baseball knocked cricket out of North America before it arrived.

288. The first war conducted by the United States was against England. In the late 19th century, America's growing prosperity and the "almighty dollar" threatened England's hegemony. As late as the 1920s, the British had contingency plans for a war with the US.

289. Corinthian columns are distinguished by the florid capitals that some stylists consider degenerate.

enclave. Peter Green[290] was the first modern English classicist who did the footwork to prove that Epipolae was the name for a steep rocky scarp rather than for some prototypical gated community.

The site of Corinth, like that of Carthage, which was flattened by the Romans at the same period, proved too attractive not to be rebuilt. Within 100 years, Corinth had a prosperous mercantile population, of Greeks and Jews, and the refined erotic amenities to excite Horace's apothegm "Non cuivis homini contingit adire Corinthum" (Not just anybody has the luck to go to Corinth). The flat modern city, in the shadow of the old acropolis, is one of the most charmless in Greece.

44.

The Persian Empire that came to threaten the Ionian Greeks, and later mainland Greece itself, was founded in the second half of the sixth century B.C.E., after Cyrus the Great had defeated first his overlord, the Mede Astyages, and then Croesus of Lydia. The Fertile Crescent as far as Babylon fell under his power. By allowing the long-exiled Jews to return to Jerusalem, he must have hoped to secure a grateful bastion in the center of the coastal plain. According to his encomiast Xenophon, he exemplified the enlightened ruler.[291] He dispensed justice in

---

290. In *Armada from Athens* (1970).

291. Unsurprisingly, Plato took issue, in *The Laws,* with Socrates' friend Xenophon and claimed that, for all his achievements, Cyrus had made a serious mistake in leaving the education of the Persian royal family to the women, with the result that his successors were "overpampered and undisciplined." Ottoman sultans were accused, with some justice, of being dominated by royal females and seraglio charmers.

accordance with what Greeks called "the law of the Medes and the Persians which changeth not." Cyrus had, in fact, reversed the previous relations between the two peoples. Cyrus was succeeded, in 530 B.C.E., by his less genial son Cambyses. Some sources claim that his first act was to kill his brother Smerdis. He had an inquisitive judge—more Mede than Persian perhaps—flayed alive and then invaded Egypt. Cambyses was said to have "killed the god Apis," the sacred bull,[292] and to have marched against Pelusium, driving a swarm of cats and dogs ahead of his army. Since the Egyptians reverenced these animals as divine, they were distracted and then overwhelmed. Cambyses died after slightly wounding himself in the thigh with his own sword, while mounting his horse. The wound was, so the Egyptians claimed, the revenge of Apis, who had died from a wound in the same quarter.

Cambyses left no heir. The throne was claimed by someone who said he was Smerdis. He was dislodged by a septet of aristocrats that included Darius, a distant descendant of Cyrus the Great who had escaped Cambyses' purge. The seven against Smerdis agreed that, after they had disposed of the usurper, whoever's horse neighed first would become king. Since Darius's groom had previously led his horse to a favorite mare, near the path which the seven would later take, the selection process is likely to have been suggested by Darius himself. As a result, according to Herodotus, "before sunrise, while they were proceeding all together, the horse recollecting the mare, suddenly neighed; and at the same time . . . a clap of thunder was heard, as if in approbation of the choice."

292. Paul Cartledge says that Egyptian records refute this claim.

The six runners-up saluted Darius. They asked only that the king's wives and concubines be chosen exclusively from their families. In addition, they should have the right of direct access to the king.[293] These conditions created, for as long as they lasted, a cross between oligarchy and tyranny. The limitation of the king's women was a modified version of the incest common among tyrants who did not care, or dare, to allow anyone outside their immediate family to have a claim on power. Claude Lévi-Strauss argued that the prohibition of incest derives from a "rule of reciprocity ... for I will give up my daughter or sister only if my neighbor does the same." Incest is "unsociable before it is morally culpable"; no genuine community, with its nexus of mutual trust and affiliation, is possible otherwise.[294] This may help to explain why tyranny was abhorrent to both democrats and oligarchs and why, in particular, the two Athenian so-called tyrannicides were so deliberately and repeatedly venerated.

Darius established his supremacy by a series of military campaigns. He captured Babylon, after a protracted siege, as a result of a ruse by a courtier called Zopyrus. According to Herodotus, he cut off his own nose and ears and fled to the enemy camp, where he told the Babylonians that he had been savagely mutilated because he had warned Darius that their defenses were impregnable. The Babylonians were gulled into appointing Zopyrus their commander, after which he was able to deliver the city to Darius. The king is reported to have said,

293. The Great King's companions were expected always to tell him the truth and were exempt, in theory, from penalty if it was unpalatable. It is tempting to suggest that the philosophical obsession with truth may have a Persian rather than a Greek provenance.
294. Cf. Louis Gernet's 1968 article "Mariages de tyrans."

many times, that he would sooner have Zopyrus intact than 20 Babylons.

Darius suffered a serious reverse when he attempted to impose his rule on the Scythians. This encouraged rebellion in the Greek cities in Ionia. Aided by a modest Athenian fleet, the Milesians and their allies took and burned Sardis. When Darius counterattacked, the Athenians sailed away, leaving their Ionian kin to take the heat. The Great King proceeded to the sack of Miletus, to which Phrynichus's play referred so tactlessly. Darius did not forget or forgive.[295] A servant was instructed to say to him every night, "Remember, O king, to punish the Athenians." In 490 B.C.E., the Great King honored his prompter and mounted a punitive expedition against mainland Greece.[296]

The shoulder-to-shoulder hoplites who confronted the Persians at Marathon confirmed that Cleisthenes' measures had engendered a new, militant solidarity, sealed by fear of what would follow the return of Hippias.[297] The Persians withdrew, but their menace dominated Greek politics for the next ten years. The infantry at Marathon was commanded, triumphantly, by the

295. History repeated itself, somewhat, in the aftermath of World War I, when the Greeks attempted to restore their Asian hegemony and were definitively ousted from the region. See *Ionian Vision: Greece in Asia Minor*, by Michael Llewellyn Smith (1998).

296. Gore Vidal's novel *Creation* (1981) dares, at mischievous length, to suggest that mainland Hellas was of peripheral, if punitive, concern for the Persians.

297. Old pieties were not abandoned: after the victory, 500 goats were sacrificed in Athens to Artemis Agrotera. Without the bloody detail, Greek religion can take on a deceptive quaintness. It may well be, however, that what was done in honor of the goddess went to feed the victorious troops.

aristocratic Miltiades, who had spent previous years in exile as the tyrant of the Thracian Chersonese and, like a condottiere, had served on Darius's staff during the invasion of Scythia. Athenian social divisions had been closed by Cleisthenes, but never healed tight. Miltiades' recovered kudos kindled the jealousy of the Alcmaeonid clan. The year after Marathon, he led a large Athenian fleet against Paros, but failed to capture it. Xanthippus, the father of Pericles, moved for the general's impeachment for taking bribes. Miltiades was fined the huge sum of 50 talents, but died, in prison, of the wounds he had incurred on campaign. Despite Cleisthenes' rebalancing of power within Athens, personal vanities and ambitions could revive antique vendettas or kindle new ones. By introducing communal rituals and ceremonies, democracy socialized confrontations it never eradicated.

45.

Themistocles was in his twenties at the time of Marathon. Since his mother was not Athenian, although his father was of ancient lineage, he benefited both from the new social climate and from Alcmaeonid support. The ambitious outsider was a useful drummer for the aristocracy: like Benjamin Disraeli, Themistocles was at once energetic and without powerful family connections. He had, however, already sponsored the development of Piraeus. The new harbor and its workforce became the base from which he pressed for investment in sea power.

In 483 B.C.E., the state-owned silver mines at Laurium produced a spectacular surplus. Aristeides, who had been Miltiades' chief of staff at Marathon, proposed that the windfall be split equally among the citizens. Themistocles appealed to them to pool the city's lucky wealth in the construction of a fleet of

200 triremes. His proposal had the immediate charm of enabling the Athenians to humble their neighbors and commercial rivals, the Aiginetans. His ulterior purpose was to be ready for a renewed Persian invasion. Darius the Great had been succeeded, in 486, by his son Xerxes. Piety and desire to assert his majesty required that he avenge his father. Themistocles' eloquence persuaded the Athenians to accept the shipbuilding policy. The ostracism of Aristeides cleared the way for the aggressive, opportunist foreign policy that naval power has often fostered.

Athens was never self-supporting in grain; barley grew more readily than wheat on Attic soil, but there was not enough of it for self-sufficiency. The nautical option was both a gamble and a necessity. Among the "liturgies" (public contributions) exacted from the 1,200 richest citizens and metics, on a rota basis, was that of contributing to build ships for the navy. The obligation could be ducked only by claiming that someone else, who had not been nominated, was better off. The latter had either to accept the charge or agree to exchange his property with that of his challenger. In practice, the case usually went before the courts. Even in the twentieth century, rich Greek shipping magnates continued to donate warships to the national navy.

Themistocles' finest hour came at Salamis. The glory accrued principally to the Athenians, both on merit and because Themistocles persuaded the Corinthians to be seen to be withdrawing their ships at an early stage. In Odyssean style, he then sent a slave called Sicinnus to Xerxes' camp on the mainland to warn him that the Greeks were escaping from the narrow waters in which they were trapped. Sicinnus had been tutor to the Great King's children and, since he could expect a big reward if he was right, he was believed. He even managed to row back safely to the Greek fleet by claiming that should his absence be noticed, the Greeks might pull out. As a reward for his performance, Themistocles persuaded the underpopulated city of Thespiae, after the war, to accept Sicinnus as a free Thespian citizen.

The Persian fleet was launched into a protracted and exhausting operation to seal the Greeks into a strategically favorable position that they had never intended to abandon. When battle was finally joined, the rested and well-trained Athenians and their allies outmaneuvered Xerxes' weary, mainly Phoenician crews. The Greek fleet included an Aiginetan ship whose captain—remembering old Athenian calumnies—called out, "Who's up for the Medes now then?" When the supposedly cowardly Corinthians returned to close the net, the Persians were trapped like tuna fish. It is said that the Great King watched the battle from Mount Aigeleos, not far from where King Aegeus had waited for Theseus to return from Crete. When Xerxes saw that Artemisia, the queen of Halicarnassus, had rammed what he assumed to be an enemy vessel, he remarked, "My men are women, my women men!" In fact, Artemisia's steersman had hit another Persian ship in the hurry to get away.

46.

The Spartans played a minor role at Salamis; although the Spartan grandee Euryblades was the titular commander of the fleet of the Hellenic League, only 16 Spartan triremes took part in the battle. The Athenians had every right, and enjoyed every opportunity, to take credit for the Persians' unlikely defeat. But the decisive battle was on land: a few months later, at Plataea, the Greek allies, commanded by the Spartan regent Pausanias, destroyed the Persian armies. Their able general, Mardonius, was killed; the war was won. Xerxes was already on his way back to Asia, having abandoned his palatial tent and heaps of treasure.[298] Athenian hoplites, commanded by Aristeides, played a gallant but secondary part (on the left wing) in the victory.

Allegedly on the same day, a Greek fleet under the Spartan king Leotychidas put an end to the remnants of Persian maritime power at the battle of Mycale, in the straits between Samos and Asia. The Peloponnesians then decided to return home. The Athenian contingent, under Pericles' father Xanthippus, sailed to the Hellespont, detached the sentinel city of Sestos from Persian control, and set the scene for Athenian hegemony in the Aegean.

The revenant Aristeides' generalship displaced Themistocles in the public eye. The victor of Salamis was deputed to go on a diplomatic mission to Sparta. Once there, Odyssean duplicity inspired him to seem eager to formalize the status quo between the two triumphant cities. The Spartans amused themselves, in their unsmiling way, by making him wait. They failed to guess that Themistocles might be as purposeful as he appeared frustrated. With Promethean foresight, he had left word for his Piraeus constituents to work full speed at extending the walls to include the harbor within the city's fortifications. By the time the Spartans were alerted to what their own delays had allowed, Themistocles was no longer negotiating from any sort of weakness. The Athenian fleet could be beached and repaired without fear of Spartan attack from the landward side. Phaleron had

298. The treasure advertised the seemingly limitless prizes to be found beyond the Hellespont. Pausanias was only the first and most famous of the Greeks to be infected by the oriental luxury that they claimed to disdain. In modern times, it has been said that few Western diplomats—Tony Blair, for conspicuous instance—fail to succumb to the robed blandishments of oil-rich Middle Eastern tyrants.

been vulnerable; Piraeus was not. The Spartans were left to resent what they were powerless to undo.

The failure of the two most powerful Greek states to build joint success into an entente, which would have allowed both to profit immeasurably from the Persian retreat, defies economic or social analysis. On the eve of the Persian invasion, in 480, Athens and Sparta made common cause in desperate circumstances, but they could not bring themselves to grant equal status to Syracuse, the paramount city in Sicily. They were no less reluctant after the Syracusan leader Gelon's victory over the Carthaginians in the same year as Salamis. Gelon demanded hegemony, but his vanity might have been assuaged by blessing him with titular leadership. Athenians and Spartans were unable to wink at each other.[299] The chance was lost. The demographic and natural resources of Sicily, and its central position, might well have enabled a union of the Hellenes' strongest cities to impose itself on the Mediterranean world.

Rome began with a population no larger than either of the great Greek cities. Although the Romans fought many wars with their Latin neighbors and were beaten in a number of battles, they contrived, in the long, hard run, to subjugate and then assimilate their quondam enemies. Despite residual grievances, the other Italians became their allies and—after the "Social War"[300] of the early first century B.C.E.—their fellow

299. The lexicon gives only *kleino to mati* (literally, "I close my eye") for "wink." Kiki Dimoula uses the phrase in *The Brazen Plagiarist*, but the complicitous aspect seems not to be Hellenic.

300. As every schoolboy used to know, the adjective "Social" derives from the Latin *socius*, meaning "ally," and has nothing to do with socialism or sociability.

citizens in the regimented mastery of the Mediterranean world and the monopoly of its profits.

What kept the Greeks apart, despite their more or less common language and gods? The Spartans were always nervous of any military undertaking that might leave their city without enough warriors to intimidate the Messenian helots. Since few in their ranks were professional, long-serving soldiers, all Greek armies wanted to limit the campaigning season to allow them to return home to help with the harvest. The Athenians also had many slaves (the most unfortunate in very harsh conditions in the silver mines in Laurium), but their workforce was of mixed, often barbaric origins; they lacked the underlying solidarity that the Spartans feared in the fellow Greeks, especially Messenians, whose lands they had occupied and whose bondage was essential to their economy and liberties.

Individuality was the charm of the Greeks, mutual suspicion their downfall. The Olympic Games and other pan-Hellenic festivals celebrated a certain unity, and sanctified truces in time of war, but the events themselves led to the glorification of competing individuals and states. Geography confirmed the standoff between cities. Their economies were seldom interconnected or interdependent; the prosperity of one was shameful or challenging to others.[301] The outstanding result of the triumphant alliance of Athens and Sparta against the Persians was, it seemed, that the two cities could afford the luxury of resumed antagonism. Lesser city-states had every reason to undermine a coalition that would render the two major powers irresistible on land and sea. Fifty years later, when Athens and Sparta finally went to war, Thucydides

301. I am grateful to Richard Seaford for observations on this topic.

was unable to furnish a convincing, prosaic reason for a conflict that, in the end, allowed Persia to recover its pride and its primacy. Mutual exhaustion, physical and economic, led the victors of Salamis and Plataea to become the Great King's sorry clients.[302]

47.

After the retreat of the Persian invaders in 479 B.C.E., the tall Cimon consolidated Athenian hegemony over Greek cities and islands in the Aegean by levying "voluntary" subscriptions in return for membership of the Delian League and the promise of joint allied action in the case of a Persian attack on any one of them. Only self-confident islands with a nautical tradition, Lesbos, Samos, and Chios in particular,[303] chose to contribute ships and men, rather than buy insurance that would leave them in annual debt, as the old Athenians had been to Minos before Theseus dealt with the Minotaur. What would become the

---

302. In his magnificent, detailed account of the supposed causes of the Peloponnesian War, as in his no-less-monumental analysis of "class war" in the ancient world (*The Class Struggle in the Ancient Greek World*), G. E. M. de Ste. Croix interpreted the remote past in accordance with a logic that chimed with his Marxist preconceptions. Such accounts, however erudite and illuminating, tend to be translations of the past into an ideologically nuanced, anachronistic language.

303. Chios combined insular pride with loyalty to Athens in the darker days of the Peloponnesian War. In the Greek War of Independence, beginning in 1821, Chios rallied to the patriotic call and, despite its proximity to the Ottoman heartland, supplied ships to the cause, provoking the punitive massacres of 1822. When freedom was achieved, even in the 20th century Chiot shipbuilders honored the old Athenian tradition of "liturgies" by constructing and donating ships to the Greek navy.

Athenian Empire began, in something like good faith, as an interdependent federation against a common danger.

In 475 B.C.E., Cimon's successes were crowned by the eviction of the pirates based on Skyros. To cap his achievement, he repatriated what were said to be the bones of Theseus. The implication that he was Theseus come again was seconded by patrician magnanimity: he kept open house to anyone who needed food. His renown was further enhanced in 466, when he crushed an attempted Persian revival in a naval battle at the mouth of the river Eurymedon, in southwest Anatolia. Always generous to his fellow citizens, Cimon was implacable with defaulting allies. The historian Stesimbrotos of Thasos reported that when Archilochus's donkey-backed island reneged on its contribution, Cimon reacted more like a Spartan than an Athenian. No compliment was intended, though the reticent Cimon, who favored amiable relations with Sparta, might have been flattered.

In 464 B.C.E., Sparta's endemic apprehensions were realized: in the wake of a disconcerting earthquake, the helots rose against their masters and fortified themselves on Mount Ithome, in their native plain of Messenia. The Spartans were sufficiently dismayed, it seemed, to call for Athenian help. Cimon was about to resume military operations against the rebellious Thasians, but he now persuaded his fellow citizens to sanction him to lead a force to assist in the siege of Mount Ithome. By the time the Athenian contingent marched in, the Spartans appeared to have recovered their nerve. They rejected Cimon's assistance and asked the Athenians to go home. Was pride their only motive? Before the earthquake, the Spartans had promised the inhabitants of mineral-rich Thasos to invade Attica, in order to head off Cimon's attack on what Archilochus had called their "thrice-wretched" city. The helot revolt precluded any dispatch of Spartan troops; but Sparta's request for Athenian aid had the effect of distracting Cimon from Thasos. Once he had marched south, instead of sailing northeast, the Spartans could claim, in effect, to have kept their word to the Thasians, who were now indeed able, temporarily, to secede from their Athenian alliance. In 463, they were subdued and severely punished for their secession.

Cimon's humiliation at Sparta tarnished his reputation. He was prosecuted, in 463, by "Pericles and other democrats for failing to take further aggressive action" against Sparta. It is unclear what he could or should have done. The *Oxford Companion to Classical Literature* implies that Pericles and his friends, led by the ambitious populist Ephialtes, formed an idealistic party opposed to the insufficiently patriotic, self-willed grandee. Who can doubt that the prosecution was fueled by envy and ambition? In the event, Cimon was acquitted, perhaps in front of the high court of the Areopagus controlled by the old aristocracy. The verdict was scarcely surprising: Cimon had been elected *strategos* (military commander) year after year by the Athenians as a whole. Pericles would hold the same office with similar regularity and military success, but his victories were all against recalcitrant allies.

Despite his acquittal, Cimon's kudos was tarnished. While the "democrats" took advantage of his loss of face to disparage the policy of rapprochement with Sparta, none doubted the propriety of assisting in the repression of the helots. In 461, Ephialtes and his friends succeeded in having the second Theseus ostracized. It lends Pericles and his friends too much honor to label them "democrats" or "liberals," as if they moved against the "conservative" Cimon and his friends out of political principle. The machinery of democracy was utilized, not least by the introduction of payment for jury service, to sweeten the rule of a faction and, in 451, to give Athenian citizenship the allure of some newly bestowed privilege.

48.

Like Cleisthenes, Pericles was an Alcmaeonid; he had as much aristocratic hauteur as communal sentiment. Ever since Themistocles persuaded the Athenians to invest their wealth in the fleet, the political balance had swung in favor of the Thetes, the least wealthy and most numerous citizens. As oarsmen, they provided the engine power of the victorious triremes that now policed the Aegean and collected its taxes. Pericles was prompt to step in to represent their interests after Themistocles' ostracism, at the instigation of Cimon, in 471. A charismatic arriviste was replaced by an aristocratic populist whose clever ruthlessness, like that of Julius Caesar, exceeded and outlasted that of his rivals.

The unforgiving Spartans now accused the hero of Salamis of conspiring with their king Pausanias, the victor of Plataea, to restore Persian hegemony in the Aegean. Since Pausanias, like not a few Spartans, had discovered a taste for personal wealth,[304] he may have been playing some kind of double game, with secret encouragement from some of his fellow countrymen, in order to frustrate Athenian expansion. It is unlikely that Themistocles was complicit with the Spartan

304. The ostentatious sparseness of Spartan diet and costume was more a form of military discipline than evidence of happy frugality. Spartan women were often their menfolk's stakeholders; they were always likely to outlive them. Back in the 8th century B.C.E., a Messenian poet accused the Spartans of caring for nothing so much as gold.

regent. Immediately after his ostracism, he went to Argos, where he did his best to rekindle that democratic city's traditional enmity with Sparta.

By accusing both him and Pausanias of Medism (an appetite for oriental self-indulgence), the Spartans leveled a charge as vague as it was damaging. Themistocles was condemned to death by the Athenians and his property confiscated. The verdict procured its own confirmation: with no future in Hellas, the victor of Salamis repaired, by a wisely circuitous route, via Corcyra, north through Epirus, and thence across Macedonia, to the court of Artaxerxes, who became the King of Kings in 464, after the assassination of Xerxes. Themistocles' energetic conduct of his anti-Persian policies before his disgrace, did more to impress Artaxerxes than to dispose him to revenge. Themistocles was made governor of Magnesia on the river Maeander (famous for its many bends) and died there in 459. The story that he committed suicide sounds like a moralist's fabrication. A master of deviousness, Themistocles is as unlikely to have had a bad conscience as his role model Odysseus. That his mother was not an Athenian may have made him less likely to pine in exile. His absence not only eased the ascent of Pericles; the Olympian's later legislation would have rendered the hero of Salamis ineligible for citizenship, as it would Cleisthenes.

Pausanias was recalled to Sparta, probably by a faction that favored his fellow king. The Spartan dyarchy avoided tyranny and encouraged caution. Rarely collegial, the kings inherited their thrones for life, but were vigilantly watched by the ephors and by each other.[305] Pausanias was first acquitted of

305. The Spartan model was somewhat mirrored in the Roman consulate, in which, from the mid-5th century, two men were elected annually as the

ill-doing and then accused of encouraging a revolt of the helots, as well as of treacherous correspondence with the Persians. The latter charge was the more plausible, but the example of Palamedes, executed for treason during the Trojan War after a trial rigged by Odysseus, suggests that it may have been fraudulent. Pausanias took refuge in a temple sanctuary where, like Sophocles' Antigone, he was bricked up and left to starve. When he was on the point of death, callous piety required his removal to ground that his corpse would not pollute.

49.

Pericles was no less a grandee than the ostracized Cimon. His mother, Agariste, was Cleisthenes' niece. Cleisthenes might be celebrated as the architect of the new, democratic Athens, but he had held high office, as archon, under the Pisistratids. If Pericles' facial and vocal resemblance to the "tyrannical" Pisistratus disposed him to egocentric populism (of a kind later imitated by the patrician Julius Caesar), it did not stop Pericles' friends from being nicknamed "the Pisistratids." Opportunism ran in the family. The wealth of the Alcmaeonids was said to have been augmented by something close to sharp practice. In the mid-sixth century, King Croesus of gold-rich Lydia asked Megacles, the son of Alcmaeon, to sponsor his mission to Delphi, where he hoped to win Apollo's endorsement.

Duly Hellenized, Croesus invited Megacles to come to Sardis and help himself to as much gold as he could carry on

---

chief magistrates of the republic. Although not always friends, their terms of office were short enough, and their responsibilities sufficiently disparate, and often pressing (and rewarding), to mitigate their rivalry.

his person. Alcmaeon commissioned a costume with commodious pockets and high, wide boots. Admitted to Croesus's treasury, he amused the king by stuffing all these coutured apertures and then rolled himself in powdered gold and filled his mouth and fundament (nature's top and bottom pockets) with the same metal.

Once Cimon was out of the way, Ephialtes and his radical friends modified Cleisthenes' constitution by reducing the powers of the aristocratic Areopagus. It was now to deal only with accusations of murder and sacrilege. The new popular courts were scarcely models of serene impartiality. All cases were settled in one day and, since juries could be composed of several hundred or even thousands of citizens, the proceedings were more a poll than a serious trial. Speeches were made, for and against, but how often was detailed evidence heard or witnesses cross-examined?[306] The changes in judicial procedure did as much to protect one set of aristocratic reformers from reactionary members of the same class as to deliver power to the people.

In 461, the unsolved murder of his colleague, the forceful Ephialtes, left the political stage conveniently clear for Pericles. Historians have suspected him, not implausibly, of complicity.[307]

306. Witnesses were, however, regularly recruited to be able to testify that loans and transactions had taken place, and on what terms.

307. As they have, for instance, Francisco Franco in the death of the previous fascist leader Gen. Emilio Mola in an air crash in 1937. Franco was left, by chance or cunning, to become the unopposed Caudillo. The rationalizing of chance into plot is an aspect of the tendency of "scientific" historians to discount what was previously attributed to providence in favor of human agency. To save the "logic" of Marxism, the failings of the Soviet system had to be attributed to traitors and wreckers, never to the inadequacy of the scheme itself. The scientific axiom that "everything has a cause" spawns claims that

He asserted his leadership by a combination of mordant eloquence in front of the citizens with ruthless treatment of reluctant contributors to the Delian League's treasury. While making
a feature of personal modesty, Pericles spent the allies' money
on public amenities such as the huge Odeon built, in the Persian
imperial style, on a slope underlying the Acropolis. The
4,000-square-meter theater, the first to have a roof,[308] was denounced, by citizens who dared to speak out, as an extravagant
advertisement for Pericles' own governance. He responded by
offering to pay for the new buildings out of his own personal
fortune, on condition that they bore his name; the demos then
insisted that the treasury pay and the credit be theirs. Public
works were not only good to look at; they also served to distribute the empire's revenues among those who worked on
them, free men and slaves.

The Olympian solicited the Athenians to love their city
like *erastai,* the grown-up lovers of attractive ephebes. They
were urged to bring their gifts to dazzle their rivals. Pericles'
own public appearances were carefully orchestrated. To keep
his emotions concealed, he never attended family funerals; he
indulged his appetite for women out of the common view, as
Franklin Roosevelt and, during his lifetime, John F. Kennedy
managed to do; and Bill Clinton did not.[309] Those wary of

---

everything—for loud instance, global warming—has an entirely *human* cause.
Inverted vanity has it that, if humanity cannot be the master of its fate, it has to
be the cause of it. This is a version of the Greek notion *sodzein ta phainomena,*
preserving—in this case anthropocentric—appearances.

308. Modeled on Xerxes' luxurious portable tent, taken to Athens as part
of the spoils after the battle of Plataea.

309. Such revelations are not always dangerous. When Benjamin Disraeli was informed, gleefully, that his political opponent, the 80-year-old

attacking Pericles personally made his un-Athenian partner Aspasia responsible for whatever they deplored in him. Aristophanes said that, after the death of his wife, Pericles was "drunk with her." Aspasia was made out to be the Helen who wanted to drag Athens into war with Sparta. It seems that at least some Athenians preferred the long, quiet life recommended by the rueful shade of Achilles when it was interviewed in the *Odyssey*.

As a public speaker, Pericles adopted the patrician style known among the Romans as *gravitas:* his hands never emerged from his robe; he mastered his audience with a mixture of barbed wit[310] and didactic solemnity, in the measured manner of the verses, if not of the offstage style, of his friend and fellow general Sophocles. Prizes in both politics and the theater were voted by the same audience. Actors and politicians were likely to use the same modulations of voice and gesture to procure applause, laughter, or sympathy. Actor-managers, such as the precious Agathon (who has a leading part in Plato's *Symposium*), presaged the ingratiating insolence of today's televised celebrities. His effeminate appearance and cute lyrics were mocked in Aristophanes' *Thesmophoriazusae*. When Agathon, like Euripides, left Athens for the court of Archelaos in Macedonia, Aristophanes lamented the loss of his pet butt.[311] Pericles affected to be indif-

---

Lord Palmerston, had been caught in flagrante delicto with a young woman while staying at Windsor Castle, and that he should therefore call a general election, "Dizzy" replied that, if the story of his octogenarian virility became widely known, Palmerston would sweep the country. So much for the myth of Victorian prudery among the general public of the time.

310. The comic playwright Eupolis said that "the most eloquent man in the world left his sting" (i.e., his prick) in his audience.

311. In 1976, Harold Wilson retired, abruptly, from being prime minister of the United Kingdom. The comedian Mike Yarwood was deprived of his favorite target and himself disappeared from public view. Yarwood's mimicry

ferent to theatrical lampoonery, but he may have been vexed
enough to have it banned during the protracted, increasingly
unpopular war with Samos which followed that island's declaration of independence from Athenian economic domination.

The Peace of Callias, in 449, formalized the end of hostilities
between Greeks and Persians, but the Athenians continued,
during the ensuing standoff, to exact tribute from their allies.
As long as his coercive leadership brought their subscriptions
punctually to the Acropolis, Pericles' tenure was unquestioned.
Despite Thucydides' remark that what was a democracy in name
was in fact the rule of one man, Pericles was subject to, and
nervous of, what could, in suspicious (and envious) democratic Athens, be a monthly audit.[312] Greeks have had good
reason to be wary of rulers with access to the treasury. The
original meaning of drachma (until recently the standard Greek
currency) was "a fistful."[313] Those with the muscle and the means
had, and have, discreet resources offshore: Miltiades, the victor
of Marathon, had interests in Thracian mines; so would Thucydides and Alcibiades. Greek shipowners have often flown foreign
flags of convenience and keep their funds out of the taxman's

---

was so close to the mark that one of his phrases—"as I said at the Brighton
conference"—came to be taken for, as it were, gospel.

312. Vincent Azoulay, *Pericles* (2015), promises that the Olympian's private estate was run so that it broke even. It also remained unencumbered by
a mortgage, which was the usual way (in Athens and, mutatis mutandis, in
Rome) for landed aristocrats to raise venture capital. Rates are said to have
varied between 12 and 18 percent. So much for the notion, propagated by Ezra
Pound, that "usury" was a Jewish invention or monopoly.

313. The drachma was divided into six obols, presumably because one
cannot grasp more than six souvlaki-style spits (the original basic metal
"coinage") in one hand at the same time.

reach: after World War II, Aristotle Onassis invested heavily, and profitably, in untaxed Monte Carlo.

In 441, democratic Samos refused to adopt the owl-faced tetradrach that, along with other Athenian coinage, Pericles and his colleagues were seeking to impose as the sole valid Aegean currency. The island was not easily reduced to docility. It was a long haul from the Piraeus; the defiance of its citizens was backed by their bold seamanship. When they captured a number of Athenians, they stamped them with the image of the trireme carried by their independent coinage. Pericles responded by embossing captured Samian rank and file on the forehead with his coinage's emblematic Athenian owl, thus literally putting his money on the islanders.

The Olympian's reputation has been sedulously polished.[314] Historians rarely find space to tell their readers that, after Samos was forced back into allegiance, its leading men were taken to Miletus, chained to planks, and left to suffer for ten days before having their heads beaten in. George Grote maintained that Athens's allies were not badly treated and "to take him all in all, with his capacity for thought, [Pericles was] . . . without parallel in the whole history of Greece." He was certainly the outstanding instance of principled and urbane greed.

When he returned home, in triumph, after the Samian campaign, Pericles honored custom by bringing the Athenian dead

---

314. See, for instance, Maurice Bowra's *Periclean Athens* (1971). Bowra was a laborious Oxford classicist with a sideline in scabrous verses, unprintable in his lifetime. He reserved his considerable wit for private purposes. He had the same sexual tastes as the great Latinist A. E. Housman, whose homoerotic elegies observed the proprieties. When Bowra heard that a gay friend was getting married to a not very comely woman, he observed, "Buggers can't be choosers."

with him. In his oration at their funeral, he compared the recent victory with the Achaean triumph over the Trojans. Cimon's sister, Elpinike, had the blue-blooded nerve to rebuke Pericles for sacrificing Athenian lives in subjugating an ally, unlike her brother, whose victories were over the Persians.[315] Never disposed to apology, Pericles was gracious enough to allow Cimon to come home from exile before the full decade of his ostracism ended. The tall revenant was, however, forbidden to take part in the battle of Tanagra in 457, when the Spartans pushed the Athenians, temporarily, from their position of power in Boeotia.

50.

After the calamitous outcome of the Peloponnesian War, Plato's Socrates could accuse Pericles, in the *Gorgias,* of having made the Athenians lazy, cowardly, gossipy, and greedy. An immoderate example of the rhetoric that Plato deplored elsewhere, the speech defaced the image of the Athenians as hard-working, inventive, and adventurous. If Thucydides' report is to be believed, the Olympian had congratulated himself for having put the city, at the outset of the war (and before the advent of the plague), in a winning position, especially from a budgetary point of view. Pericles never pretended to, perhaps could not afford, Cimon's boundless generosity. He did, however, introduce what amounted to the first welfare payments, out of

---

315. The upstart Roman emperor Vespasian (9–79 C.E.) confirmed his accession by giving himself a triumphal procession through Rome, after the suppression of the Jewish revolt of 67–70. No one had previously celebrated a triumph for the repression of a provincial uprising.

public funds, when he instituted a daily rate for jury service. Athenian juries were of almost unlimited size. Daily handouts sealed their recipients' loyalty to the new democracy and to its leader. When Cleon increased the payments, by a half, he began the process whereby politicians are tempted to promise enhanced state benefits and bank on fears that austere opponents will withdraw them.[316]

The greatest, if inadvertent, disservice Pericles rendered to his city was the law, enacted in the mid-fifth century, limiting citizens' rights to those with two "autochthonous" parents. This was designed, at least in part, to keep any share in windfalls, such as the king of Egypt's gift of 40,000 measures of wheat, out of the hands of the thousands of residents with only one Athenian parent. Like today's immigrants into prosperous societies, the metics did much to bolster the economy. To enfranchise them, however, was likely to dilute the privileges and reduce the benefits of current full-blown citizens. The unforeseen consequence of limited citizenship was demographic: losses in war and natural wastage diminished the city's manpower; electoral exclusivity offered outsiders, even those in the Delian League, no incentive for sustained allegiance.[317]

316. When the French right-wing statesman Adolphe Thiers (1797–1877) was attacked, in the wake of the 1870 Paris Commune, for disenfranchising the poor, the historian/politician responded by recommending, "Enrichissez-vous" (Get rich). George W. Bush relied on the contributions of what he called, skittishly, "the haves and the have-mores."

317. The issue of immigration currently dominates European and US political debate not least because of the fear that unlimited access to state benefits will lead either to their reduction or to economic ruin of the "developed" world. Citizens who feel threatened tend to desert traditional "left-wing" parties and rally to exclusive nationalist groups such as UKIP and the Tea Party. The most reliable supporters of the English (socialist) Labour

Pericles' decision, at the outset of the Peloponnesian war, not to meet Sparta in a land battle was strategically prudent, politically ill judged: it avoided needless casualties, but it required the peasantry to withdraw behind the city walls. Meanwhile, the unopposed Spartan forces burned the Athenians' homes, cut down their slow-growing olive trees, and pillaged their livestock. Enough of the Homeric tradition of philoxenia survived for Pericles to fear that the Spartan king Archidamos II might have the malicious grace to leave his own estates undamaged. He took steps to share the common misfortune by ceding the ownership of his rural property to the city. After all his legitimate sons had been killed in the war, the great man was moved to uncharacteristic tears; he then petitioned that his son by Aspasia, Pericles junior, be given citizenship and so become eligible to be a general. The request was granted, with the ironic result that, years after Pericles' own death, the young Pericles was among the six admirals convicted, after their victory at Arginusae, in 406 B.C.E., for failing to rescue Athenian sailors from an increasingly rough sea, and executed. The illegal, because wholesale, verdict (to which Socrates took gallant exception) testifies more to popular disillusionment with the war than to any honest assessment of what the naval command could have done under the conditions. The admirals' executions disposed their replacements to the

---

Party are the million or more Muslims admitted to unqualified citizenship by Tony Blair's government in order to supply ballast for their electoral prospects. The anti-Semitism now fashionable in parts of the Labour Party is an unadmitted consequence of the desire to retain the allegiance of Muslim voters.

nervous tactics that led to the catastrophe at Aegospotami a
year later.[318]

51.

Athenians were not alone in the self-inflicted reduction of their
own manpower. Casualties also contracted the exclusive Spartan élite. By the time of the battle of Leuctra (in 371 B.C.E.),
scarcely 1,000 red-cloaked Spartiates were available to confront
the military genius of Epaminondas. After the thrust of the
bristling Theban phalanx had put an end to Sparta's military
ascendancy, the Theban general restored the liberated helots to
their own, rebuilt city of Messene. He also installed a large
number of Arcadians, who had also been subjugated by the
Spartans, within the still visible wide walls of a federated capital called Megalopolis (Big City), in the southern Peloponnese,
not far from the still succulent olive groves of Kalamata. Plato
is said to have been invited to supply Megalopolis with a constitution; but after his experience in Sicily, he was averse to
another dose of practical politics.

    Megalopolitans left no bright mark on Greek history.
One of them, Polybius, born at the end of the third century
B.C.E., became the historian, more thorough than readable, of
the spectacular rise of Rome. Having been an officer of the

---

318. In 1757, the English admiral Byng was court-martialed for failing to
do all he could to keep the island of Minorca under his control. Although
his ships were not seaworthy and he had been an exemplary officer, he was
convicted, doubtless to appease opinion at home. This occasioned Voltaire to
remark that the admiral's execution, by firing squad on his own quarterdeck,
was conducted "pour encourager les autres." Voltaire did not fail to observe,
elsewhere, how perishable Pericles' fame would prove.

Achaean Confederacy, he was taken to Italy, as an aristocratic hostage for Greek good behavior, after the Romans, under Aemilius Paullus, defeated the Macedonians at Pydna in 168 B.C.E. Victory primed Rome's mastery of the Hellenistic world. Polybius became tutor to the conqueror's second son, Publius Scipio Aemilianus. As Scipio's companion when he was in command during the Third Punic War (149–146 B.C.E), Polybius witnessed the destruction of Carthage. He described the seemingly inexorable ascent of his patron's city, with rented admiration and, of course, in Greek. Two centuries later, another degraded enemy dignitary turned Roman pensioner and historian, Joseph ben-Mattathias, renamed Titus Flavius Josephus, would describe, in Greek and at length, Vespasian's crushing of the revolt in Judaea, culminating in the siege and sack of Jerusalem in 70 C.E., a year after that triumphant general's assumption of the purple.[319]

As Aemilius Paullus's victory proved, the conquests of Alexander the Great were, in the long run, a triumphant disaster for his homeland. He kept his army on the march for so long that the virile population of Macedonia itself shrank to a low level. The offer of bounties to soldiers who married Persian women and settled on warm conquered land discouraged their return to the rugged uplands of northern Greece. By contrast, the Roman policy of enrolling other Italians into their social and economic sphere meant that, until its last years, the empire never lacked recruits for its armies. There was no likelier way for an ordinary man to get rich. Long-serving rank and file could look forward to a share of the spoils and an allotment of land. The process of enfranchisement culminated in Caracalla's

---

319. See my *A Jew among Romans* (2014).

decree, in 212 C.E., bestowing Roman citizenship on all free inhabitants of the empire.[320]

For Maurice Bowra and his school, Pericles impersonated the stylishness of fifth-century Athens. In the *Federalist Papers*, however, Alexander Hamilton alleged that Pericles destroyed Samos "to appease the resentments of a whore" and that he was responsible for the ruin of his city. Pericles promised that Athens had the power and more than enough financial resources to prevail against all comers.[321] He could not have foreseen the plague, still less his own death from it, in 429 B.C.E. His disappearance left the conduct of the war to a succession of chancers, from Cleon to Alcibiades, reliant for power, as their predecessor had been, on promises of sustained success. Democracy is more a business than an ideology.

Vincent Azoulay maintains that Pericles' death was not a "game-changer" in Athenian history. The terms of the game itself, however, were determined by his less than steady political line. At the outset of the war, he stated that Athens had no need of further territorial acquisitions to maintain its hegemony;

320. Cassius Dio said that Caracalla's less than generous purpose was to expand the empire's tax base. The British, at the zenith of their power, made a similar declaration of imperial citizenship, at a time when travel was by sea and expensive. The post–World War II influx of citizens to the UK, seeking work and entitled to welfare, put a strain on the economy and, in the case of politician Enoch Powell, the tolerance of the natives. Caracalla gets a bad press, especially in Christian sources, but before he died, at the age of twenty-nine, he gave Rome some handsome baths.

321. Robert McNamara's defense of the US involvement in Vietnam, in the presidencies of John F. Kennedy and Lyndon Johnson, was similarly based on the presumption that logistics alone could be relied on to determine the outcome of war.

early misfortunes, and public disquiet, impelled him to suggest that further sacrifices would yield rich pickings. From the outset of his supremacy, the Olympian's attitude to Sparta and its allies combined condescension with violence. The Athenians made no friends abroad and, when things went badly, became divided among themselves. For all the obstinate hostility of the Spartans and their auxiliaries, the Athenians were undone by their own failure to agree on when and how to make peace, even in favorable circumstances. After Cleon's capture of 120 Spartiates and 172 of their allies on the island of Sphacteria, in 425 B.C.E., peace was within view. The all-or-nothing gamblers—Pericles' nephew Alcibiades at their head—elected to play on.

52.

Nothing has done more serious damage to the reputation of post-Periclean Athens than the Melian Dialogue. Set out in book 5 of Thucydides' history, it reads quite as if it were a transcript of the negotiations (in 416 B.C.E.) between the Athenian admirals and a Melian delegation that met, in seclusion, to negotiate the fate of the Cycladic island, which the Athenians were determined to enroll into their coalition against Sparta. On Thucydides' warrant, the democratic Athenians, incited by Alcibiades, are routinely depicted as callous aggressors, the Melian oligarchs as courageous defenders of freedom. It requires no great stretch to read the former as playing the traditional Greek male role. They claim that the weak, by their nature, have no choice but to yield, hence no need to feel ashamed. If philosophy and "science" liberated the Greeks, and then mankind in general, from superstition and fatalism, they also lend plausibility to the apparently irrefutable force of self-justifying systems, left and right, that appear to leave inquisitors with no choice but to implement them. Logic knows no mercy.[322]

Pericles' nephew Alcibiades, who had been his ward until he came of age, played a leading part (including the acquisition of a local female by whom he had a child) in the flotilla sent to intimidate the Melians. He proved as callous as his uncle, perhaps with better cause: Pericles' brutal treatment of the Samians was meted out to a supposedly voluntary ally, at a time when Persia was no longer a palpable menace. The ultimatum to Melos was served, in the course of a major war, on a city whose spokesmen affected neutrality but clearly hoped for Spartan support and victory.

Had the Athenian proposals been put to a full assembly of the islanders, they might well have voted to accept them. Such a decision would probably have been followed by the eviction of the ruling oligarchs; very possibly—as the precedent of Corcyra suggested—by their murder. Whether from pride or self-preservation, the Melian oligarchs condemned their citizens to play the gallant role. Their decision led, after a six months' siege, to the execution of all the island's males and the enslavement of its women and children. Thucydides ignores the possibility that the Melians' mineral wealth might have been

---

322. The "logical" discounting of the significance of particular sensations and of the value of ritual leads to abstract reason becoming, in Leopardi's phrase, "the true mother and cause of nothingness" (*Zibaldone* 2943). The lack of humor, as opposed to irony or sarcasm, among philosophers (Democritus alone has a happy reputation) is an aspect of the detachment of logical constructions from humane levity. Gershon Legman's *Rationale of the Dirty Joke* (1968) is not a lot of fun; Legman seems not to have been amused by the comedy of his own name as the author of such a study.

a motive for the Athenian ultimatum. His inherited share in Thracian gold mines allowed the exiled historian to spend 20 years in cushioned discomfiture while he wrote his variously interpreted, originally unpunctuated and unaccented, all-in-capital-letters account of the decline and fall of Periclean Athens.

What moralists like to label as Athenian hubris is said by them to have met condign retribution after a similar diktat was delivered, later the same year, 415, to the Syracusans in Sicily. Its rejection, by a rich and well-defended city, was followed by the annihilation of the original Athenian fleet and of its expensive reinforcements. It is less often remarked that Brasidas (who, as Thucydides conceded, was a good general and not a bad speaker "for a Spartan") served the citizens of Acanthus, a city near Mount Athos in the northeast of Greece allied with Athens, with an ultimatum pretty well identical with that of the Athenians to the Melians. By their immediate submission, the Acanthians avoided becoming exemplary.

What great power down the ages has not at some stage made ruthless overtures to smaller ones? Geoffrey Hawthorn[323] would have it that institutions such as the United Nations and "international law" have rendered brute force obsolete. Recent events in both the Ukraine and Syria, where Russian power has been used with grim partiality, suggest that, as the Athenians argued, little is likely to be done, at any period of history, when a strong power elects to impose its purposes on a weaker. International agreements, when not backed by determined force, are as vacuous in the modern as in the ancient world: why else are the Turks in northern Cyprus, the Chinese in Tibet, the

323. In *Thucydides and Politics* (2014).

Russians in the Crimea and eastern Ukraine? And how morally distinct from ancient practice was the "shock and awe"
visited on Baghdad by the "coalition" of the United States and
its client states in 2003?

53.

The Greek financial crisis that, in 2015, threatened imminent
national bankruptcy excited Robert Zaretsky, a professor of
literature from Houston, Texas, to synopsize Thucydides' Melian
Dialogue as follows:

> A foreign delegation representing a powerful alli-
> ance confronts a small Mediterranean country with
> an ultimatum. Either join our alliance, pay ruinous
> dues and cede your national sovereignty, or you
> will be destroyed. Unwilling to allow the delegation
> to present its case to their fellow citizens, the coun-
> try's political elite tries to buy time. But appeals
> to reason, pragmatism and common decency fail
> to budge the visitors.[324] When the elite finally re-
> plies that it is not prepared to surrender its nation's
> freedom, the delegation withdraws and, true to its
> threat, crushes the rebellious country.

Zaretsky promises that "there are sobering parallels between then and now that may offer insight into our current

---

324. Paul Cartledge points out that the Melian oligarchs were in fact said
by Thucydides to have been *unreasonable* since they relied on "sentiment
(alleged filiation with Sparta) and unjustified hope."

predicament. . . . The Melian Dialogue . . . depicts the endgame [of] what Victor Davis Hanson has called Athens's 'reign of terror.' The war between Athens and Sparta was already nearly two decades old, yet no end was in sight. With its citizens weary and restless, Athens adopted a brutal political calculus, declaring that those city-states not with them were, quite simply, against them." Victor Davis Hanson indulges in what has become, in meta-Marxist cant, the identification of the West with "terror." The sprinkle of journalistic clichés—"no end in sight . . . weary and restless . . . quite simply"—is characteristic of academics on secondment to the Department of False Analogy. Zaretsky's distinction between "its citizens" and "Athens" is markedly tendentious: as Pericles had insisted, Athens *was* its citizens; its policies required their frequent endorsement; they pulled the oars that propelled the fleet to Melos.

Having conceded that "the parallel falls short in many ways," Zaretsky proceeds as if it were still valid:

> what was at stake then and now is, first of all, the issue of national sovereignty versus supranational organizations. "Europe" was born, in part, of the fear of Stalin's Russia, no less threatening and grim than Xerxes' Persia. But, like the Delian League after the evaporation of the Persian threat, the original basis for unthinking allegiance to Europe disappeared with the Soviet Union's disintegration. (The Greek prime minister Alexis Tsipras's . . . fruitless meeting with President Vladimir V. Putin echoes the Melian hope that Sparta would fly to their rescue.)
>
> . . . the prospect of a different kind of auto-cratic rule has unsettled a growing number of

Europeans. Looming behind the euro has been the blunt fact of Germany's strict monetary and economic policies, the edginess of a European Central Bank preoccupied by the spectre of inflation and the eagerness of the European Union's Council of Ministers to make policy in what is the near-total absence of democratic process.... Brussels bureaucrats are little different from the Athenian delegation. Both come making offers their friends can't refuse....

...we are not that far from the Athenian claim at Melos that "the strong do what they have the power to do and the weak accept what they have to accept." In this light, the resistance of today's Greece on behalf of freedom and dignity recapitulates the earlier response of the Melians. The difference, perhaps, is that force then came with phalanxes and triremes, not economic diktats and monetary threats.[325]

The suggestion that "democratic process" of itself will procure sound policies was put in question by Thucydides' neat, if debatable, antithesis that Periclean Athens was "in theory" a democracy, but in fact the rule of one man. Zaretsky conflates Europe's ministers (whose mandate derives, at whatever distance,

325. The misfortunes of Melos were not without sequel. Philip Mansel reports that the so-called Venus de Milo was seized on the island in 1820, a year before the outbreak of the war of Greek Independence, by the second councilor at the French embassy, the Vicomte de Marcellus, and taken to France after the statue's then owner, Nicholas Morousi, grand dragoman of the Ottoman fleet, had been executed by the sultan.

from the electoral process) with the "bureaucrats" whom he vilifies as the callous agents of Europe's central bankers. He can then contrast the outgoing Greek government with the populist opposition that displaced it, by implying that "austerity" could be legislated into its opposite. Today's left-wing populists and the ancient Melian oligarchs are classified in the same heroic bracket as "defenders of freedom and dignity."

The analogy is specious. Today's Greeks have responded to the economic situation, brought about by their leaders' false accountancy, with something very like the *stasis* that divided Corcyra at the outset of the Peloponnesian War. Thucydides' claim to be making a record for all time is borne out by his description of the consequences of civil war: "Reckless audacity came to be held comradely courage, far-sighted hesitation was cowardice; moderation unmanliness; to show understanding was doing nothing . . . opposition was as fierce within parties as between them."

In the 2015 crisis, however rhetorically coercive the Germans appeared to be, no one threatened Greece with anything but the exit from the euro that Alexis Tsipras seemed to favor, until, having achieved the leadership of his country, he flinched, not foolishly, perhaps with neo-Odyssean guile, from its enactment. The Achaeans pretended to be withdrawing from Troy, the better to deceive the Trojans into hauling the wooden horse within their ramparts.

There was a direct, less salable analogy: Thucydides' account of the Athenian treatment of Samos[326] when Pericles forced the Samians to accept the Attic tetradrach. The Europeans might have been damaged by Greece's exit; none denied the

---

326. See section 49 above.

Greek right to revert to the drachma. Zaretsky's inapposite erudition is a recension of the long habit of preachers and evangelists to lend force to half-truths by references to sources that most readers or listeners lack the aptitude to verify. Tendentious translation of key terms, "democracy" not least, is integral to the "treason of the clerks."[327] Liberated from the vigilance of professorial peers, academics on the make lard their pieces with travesties of chapters and verses beyond their audience's corrective scope.[328]

54.

Alcibiades was regarded by his contemporaries as the most charming and the most attractive man in Hellas. He shared their opinion. From his earliest years he presumed that he would have his way. Plutarch tells how, as a boy, Alcibiades was playing knucklebones in the street and signaled to a carter to stop. When the cart rolled on, the small aristocrat threw himself in front of the wheels, calling out, "Now go on, if you dare!" The carter pulled up abruptly and everyone ran to raise the unharmed

327. In *La trahison des clercs* (1927), Julien Benda accused interwar intellectuals, especially French, of sacrificing their duty to tell the truth by the opportunism which led them to subscribe to the current ideologies, communism and fascism. Benda was a classical scholar. His novella *Les Amants de Tibur* dealt (somewhat sentimentally) with an ancient Roman love affair between Ezra Pound's favorite Latin poet, Sextus Propertius, and his mistress. Pound's versions of Propertius set the style for "creative" translation.

328. There is an additional, petty treason to be found in, for instance, Daniel Mendelsohn, whose self-esteem allows him, in his version of Cavafy, to translate the modern (and ancient) Greek for eight, *oktō*, as seven with little likelihood of exciting the derision that Pound's inventiveness provoked in Robert Graves's young son.

child. He refused to learn to play the aulos, a wind instrument somewhat like today's oboe, as other well-brought-up children did, because, he claimed, it deformed the face (the young goddess Athene showed the same reluctance) and hampered vocal performance. Alcibiades was someone who expected to be listened to.

In 447 B.C.E., when Alcibiades was three or four years old, his father Cleinias was killed at the battle of Coronea, against the Boeotians. The boy then became the pampered ward of his uncle, Pericles.[329] His looks and wit allowed him to take precocious liberties. Once, when wrestling, he bit his opponent's arm; accused of biting like a girl, he said he bit like a lion (Aeschylus, in *Agamemnon,* had warned of the danger of raising a lion cub that later turns on those who petted it). When he came upon Pericles frowning over the annual accounts that he was due to deliver to the Athenian people, the young Alcibiades said, "You'd do better to work out how not to have to present them at all." Ribald rumor had it that he went with Pericles on an expedition to Abydos, at the mouth of the Hellespont, where local custom sanctioned them both to marry the same woman. If a daughter was born, no one could be sure who her father was and so both could share her favors.[330]

In the pseudo-Platonic dialogue *Alcibiades,* Socrates accuses the young charmer of thinking that he had "only one day to address the people and he would, at one stroke, become a

329. Alcibiades' presumption of entitlement, in the light of his uncle's supremacy, was somewhat matched by that of Octavian, the great-nephew of Julius Caesar. Octavian was also precocious (he claimed his questionable inheritance at the age of nineteen), but he was less reckless and much more devious than the glamorous Athenian.

330. Jacqueline de Romilly, *Alcibiade* (1995).

second, omnipotent Pericles." Socrates is presented as the only person who had a chastening effect on Alcibiades. "When I hear him," Plato has the golden boy say, "my heart beats more than the corybants[331] in their ecstasy . . . it no longer seemed possible to live in the same style."

His style was, however, the man: smart young contemporaries followed Alcibiades' lead and his taste for purple robes, cockfights, and the hand-made shoes that (like Roger Federer's) advertised his name. He had his dog's tail cut off, so that people would gossip about that rather than other things, such as his publicly hitting a rival theatrical producer in the face for saying that he had put a noncitizen in the tragic chorus.[332] What might have been insufferable in someone less handsome or less well heeled was irresistible sexually and socially. Socrates, whom he described as "Silenus without a pipe," was alone in rejecting his sexual favors. In his eulogy of the philosopher, Aeschines of Sphettus[333] said that when, in later days, Socrates compared Alcibiades to Themistocles, disparagingly in terms of both wit and success, the comely charmer put his head on Socrates' knees and wept.

On the other hand, when the comic poet Eupolis, in a satire on the licentious rites of the Baptoi, followers of the goddess Cottyto (a Thracian variant of Persephone), said that

---

331. Originally Phrygian, then Cretan priests of Cybele who, in their festivals, beat cymbals and behaved as if crazed. They were said to have had a hand in educating the infant Zeus.

332. P. J. Rhodes, *Alcibiades* (2011).

333. Not to be confused with Aeschines the ex-actor and eloquent opponent of Demosthenes. Greeks appear to have set no great store by nominal individuality; to give a child a name already current in its family implied the wish for another of the same quality.

Alcibiades had been "baptized in the sea" (suggesting that Alcibiades was effeminate[334]), the latter is said to have responded by drowning him. Lemprière cites the more likely story that the poet died in a Hellespontine sea battle with Sparta and that, sorry to have lost him, his countrymen voted that henceforth no poet should go to war.[335] It is plausible to guess that someone alleged that Alcibiades had had Eupolis sent into action and hence that he had drowned him. What is certain is that Alcibiades' first quality was not an aptitude for taking things lying down.

Elected general in 420 B.C.E., at the earliest possible age of thirty, Alcibiades had the Achillean insolence to commission a gilded shield depicting Eros wielding a thunderbolt. He had already been diplomatically precocious. Thucydides mentions him first when in 421, during what came to be known as the Peace of Nicias, he sent personal messages to friends in Mantinea, Elis, and Argos to come to Athens and form an alliance against the Spartans, who were being slow to implement all the terms of the truce. The suspension of hostilities had come about only because Cleon, a demagogue with no military experience, had denounced the incompetence of the generals who,

334. I.e., that he allowed himself to be penetrated by another man, which was unworthy of a citizen.

335. Robert Graves, who won a Military Cross in the Great War, despised the poets of the 20th century who shirked military service. See, in Graves' Clark Lectures, the chapter entitled "These Be Thy Gods, O Israel" (*Crowning Privilege*, 1955). The equally gallant Richard Aldington denounced Ezra Pound as a two-time shirker. The American poet Karl Shapiro, who had a long period of active service in the Pacific, had his reputation ruined by Pound's supporters when he voted against an admirer of Mussolini and Hitler being given the first Bollingen Prize in 1949.

by chance more than skill, had cornered a battalion of élite Spartiates on the island of Sphacteria, off Pylos, on the west coast of the Peloponnese, but lacked the wit or the nerve to finish them off. Perhaps for the pleasure of embarrassing the inexperienced loud-mouth, the Assembly voted that Cleon should go and do the job himself.

And so he did, promptly, bloodlessly and gracelessly, by literally smoking out the Spartiates and taking them prisoner. Stunned by the capture of so large a contingent of their best men, the Spartans immediately sued for peace. The Athenians never had a better opportunity to end the war on their own terms, but they were gracious (or complacent) enough to allow the captives to return home before a binding treaty had been sworn. It may be that the Spartans acted against character and made an Odyssean show of submission. If so, it was abandoned once the Spartiates were home again, to what we can guess was a sarcastic welcome.

The news of Alcibiades' hostile initiative, however, prompted a Spartan mission to Athens, allegedly with full powers, to confirm the peace terms and avert the impending coalition of lesser powers. The delegation was led by a hereditary guest-friend of Alcibiades called Endios, whose father was also called Alcibiades (the name carried Spartan connotations). Endios's urgent concern was to get the Athenians to hand back the captured bastion of Pylos, which lay in tempting range for fugitive helots. The day before the Spartans were due to make their case to the Athenian demos, Alcibiades proposed a secret deal to Endios: if the latter denied in public that he had plenipotentiary powers, Alcibiades would ensure that Pylos was handed over and any other problems resolved. If the offer was attractive to Endios, it has to be because it would head off the risk of a vote against the truce itself.

No doubt as expected, the Athenian audience was outraged by Endios's sudden confession of impotence. This gave Alcibiades his cue to step up and denounce the Spartans for wasting the people's time. The ruse seems to have been devised to make sure that the alliance with Argos was confirmed; but it would, in the best Odyssean tradition, have worked in Alcibiades' favor in either case. He did not foresee that Odysseus's old enemy Poseidon, the earth-shaker, might interrupt the proceedings. The tremor was violent enough to panic the public and suspend the session. Nicias, the conservative leader, as superstitious as he was distrustful of Alcibiades, declared the earthquake divine intervention. The suspension gave him time to send an urgent deputation to Sparta to seal the peace process. The Spartans, as so often, were in no hurry to act, even in what seemed their own interests; their coolness embarrassed Nicias just as their fathers' had Cimon half a century earlier.

That Endios incurred no loud reproach on his return home indicates that at least as many Spartans as had snubbed Nicias had no sincere wish for permanent peace. If Endios was of their party, he may never have intended to make a formal contract with the Athenians. Alcibiades had provided a ruse that took care of both of their interests. Thucydides was one of the few men immune to Alcibiades' glamour, but the accusation of bad faith, in this case, ignores the wit and *tolmē* (daring) that were to keep his ambition buoyant for so long.

Alcibiades was now clear to induce the Athenians to seal the pact with Argos and the other cities. He was promptly elected one of the ten generals for the following year. The principal plank of his strategy was to march into the Peloponnese and construct fortifications to contain (and vex) the Spartans. For reasons that Thucydides leaves unexplained, Alcibiades' apparent deception of Endios did not lead to any noticeable breach in their friendship. When, later in his sinuous story, Alcibiades sought asylum in Sparta, Endios greeted him with traditional philoxenia. This suggests that the original Spartan delegation may indeed not have had (or not have wanted to have) full authority to come to conclusive terms with the Athenians.

55.

Like many playboys, Alcibiades acted as if he had all the money he needed. Although he was well connected, his estates did not exceed some 80 hectares, a large holding by Attic standards but insufficient to fund his appetites. In the late 420s, he negotiated to receive a huge dowry, of ten talents, when he married Hipparete, the daughter of the rich Hipponicus. Another ten would be delivered when their first child was born. He rewarded his wife with blatant infidelity. Too blue-blooded for meekness, she left him to go and live with her brother Callias. When she applied for a divorce, which entailed return of her dowry, Alcibiades seized her and dragged her back to his house. She died not long afterward. The happy widower suffered no marked damage to his reputation. Callias was so afraid of Alcibiades' purposes that he made a will stipulating that, if he died childless, his property should go to the state.[336]

The Athenian demos took pleasure in Alcibiades' handsome insolence. The resumption of the war was less to the public taste. He was not reelected general in 418. His much older rival Nicias lacked glamour, but appeared as reliable as he was unglamorous. Most of his modest and effective soldiering

336. See Rhodes, *Alcibiades.*

had—like that of Pericles—been directed at extracting protection money from Athens's putative allies. If Nicias lacked grand credentials and property, he derived rich revenues from his investment in the Athenians' silver mines at Laurium. He also owned 1,000 slaves, whom he rented to other concessionaires and who crawled to work in abysmal conditions. No one ever reproached their master for the source of his wealth, as Aristophanes did Cleon for being a tanner.

Alcibiades' stock with the electors rose after the battle of Mantinea in 418, where—in his absence—the Athenians and Argives had the worst of it against the Spartans. Soon afterward, Argos made peace with its ancestral enemy Sparta and ejected its pro-Athenian democrats. Alcibiades must have been able to imply that things would have gone differently under his own leadership. In 416, he became the only man ever to enter seven four-horse chariots in the big race in the Olympic Games. His runners gained first, second, and fourth places. Although he did not take the reins in any of them, and there were rumors of sharp practice, success made him the man of the moment. He now proposed that Athens implement the big idea of an expedition to bring Sicily under Athenian control.

Few of his listeners can have known the complexity of that island's politics or the power of its major city, Syracuse. Alcibiades proposed to raise a coalition of lesser states. Such a daring stroke would secure more accessible corn supplies than the long haul through the Hellespont, and also outflank the Spartans from the west. The idea was opposed by Nicias. He had good, boring reasons to be wary of unnecessary and distant gambles; but tolmē—the bold stroke—was integral to the Athenian self-image: the ascent of Athens had begun with Themistocles' plan to abandon the city and embark on the ships that, soon afterward, triumphed at Salamis. Seagoing enterprise had liberated citizens from the stenochoria (narrowness) of Attica and allowed them to make their fortunes.

Elizabeth I of England encouraged the practice of privateering, which promoted the opportunism of her captains and enriched her treasury. Sailors are likely to show individual initiative: before defying the odds and his nervous superiors, Horatio Nelson put his telescope to his blind eye. When the now infamous Colonels led their tanks into Athens in 1967, young King Constantine, who liked to wear naval uniform, failed to take advantage of the willingness of his naval commanders to use their guns against the fascistic Georgios Papadopoulos, with unfortunate results for Greece and for Constantine: he went, by ship, into unredeemed exile.

The standoff between Nicias and Alcibiades precipitated the him-or-me stalemate that ostracism had been devised to resolve. The machinery was put into process on the initiative of the radical Hyperbolus, whom Aristophanes ridiculed as a "lamp seller." The proposer's name was added, as custom required, to the list of candidates for eviction. Had Cleisthenes' device operated as intended, Athens would have been left with a single leader, cautious or otherwise, decisive in either event. Anyone else might have abided the verdict of his peers; Alcibiades was nothing if not peerless. It must have been on his cynical initiative that he and Nicias each urged their supporters to mark their ostraka (potsherds) with the name of Hyperbolus, who was duly, legally, and pointlessly voted into a decade of absence. No other single event was more determinant in the history of democratic Athens.[337] The fix resulted in the nomination of

---

337. See *Une cité divisée*, Nicole Loraux (2005). "Democracy" was less a political creed than a means of civilizing division, not least by the prospect

Alcibiades and Nicias in a troika with the experienced, lackluster Lamachus, as commanders of the Sicilian adventure.

No sooner had Nicias and Alcibiades disposed of their
scapegoat than they resumed their rivalry. Nicias accelerated
what he least wanted by declaring that a fleet of the size first
voted could never achieve what was asked of it. He hoped that
the demos would flinch at the extravagance of the whole
enterprise; instead, they served him right and doubled their
bets. While Nicias was wrong-footed by his own clumsiness,
Alcibiades was involved in a scandal that might have been, and
perhaps was, tailored to fit him. Soon before the fleet was due
to sail, the Athenians woke to find that nocturnal vandals had
broken off the phalluses from a large number of herms, the
statues of Hermes that many put at the doors of their houses,
stone sentries against bad luck. Fingers were pointed immediately at Alcibiades and his larky "Dionysian" clique as likely
"Hermokopids" (herm-choppers), but there was no plausible
evidence of their guilt.[338]

The armada sailed, Alcibiades still its elected joint commander, while investigations continued. The many young men
in the fleet's complement were fired with the erotic fervor that

---

of communal enrichment. The European Union, and its flawed project of
a common currency, has sought to create economic prosperity as a happy
prelude to the political homogeneity which, it could be said, is capitalism's
version—a stateless rather than a classless state—of the Marxist "paradise."

338. Steven Forde, in his study of Alcibiades, *The Ambition to Rule* (1989),
suggests that the genital mutilation of the Herms was the work of those opposed to the Sicilian expedition and to the erotic thrust of Athenian policy
of which Pericles was the primer and his nephew the randy advocate. The
Herms were, Forde says, symbolic of the Pisistratids, whose rule, if officially
discredited as tyrannical, was regarded with nostalgia by Athenian conservatives (Thucydides among them).

Periclean rhetoric associated with love of the city. They also hoped for riches that would supply what Steven Forde calls "everlasting pay."[339] Athens was left in the control of the older generation. A quality witness named Agariste came forward to say that Alcibiades and his fancy friends had mounted parodies of the Eleusinian mysteries in which, as the hierophant, he camped in the principal role. In times of stress, even sophisticated Athenians were liable to lapse into atavistic superstition. Human sacrifice, literal or judicial, was common in Carthage and not unknown in Rome.[340] While Alcibiades and his colleagues sought, in a confusion of tactics, to bring Sicily, outside Syracuse, under their control, reactionaries at home tried him, in absentia, on a charge of impiety. The jurors likeliest to have acquitted him were away on active service under his command. The stay-at-homes found him guilty. *Salaminia,* one of the state's official triremes, was commissioned to arrest and bring him back to Athens.

Nothing if not stylish, Alcibiades had traveled to Sicily in his own vessel. He appeared not to question the summons, but he did insist—imagine the winning smile, if not the drinks all round!—that he be allowed to return to Greece under his own smart sail. When the flotilla put in at Thurii, in southern Italy,

339. See his *The Ambition to Rule.* Thucydides uses the term "misthos aidios," endless income. It is tempting to draw an analogy with the Greek state in the period before the euro crisis of 2015, in which citizens drew large, early pensions and expected to pay little or no tax.

340. After their calamitous defeat by Hannibal at Cannae in 216, the Romans ritually slaughtered a number of Carthaginian prisoners of high social rank. This may have been done less to please the gods than to prove to any timid citizens that surrender was not an option, since Hannibal would certainly take pitiless revenge (his reputation for barbarous cruelty was probably deliberately exaggerated).

he gave his escort the slip. Pausing to tip off the Syracusans that democrats in Messana (today's Messene) were conspiring to join the Athenians, he crossed to the mainland and headed for Argos, where he had reliable friends. There he heard that he had been condemned to death in Athens; his enemies were demanding his extradition. "In that case," he said, "I shall show them that I am well and truly alive!" He repaired to Sparta, where he received a warm, if frugal, welcome from Endios and others.[341]

Plutarch says that in Sparta Alcibiades shaved hard, bathed in cold water, and ate black porridge "as if he had never had a cook or perfumer." To prove his worth and his good faith, while it lasted, he gave the Spartans some intelligent advice: they should send a general to organize the defense of Syracuse (they did, in the person of the experienced Gylippus) and also fortify the town of Decelea, in northeast Attica, midway to the Boeotian border, so that runaway slaves from Athens would have a place of refuge. Slaves were to the ancient world like oil to the modern: the machinery of peace and of war relied on their energy.

With entertainment in short supply, Alcibiades amused himself with seducing the wife of the absent Spartan king Agis, Timaea, from whose bed he emerged when an earthquake disrupted their pleasures.[342] Agis had been the commander at

---

341. Mansel, *Constantinople*, p. 211, notes that, in 18th-century Europe, for instance, it was common for ambitious men to regard "a country as a career rather than a cause."

342. "Seduction" may be a courteous term. Spartan women were not chided for distributing their sexual favors. What mattered was to bear male children. The story, cited by de Romilly from Plutarch, is that Agis's wife had a child by Alcibiades, whom she called Alk when (she thought) no one was listening. The boy received the Eurypontid royal name Leotychidas, but was later declared illegitimate.

Mantinea a few years earlier, when Alcibiades' plans for an anti-Spartan coalition in the Peloponnese were among the casualties. Agis was not regarded with unqualified deference in Sparta: during the eventually successful battle, two of the polemarchs (lieutenant generals) had refused to adhere to his plan and he was heavily fined for his deficient strategy. To sleep with Agis's wife and screw the king at the same time was in economic keeping with Alcibiades' idea of a good time. His remedy for having gone too far was always to go further. He now decided on a change of climate and, no doubt, of diet. The revelation of his affair with Timaea both accelerated his exit, in bad odor, from Sparta and impelled him to repair his reputation with the Athenians.

He could hardly have been in deeper, rougher, or hotter water, but he had the instinct that kept the solitary Odysseus afloat and determined to survive. First, Alcibiades had the nerve to put it about that he had been betrayed by Athens: "You are at home," phemē (rumor) is reported as having him say, "where you have rights and can enjoy them; when denied, you cease to be a patriot and think of reconquering the country by force."[343] He now had the insolence to suggest that love of Athens impelled him to attack its present regime. Nothing shows up less clearly in historical records than charm of the kind that made Alcibiades irresistibly attractive. *Liaisons dangereuses* were always his favorite sport.[344] He proceeded to make his mark both

343. De Romilly, *Alcibiade*.
344. In *Les liaisons dangereuses*, Choderlos de Laclos (1741–1803) cites an ancient Athenian architect whose watchword was "What you talked about, I did." Alcibiades qualified for the same tag.

with Persian satraps and with the Athenian garrison on Samos. His tactics were so mischievous and so cool that he seemed able to sit on both sides of the checkerboard at the same time. Since he alone seemed to know what was going on, or was likely to happen next, he contrived to have a free hand in all directions.

Athens had recovered with remarkable buoyancy from the Sicilian disaster, but the war was not going well, not least because the Spartans had appealed to the Persians to refresh their treasury. Geography rendered their application plausible: the Athenians, if buoyant, were a persistent naval threat in the Aegean; Sparta no threat at all. Without trumps, Alcibiades psyched[345] the Persian satrap, Tissaphernes, by advising him, as if impartially, to allow the Greeks to exhaust each other: sponsor a quick victory for the Spartans and they might have the energy and confidence to turn on his fiefdom in the hope of easy pickings.[346] Tissaphernes listened to Alcibiades with one ear: he reduced the subventions to the Spartans, but made no concessions to the Athenians. This small gesture gave Alcibiades a credible claim to an irreplaceable role in the diplomatic game of bluff and double-bluff. Loyalty and grievance were indistinguishable: his

345. In contract bridge, to "psych" an opponent is to lead him, by your bidding and attitude, to believe that you hold more high cards than in fact you do.

346. Nothing recommended the Spartans to old-fashioned schoolmasters more than their supposed disdain for money. Pupils were told that they used only iron bars as small change. In truth, their appetite for loot was age-old. The poet Alcaeus, of Mytilene, quotes Aristomenes, a legendary Messenian hero of the 8th century B.C.E., as saying that "at Sparta, wealth is the man, and no poor man is good or honorable." Spartan self-denial was a tactical, not a moral, practice.

Achillean revenge on Athenian injustice would lie in making himself indispensable to them.

The leader of those on Samos who blocked his return to power was the very intelligent Phrynichus.[347] Having originally favored the anti-oligarchic Athenians in his Samian garrison, Phrynichus came to realize that the rank and file were tempted by the Persian subsidies that Alcibiades, on a lightning visit, promised them if they would rally to the oligarchs, under Plato's uncle Critias, who had seized power in Athens. Phrynichus warned that Alcibiades was interested only in self-advancement, even if it meant civil war, but the troops were keen to take the money. With good reason to fear that, if Alcibiades came to power on Samos, he himself was liable to suffer the fate of a latter-day Palamedes, Phrynichus sent word to warn the Spartans of his rival's double game.

The Spartan admiral, perhaps because he was out of his depth, perhaps for a laugh (an underrated motive among historians), revealed Phrynichus's ploy to Tissaphernes and Alcibiades, who were together at Magnesia, where Themistocles had ended his days in Persian employ. Phrynichus's smart riposte was to compose a covert letter to the Spartans, offering to help annihilate the Athenian force on Samos. As soon as the text was on its way, he ordered the Samian garrison to strengthen its defenses with all haste and supervised their efforts with urgent enthusiasm. As a result, when—as expected—Alcibiades

347. Thucydides calls him *sunetos*, quick-witted, a term he applies elsewhere only to Theseus, Brasidas, and Themistocles. This Phrynichus is, of course, quite distinct from the playwright of the same name.

disclosed Phrynichus's treasonous letter to them, the Athenians on the island had every reason to read it as a forgery.[348]

Phrynichus had contrived an elaboration of the trick that Odysseus played on Palamedes. He had only brief success with it. When Alcibiades arrived in person on Samos, Phrynichus was deposed by the star-struck democrats whom he himself had commanded. He fled to Athens. In 411, he was dispatched to Sparta, to negotiate a peace treaty on behalf of the oligarchs whom Alcibiades had earlier favored. On his return, with a dusty answer, Phrynichus was murdered in the agora. Alcibiades' personal enemies (the waspish Androcles was another) had a way of disappearing with the convenient punctuality that attended the timely, sudden death of his uncle's rival Ephialtes.

56.

Elected general, in 411, by the citizen-soldiers on Samos, Alcibiades displayed untypical caution. Before he could think of returning home, he had to position himself as spokesman for the democrats. When a deputation came from the oligarchs

348. For a modern example of diplomatic bluff and double-bluff, there is the story of the Zimmermann telegram, sent by the German Foreign Office in the autumn of 1917. The technology and the stakes may be different, but the logic of deception remains largely unchanged. John Le Carré's 1963 novel *The Spy Who Came in from the Cold* is a variation on the same plot. The 1924 "Zinoviev Letter," purporting to be a Soviet document favoring the election of a Labour government in England, was published in the London *Daily Mail* to deter voters from playing into Moscow's hands. *The Protocols of the Elders of Zion,* first composed in Russian in 1903, was recognized as a forgery soon after its publication in the London *Times* in 1920, but so perfectly encapsulates anti-Semitic fantasies that it has been treated, especially by Arab and Iranian propagandists, as a genuine fake.

at Athens, he selected the populist card by insisting that Cleisthenes' version of the Assembly be reinstated and the current
junta replaced by a moderate, centrist administration. The
frowning Thucydides concedes that in this way he rendered a
service to the city "for the first time."

Alcibiades was wise enough not to present himself in
person as a candidate for Athenian applause until four years
later. Meanwhile, against the odds and under his flag, the war
in the Aegean turned in Athens's favor. A series of small naval
victories was crowned in 410 when 60 Spartan ships were seized
or burned at Cyzicus, close to the Asian coast. The Spartan
admiral Mindaros was killed, and word was sent to Sparta that
the troops were hungry and no one knew what to do. Alcibiades
was seldom in that condition. His relations with Tissaphernes
were now cordial, or so he chose to announce. While he still
dared not risk a return to Athens, he made sure that the city
did not lack news of his exploits.[349] In 409, the *Philoctetes* of
Sophocles depicted an abandoned figure who was wooed back
into active service in the Trojan War because the Achaeans could
not prevail without his unique bow and arrows.

The capture of Byzantium from the Spartans gave Alcibiades
sufficient kudos and funds (extracted by force from rich sources
in Caria) to be a candidate, in his absence, in the Athenian poll
for generals for the following year. After he was elected, if by no
means unanimously, its prodigal son was clear to return in some

---

349. The 1st-century B.C.E. Roman historian Cornelius Nepos attributed
the victories in the Aegean principally to Alcibiades' able colleague Thrasybulus. Nepos describes the former as "luxuriosus, dissolutus, libidinosus,
intemperans" (luxury-loving, dissolute, lustful, uncontrolled).

sort of triumph to the city where he had been condemned to death eight years earlier. His flotilla of 20 ships sailed under the cliffs of Sounion loaded with booty and decorated with the prows of enemy ships. The admiral's ship flaunted purple sails, as if in ironic tribute to Theseus. The pipe player (*aulētēs trieraulēs*) who gave the rhythm to the oarsmen was Chrysogonos, a popular prize-winner at the Pythian Games. Orpheus had had that role when the Argo brought home the golden fleece.[350] The whole gala, as they rowed into the Piraeus, was directed by the tragic actor Callippides. According to Plutarch, the leading players wore straight-cut tunics, long robes, and festive costumes. Theater and politics were almost indistinguishable.[351]

Triumphal mise-en-scène masked apprehension. Alcibiades did not disembark until his cousin Euryptolemus and a posse of friends and relatives gave him a promising signal. Within a few days, his goods and possessions were restored, the maledictions against him publicly rescinded, gold crowns voted to honor him. In September 407, he supervised the annual procession to Eleusis. It had had to go by sea in recent years, because of the menacing

350. For a lively, fanciful account of his chaste, quasi-divine myth, see Ann Wroe's *Orpheus: the Song of Life* (2011). In his *Georgics*, book 4, Virgil inserted a neat digression about Orpheus's descent to Hades to retrieve his dead love Eurydice. His music seduced the powers below into allowing him to lead her back to the upper air, on condition that he did not look round before they were both above the surface. At the last moment, he turned and she vanished "ceu fumus in auras" (like smoke in a breeze). One of Jean Cocteau's most famous films is entitled *Orphée* (1950). Marcel Camus' *Black Orpheus* won the Palme d'Or at Cannes in 1959.

351. Religion, however, seemed forgotten. Only later was it recognized that Alcibiades' return coincided with the festival of *Plynteria*, the spring cleaning of the wooden statue and adornments of Athene Polias. It was traditionally an inauspicious day for any Athenian to begin an important enterprise. See Parker, *Miasma*.

presence—originally recommended by Alcibiades himself—of the Spartan garrison in Decelea. It was commanded by King Agis, who had to watch helplessly as the Athenians marched out, led by Alcibiades in the role of mystagogue and hierophant, which he had been convicted of profaning a few years earlier.

If Alcibiades was back at the top, the pole was greased with the expectations of the demos. When he returned to command the fleet in the Aegean, he was confronted by a new Spartan admiral. Lysander was a mothax, son of a déclassé Spartiate, and a careerist of vengeful ambition. His energetic presence won the favor of the Persian crown prince Cyrus, who funded a raise in wages for the Spartan crews. Alcibiades led the Athenian fleet to make its presence felt by the Spartan base at Notion, then left his friend Antiochus in charge, with orders to do nothing remarkable, while he went to raise money.

An early port of call was Herodotus's birthplace, Halikarnassos (today's Bodrum). It was to become the showy capital of the ostentatious King Mausolus. Doubling as a subsatrap of the Great King of Persia, he would rule Caria from 377 to 353 B.C.E. He and his sister/wife Artemisia built a tomb intended forever to advertise their fame and flaunt their fortune. The first ambition alone was achieved: the Mausoleum became synonymous with incautious folly. Listed by Alexandrian tabulators as one of the Seven Wonders of the Ancient World, it survives only as the stone hub of its once bejeweled and richly sculptured original. The incestuous couple[352] had the revenue to hire the

---

352. Artemisia is said, when widowed, to have consoled herself with a tonic containing the ground bones of her deceased spouse, thus herself becoming a supplementary, two-legged mausoleum.

best Athenian artists to decorate it in a showy amalgam of styles, but their city lacked the muscle to protect its precious embellishments from plundering pirates.

In Alcibiades' absence, Antiochus—with more ambition than wisdom—sailed into Ephesus harbor. He lost some 20 ships in the resulting battle. Alcibiades returned and was eager to reengage, but Lysander backed away. The reverse at Notion was not a catastrophe, but it might as well have been: Alcibiades' stock plunged; he failed to be elected strategos for the following year. In the first month of 405, Aristophanes' *Frogs* won first prize at the drama festival of the Lenaea. While it lampooned Alcibiades' main enemy, Cleophon, it also parodied Euripides, who was made to denounce "a citizen slow to serve his country but quick to do it harm, ingenious for himself but without wit for the city." No prize was offered for identifying the target.

Like Thucydides, after his disgrace, Alcibiades took refuge in Thrace. Thanks to a stash of booty from earlier operations, he raised a private army and bided his time, yet again. The Athenian admiral Conon took command in the Aegean and won the victory at Arginusae that might have turned the war. Failure to rescue his own side's shipwrecked sailors in increasingly rough seas led to the execution of six of the eight victorious admirals. Conon was disgraced and absented himself from Athens to make a privateering fortune. Lysander was able to seize the initiative, carefully. He teased and tired the Athenians by refusing to come out to fight them at Aegospotami in the Thracian Chersonese. Alcibiades made a sortie from his adjacent redoubt to warn the new, guileless Athenian commander about Lysander's stealthy tactics and to offer help. He was repulsed on both counts. Soon afterward, Lysander destroyed the entire Athenian fleet.[353] It was at this point that those 3,000 captive Athenian prisoners had their throats cut at Lampsacus, a town north of Abydos, notorious for vinous debauchery.

Alcibiades tried to mend his fences with the Persians, but in 404 he was murdered, on the orders of the satrap Pharnabazos, in a village called Melissa in Phrygia, where he was hiding with a golden-hearted beauty called Timandra. He had a dream in which he was dressed in female clothes and made up like a woman. When he woke and saw that the house was surrounded by killers, he rushed out with such menace that they backed off. As he tried to get away, he was shot down by their arrows and javelins. Timandra buried him in brave style. She was said to be the mother of the great Corinthian courtesan Lais, who "filled all Greece with desire." P. J. Rhodes suggests that Alcibiades' fate was determined by fear that, in order to find new allies, he would betray his knowledge of Cyrus's plans, backed by the Spartans, to challenge his brother Artaxerxes II for the Persian throne. Despite what Plutarch called his *aphrosune,* lack of prudence, Alcibiades' handsome allure did not fade. In the second century C.E., the Roman emperor Hadrian was enough in love with him to have a monument erected at Melissa in his honor.

353. Lysander is the first historical figure in the Greek world to be given divine honors in his own lifetime. The restored oligarchs of Samos almost certainly declared him a god for delivering them from a repetition of Periclean vindictiveness in 439. Memory is also the mother of resentment.

57.

In *Parallel Lives,* Plutarch paired Alcibiades with Coriolanus, whose pride caused him to join his old enemy, the Volscians, and march against Rome, only to change his mind and be killed by them. The similarity is as clear as the difference: the mythical Coriolanus was a prig, Alcibiades a mercurial charmer bright enough to win the admiration of Michel de Montaigne, no stranger to political ups and downs. Although he lacked Coriolanus's battle honors, Lucius Sergius Catilina (the target of Cicero's Catilinarian orations) was probably more like Alcibiades than Coriolanus was: tailored turncoats, both had the upper-class chancer's *superbe* that led them to play for the highest available stakes.

Defending and attacking Alcibiades became an academic exercise for many centuries. Moralists have frowned on the mutable playboy; even the rarely severe Peter Green says, in a Texan metaphor, that he was "all hat and no cattle." Did Alcibiades behave markedly worse than other Greeks? His changes of allegiance were an opportunist's revision of the epic vanity that made an enemy of anyone who stood in a great man's way. Achilles may not have fought for the Trojans, or even offered them advice, but his petulant withdrawal from the battlefield led to many deaths among the Achaeans. Themistocles had no shame in finding employment with Artaxerxes; the dethroned Spartan king Demaratus had already shown him the way by literally fellow-traveling with Xerxes, though he rarely told the Great King anything he would be glad to hear: for instance, he warned that, being free men, the Greeks would fight to the death for their liberty against slaves who had to be whipped into battle.

The idea of patriotic loyalty, regardless of who might be in power, was—like graciousness in defeat—at odds with the heroic notion of manly pride.[354] No Roman of consequence sided with Hannibal or Mithridates, but aggrieved or arrogant Roman generals from Cornelius Sulla to Julius Caesar, and in countless cases under the empire, marched on their fellow countrymen without incurring any loud obloquy, provided they were victorious. Raymond Aron claimed that it was a "twentieth-century conviction [that] no one can have two countries."[355] If Alcibiades stands out as the biggest bad boy of ancient Athens, it is not because his ambition was more immoderate than that of Pisistratus or more insolent than that of Pericles.[356] His greatest failing was to have failed.

Alcibiades' persona fits remarkably into Robert Blake's analysis of dandyism:

354. Greeks and Romans would agree with John McEnroe's dictum: "Show me a good loser and I'll show you a loser."

355. Cited by Philip Mansel in *Constantinople*. The multifaceted diplomacy of the Mavrocordato family under the Ottoman sultans illustrates the Odyssean duplicities of clever Levantine Greek Phanariots in perilous or opportune circumstances. In the 1850s, Alexander Mavrocordato, head of the "English party" in "chaotic, nationalistic Athens," was said to be the only Greek politician who wanted "a regular government as . . . understood in Europe."

356. Azoulay (*Les tyrannicides d'Athènes*) suggests that expansion of Athens's overseas interests was hinted at by Pericles when he was seeking to reinvigorate Athenian morale early in the war. Alcibiades was reckless, but he was also hampered by the helping hand of Nicias, and then became the scapegoat for the final disaster at which he was not present. Lyndon Johnson has been widely blamed for the US's disastrous involvement in Vietnam, a policy initiated by John F. Kennedy, whose rise to power was based on his family's dubiously acquired wealth and whose personal hero was James Bond, an Alcibiades recycled for the simpleminded.

characteristic of an era of social flux, when aristocracy is tottering or uncertain, but when radicalism
has not yet replaced it with a new set of values. It
flourishes ... when manners are no longer rigidly
fixed, but have not yet degenerated into mere anar-
chy, so that there is still a convention to rebel
against, still a world to be shocked and amused by
extravagance and eccentricity. The dandy must
have a framework in which to operate.[357]

Pericles' combination of ruthlessness and bluff had furnished
Alcibiades with a stage on which style itself was a form of content. Athens recovered its prosperity, but never the swagger that
fostered and then died with Alcibiades.

58.

Alexander the Great succeeded so outlandishly that old-style
classicists viewed him with distaste. In addition, his unique
achievements failed to be recorded by any historian with a
recommended prose style. He did take embedded writers with
him, but none are said to have delivered anything like Thucydides' monumental, and cautionary, *ktema es aei* (timeless
work). Thucydides' claim to have described the greatest of
wars could have been ridiculed, had a scribbler of genius lasted
the course with Alexander.[358] His most competent attendant

357. Robert Blake, *Disraeli* (1966), cited by Richard Jenkyns, re Catullus,
in his *Three Classical Poets* (1982).
358. The fictional *Alexander Romance*, although popular, lacked the grim,
if not prim, qualities that made Thucydides a classic. The first version of a saga
much embellished in later centuries was written in Alexandria in the second

reporter was Callisthenes, who had previously been a research assistant to Alexander's tutor, Aristotle, in collating a list of victors at the Pythian Games "from the earliest times" (tabulating lists of names and laws was an early use of literacy).

Aristotle's influence on Alexander has probably been exaggerated (Homer was his great source book), but it was timely of the philosopher to declare all barbarians to be natural slaves, so supplying an ethical license for invasive subjugation.[359] Suitably reupholstered, the Stagirite's presumption would lend moral sanction to Christian crusaders, European imperialists, and Muslim conquerors. The Catholic Church gave Aristotle a prim dignity it became amusing to puncture: a thirteenth-century scandalmonger retailed the story that Alexander the Great discovered Aristotle having sex, from behind, with a slave girl.[360] Anything *ben trovato* in writing, however flippant or biased, is likely to be seen by at least some scholars as worthy of a measure of credence.[361]

---

century C.E. by a Hellenized Egyptian. The *Alexander Romance* contains early instances of fictional correspondence. The epistolary novel became a convincing means of persuading readers that a text was genuine. Most of the letters attributed to Plato are said to be fakes, although the seventh, a detailed account of the philosopher's misfortunes in Sicily at the court of the tyrant Dionysius, is so plausible that it is tempting to suspend disbelief.

359. Alexander later married three "barbarian" wives, but his "philosophy" with regard to the inhabitants of the Persian Empire changed markedly in accordance with pragmatic purposes, hence the alarm expressed by unreformed Hellenists such as Callisthenes and "black" Cleitus.

360. Richard Seaford reminds me that the episode is illustrated on the wall of the podesta's bedroom in San Gimignano. Another academic, who chooses to remain anonymous, has suggested that this story is a play on the words of Aristotle's philosophical work known as the *Posterior Analytics*.

361. French pedants used to be in the habit of asking, "Vous avez un texte, monsieur?" (Do you have a text, sir?).

Callisthenes was unwisely sure that he and his pen were indispensable. On the road to the East, in 327 B.C.E., he dared to question Alexander's policy of enrolling Asians in the élite formations of the Macedonian army. When a young officer called Hermolaos was reproached by Alexander, during a hunting party, for throwing his spear at a boar before the king had time to throw his, Callisthenes was presumptuous enough to make reference, however skittishly, to Harmodius and Aristogeiton. He acquiesced in declaring Alexander a god, in Asiatic eyes at least, but refused to honor a new ordinance and cower like an oriental dog before the new King of Kings. His insolence was soon interpreted as treason, not least because it was infectious: a number of leading Macedonians resented being demoted to equality with Persians. After his scribe's execution, Alexander incurred collateral disparagement by Aristotle's other pupils and associates. On the other hand, following his capture of Constantinople in 1453 C.E., Mehmet II—still in his early twenties—identified so keenly with Alexander that he commissioned a eulogy of himself in Greek, the language of common record. His meta-Alexandrine ambition was to advance from east to west in order to impose a single faith, Islam, and a single sovereign, himself, on the Mediterranean world.

Thucydides' history of the Peloponnesian War has remained the classic ground for wars of interpretation.[362] His knotty prose has little charm (Erasmus preferred Herodotus, Lucian, and Demosthenes), but its bleak intelligence has never

362. His first (elegant and tendentious) translator into English was Thomas Hobbes (1588–1679), for whom Thucydides served as evidence of the necessity of a formal head of state who would be the guarantor of moral continuity and social stability. Hobbes lived through a period of abrupt transitions and the *stasis* of the English civil war between monarchists and republicans.

lost quasi-scriptural authority. Neville Morley[363] tells of a meeting in the Charlottenburg Palace in Berlin in 1881, at which Oelssen, the head of the German imperial finance ministry, was defending an issue of paper money to cover national debts. The historian Friedrich von Raumer responded, "But, Privy Counselor, do you not remember what Thucydides tells of the evil that followed from the circulation of too much paper money in Athens?" According to Raumer, Oelssen then said, "This experience is certainly of great importance," after which he "allowed himself to be persuaded in order that he might retain the appearance of learning." Paper money (like the "science" of economics[364]) was unknown in Thucydides' time.

During the French Revolution, the Jacobins chose, like America's founding fathers, to visualize themselves as Romans or Spartans rather than democrats on the Athenian model. The young and idealistic Camille Desmoulins dared to disagree with his comrades: in his view, the "science" of the Spartan lawgiver Lycurgus "consisted in nothing but imposing suffering on his citizens . . . like Omar who made all the Muslims equal and equally wise so that they burned the libraries. That is not the kind of equality we envy." Desmoulins favored intelligent diversity over a doctrinal party line. During Robespierre's reign of terror, he was arrested and executed. Today, no doubt, he

363. In *Thucydides and the Modern World* (2012), edited by Morley and Katherine Harloe, from which several of the examples cited in this section have been drawn.

364. Xenophon's *Oeconomicus* was a country gentleman's treatise on estate management. His *Poroi* (Ways and Means) suggests the means by which 4th-century Athenians might procure social stability and avoid aggressive imbroglios by more equable distribution of national income, in particular from the silver at Laurium.

would be denounced, in politically correct (or opportunist) circles, as an Islamophobe.

Abraham Lincoln was neither the only nor the first speaker at the dedication of the Gettysburg memorial. He was preceded by Edward Everett, a German-educated Harvard professor. The latter's two-hour lecture cited Pericles' Funeral Oration, but also challenged the Olympian's dismissive attitude to women. Everett saw females as worthy mourners; he harped on messages to mothers and sisters from sick or dying soldiers. It was, he said, characteristic of Americans, unlike Greeks, to treat women with respect. Lincoln's brevity then consigned the professor's disquisition to the oubliette.

Simon Stow maintains that Pericles' "decidedly masculine" tone was implicit in George W. Bush's "shallow and unquestioning patriotism" in reaction to the terrorist attacks on the Twin Towers.[365] Thucydides' underlying wish, Stow claims, was for "a more balanced, less hubristic perspective . . . a model of public mourning that offers the possibility of avoiding further tragedy." It is a very pretty moral, but is it any more present in Thucydides than the mention of paper money? If Brasidas had been headed off by a bold stroke at Amphipolis, Thucydides might never have had time, or inclination, for sage reflection. Steven Forde notes that, almost five centuries before Ground Zero, Macchiavelli doubted the distinction between aggression and defense, "the bedrock principle of any *moral* approach to international politics. The Romans conquered not only Greece but the entire world out of self-defence . . . *failing* to expand is irrational. If so, how can moral restraint have any place in international politics?"[366]

365. *Pericles at Ground Zero* (2007).
366. Forde, *The Ambition to Rule.*

George W. Bush's secretary of state, Colin Powell, displayed in his office a framed quotation from Thucydides: "Of all manifestations of power, restraint impresses men most." It was, in truth, a very loose version of a remark attributed to Nicias, hardly the most effective of Athenian leaders. As Mary Beard has observed, "the catchier the slogan, the more likely that it's the product of the translator rather than of Thucydides himself." During his period out of office in the 1920s, Eleftherios Venizelos rendered Thucydides into *katharevousa*, the version of classical Greek resuscitated to enhance the diction and dignity of modern, independent Hellas. Venizelos sought to confirm the continuity between ancient and modern Greece, for instance by translating *ergon* (work or action) as *ekstrateia* (expedition), which has a solely military connotation. In this way, he enlisted Thucydides as an involuntary advocate of, in particular, the Big Idea that ended in the catastrophe of 1922.

In truth, Greek nationalism was far less attractive to many Greeks than Woodrow Wilson's cant about "self-determination" came to proclaim. According to Philip Mansel, "Preferring the Ottoman Empire to an independent Greece, many Greeks voted with their feet and emigrated to Constantinople. The census of 1881 said that over 50 percent of the 200,000 Greeks in Constantinople were born outside the city."[367]

Modern academics tend to editorialize rather than construe dusty texts or unravel obsolete detail. Geoffrey Hawthorn, for example, asserts that today's media are involved only in delivering "praise and shame." He can accuse ancient auguries of being venal or corrupt, but the purposeful and crowd-pleasing partiality of today's press, radio, and TV networks

---

367. Mansel, *Constantinople*, p. 278.

escapes his attention. He is, however, illuminating on pressures exerted on the Spartans by less powerful elements in their alliances: in 421, the Corinthians made noisy trouble when the prospect of a reconciliation between Sparta and Athens threatened to pinch them in an uncomfortable vice; Thebes behaved similarly with regard to Plataea in 427 B.C.E.

The Athenians were never disposed to accommodate the counsels of anyone else. This liberated their initiative; it also serviced their delusions. If they had had any practical objective in going to war, they might have achieved it and been content. Since they had persuaded themselves that they were invincible, unjustly envied, and ubiquitously potent—a recurrent illusion of naval (and now aerial) powers—they contrived to be both domineering and overstretched. Even Thucydides indulged in Athenian conceit when he described a vain war between two small states (neither with a population a tenth as big as Brooklyn's) in grandiose, geopolitical terms.

The Melian Dialogue somewhat resembles Julius Caesar's conversation, on the banks of the Rhine, with Vercingetorix, a Gallic nobleman few of whose compatriots had provoked the Romans or wished them harm.[368] A million Gauls died for no better reason than to satisfy Caesar's appetite for gold and glory. He first paraded a far-fetched excuse for invading Gaul, as had

---

368. In Virgil's *Aeneid,* the Latin leader Turnus would play the Vercingetorix part: he had to die, although he had done nothing directly to offend Aeneas. His only literary consolation is that he is portrayed as a nicer man than his killer. Perhaps Virgil's imagination inhabited a victim with more warmth than his synopsis demanded. Vercingetorix was executed after appearing in Caesar's triumph (at which, according to Mary Beard's *The Roman Triumph* [2007], only one tribune failed to stand up in fawning tribute to the conquering hero).

Alexander when he attacked the Persian Empire: in 390, the Gauls had sacked Rome; a good number sided with Hannibal more than a century and a half later. Since Caesar's campaign was successful, few commentators pass censorious judgment on his callousness. The Gauls were quite quickly assimilated into the Roman imperium (even their Druidic religion lost its hold on the Latinized population).[369] Learning from Alexander, Caesar had had the wit to recruit to Roman service many who might otherwise have retained their national allegiance. Innocent of antique guile, Bush and Blair's policies roused Iraq's population against its "liberators." They had, it seems, no plan for winning the post-war support of enough Sunni or Shi'a to restore the lineaments of a viable society.

Neville Morley's study of the various views taken of Thucydides' history finds nothing to reproach in postwar German scholarly attempts, for instance by Ernst Nolte, to lend excusing "perspective" to Nazi practices. Is there nothing anomalous, if not dishonest, in comparing Hitler's attack on Russia with the precipitation with which Pericles provoked and legitimized war with Sparta? The principle "Better our sooner than their later" is taken to be applicable in both instances. Ernst Topitsch may be chided for far-fetched analogizing; yet he never broaches the intrusion of totalitarian "logic" among modern motives. His silence on that topic is flagrant and loud. The "return" of religion is mentioned, if at all, only as a courtesy during the creation of the United Nations. In 1945, who among the victorious leaders guessed that aggressive Islamic monotheism might become a metaphysical lever, seeking to move the world from a platform outside the Western *oikoumene*? Morley ignores the tendency of

369. Jean-Louis Brunaux, *Nos ancêtres les gaulois* (2015).

some modern historians—influenced by the Hegelian/Marxist model—to lend dialectical logic to chance by postulating an impersonal agency that can be held to be driving mankind toward some redemptive, inescapable conclusion. Arnold Toynbee's schematic *Outline of History,* drawn from convenient data and delivered in preconceived terms, was edited to seem objective, its issue inevitable.[370]

Although one seems cheerful and the other glum, nothing in Herodotus or in Thucydides indicates that the world is going somewhere in accordance with a divine plan or inevitable logic. Neither democrats nor oligarchs, neither tyrants nor heroes, among Greeks and Romans, affected a motive finer, or more reliable, than the power and the glory later laid, with whatever sincerity, at the feet of God. Monotheism—once it was institutionalized—channeled events into a purposeful direction. Christian and Muslim apologists commandeer the speculative playfulness of Plato and attach it, joylessly, to notions of otherworldly salvation for the faithful. We can presume that Thucydides observed the ritual religious calendar, for civic reasons, but his scorn for Nicias's ruinous delay in retreating from Syracuse, after a total lunar eclipse, indicates that between formal respect and nervous superstition lay the distinction between the worthy and the foolish leader.

The accusation that Thucydides is obsolete has at least as much to do with his relegation of the gods, and supernatural

---

370. Hugh Trevor-Roper ridiculed Toynbee's pretensions to being history's rector in a famous article in *Encounter.* Trevor-Roper himself later proclaimed the "law" that defeated powers (he had Germany in mind) were known to return to fight on a second occasion, but that they never did so for a third time.

machinery, to irrelevance (a prefiguring of Epicurus) as with any
want of jargon-braced sophistication. Morley insists that *to
anthropinon* (human character) is an obsolete, essentialist concept. Have today's human motives nothing in common with
those to be observed in the ancient world? In what definitive way
have "we" distanced ourselves out of comparative range with the
Corcyrans or the Athenians when the plague dismantled their
civility? Contemporary divisions are still as arbitrary as they are
murderous: Hutu and Tutsi, Shi'a and Sunni, us and them.

The intrusion of Christianity and then of Islam, alike at
least in their schisms and self-righteousness, followed the uni-
versalizing processes of Alexander the Great. His demand that
he be recognized as personally divine led, by a short path, to the
effusive speech and fawning posture in both Hellenistic courts
and later (Christian and Islamic) scriptures. Since Hellenistic
kingdoms had no manifest geographic or ethnic boundaries,
and no machinery to encourage patriotic solidarity among the
common people, the veneration that Alexander concentrated on
himself stood for the patriotism that, in a widely diverse population, was likely to have little social or ethnic basis. His affectations of divinity were taken on by domineering successors whose
titles often incorporated claims to supernatural, and super-
national, authority. The end of free speech and argument came
with the episcopal presumption that would make heresy a
capital crime both in Christianity and in Islam. Which monotheism ever gladly accepted the right of choice, heresy's first meaning? The doctrine of free will was perverted to allow ecclesiastic
authorities to treat the "wrong" choice as deliberate treason.[371]

371. This alone justifies Charles Freeman's title *The Closing of the Western
Mind* (2003).

59.

In the traditional taxonomy, the triumph of Macedonia, under
Philip II, the father of Alexander the Great, put an end to
Greece's Golden Age, both in literature and in politics. The
Philippics of Demosthenes (384–322 B.C.E.) have, however, been
construed as a swansong of rare eloquence and of greater poignancy even than Pericles' Funeral Oration. In attempting to
rally the Athenians to lead Hellas against the titanic outsider,
Athens's supreme orator portrayed Philip II and his Macedonians as boozy predators.[372] They were also held to have lacked
the redeeming quality of being genuine Greeks.[373]

During his long and profitable leadership of Athens before
the Peloponnesian War, Pericles impersonated and licensed the
ambitions of his fellow citizens. Demosthenes never enjoyed
the same unrivaled leadership. Although Isocrates was no public orator, his elaborately composed writings[374] had made a
convincing case for an alliance of convenience with Macedon.
Athenian self-sufficiency was a thing of the past; it was time for
practical considerations to banish principle; hence Plato stigmatized Isocrates as morally subversive.[375] The latter's influence

372. In fact, Macedonian wine cups were smaller than those commonly
in use in Athens.

373. After the breakup, in the 1990s, of what had been Yugoslavia, the
province of Macedonia proclaimed its independence. The modern Greeks
disputed the Macedonian claim to be entitled to consider themselves other
than Hellenes and have made no marked show of good-neighborliness.

374. Plutarch reports that Isocrates spent as much time writing his *Pan-
egyricus* as it took to build the Parthenon (15 years).

375. Isocrates' "realism" had something in common with the attitudes of
modern economists who regard the scheme of things as best left to "market
forces" on which moral scruples and pious purpose have little or no effect.
Marx inverted Hegel; the advocates of market forces invert Marx.

was divisive enough to oblige Demosthenes to inflate himself, with a measure of rhetorical hot air, into what Hegel would call (in the case of Napoleon) "a world-historical figure."

Until the rise of Philip II, Macedonia's position—astride the corridor that led from Asia into northern Greece—had given the insecure rulers of its fractious population little choice but to make their peace with whatever power marched closest to their gates. In the late sixth century B.C.E., King Amyntas married his daughter to a Persian general. Salamis and Plataea dissolved the menace from the East, but it was replaced first by the demanding imperialism of Athens, then by contradictory demands from both sides in the Peloponnesian War. After the victorious Spartans had been exhausted by the long war, their ascendancy was sapped by jealous allies and ended, forever, at Leuctra (in 371 B.C.E.), by the Thebans under the great Epaminondas. The bristling weight of the phalanx broke the previously all but ritualized routine of land warfare.[376] The teenage Philip, who had been delivered to the Thebans as a hostage for Macedonian docility, watched and learned.

At the end of three years of exile, the young prince returned home and in 359 B.C.E., after the death in battle of his brother Perdiccas III, became king, at the age of twenty-three. He accelerated the removal of the capital of Macedonia from Aegae, an unimpressive collection of villages in the Spartan style, to Pella, where he expanded the palace begun under King Archelaos (413–399). Designed on Pythagorean principles of

---

376. The phalanx had an influence resembling that of the tank on the western front in 1916. In 1940, the German blitzkrieg, conceived by Heinz Guderian, used massed tanks as a mechanized phalanx to punch through the French lines.

harmony,[377] it rivaled the majesty of the Parthenon. Under Philip's urgent instruction, Macedonian infantry was reorganized on Theban lines, with the formidable local cavalry as an additional strike force.[378] Philip avenged his dead brother, then, during the 350s, set about evicting the resurgent Athenians from key cities in his region. He celebrated the capture of the Thracian gold mines with the issue of gold coins, and—as a proclamation of panhellenic ambitions—adopted Attic *koinē* as Macedonia's official language.

The neat charm of coincidence has led to the claim that the monumental temple of the virgin goddess at Ephesus was consumed by a fire started, by an Ephesian called Herostratus, on the same day in July 356 B.C.E. on which Philip's son Alexander was born. Herostratus solicited immortal fame by destroying the beauty he could not create.[379] It was decreed to be a crime even to mention his name, but he achieved lusterless immortality by becoming the by-word for a cultural vandal. Parts of the temple survived the arson, but some seven and a half centuries later, in 401 C.E., a Christian mob led by the rabid St. John Chrysostom (the Man with the Golden Mouth), leveled

377. Dionysian appetites combined with cultural refinement. At the royal drinking parties of Perdiccas III, in the 360s, entry was forbidden to those not conversant with Pythagorean geometry. See Angeliki Kottaridi in the catalogue of *Heracles to Alexander the Great* (2011).

378. The image of the *Hippocharmes,* the emblematic cavalryman, proclaimed the long connection between Macedon and horsemanship. Philip made fresh grants of land to horse breeders.

379. When, in late 1944, Adolf Hitler asked, "Is Paris burning?" as he had ordered, he played the Herostratan part, as the leaders of ISIS have by blowing up the great temple of ancient Palmyra in 2015 and other acts of provocative and newsworthy barbarism. Jean-Paul Sartre's story "Erostrate" modernized the image of the egocentric psychopath.

it beyond repair. One pillar is still standing, on which, when I last saw it, a seemingly one-legged stork was nesting.[380] Close to the site is a modest, not very ancient-looking house in which local guides promise that the Virgin Mary once lived.

While the Athenians applauded Demosthenes' eloquent scorn for the semibarbarian Philip, they were slow to take up arms against his intrusion into the Greek heartland. The Macedonian's tactical skill was supplemented by purposeful diplomacy. He fought when he had to (and lost an eye at Methone, in 354), but he also observed that no city in Hellas was impregnable so long as he could get a donkey laden with gold up to its gates. When Demosthenes did at last persuade the Athenians to confront Philip by making common cause with their old enemies the Thebans, it was in time for their joint forces to be routed at Chaeronea in August 338.[381]

At once aggressive and cunning, Philip expanded Macedon's military menace and offered the Greeks, especially the Athenians, the prospect of a privileged, if junior, collaboration in what he intended to be his crowning glory, the overthrow of the Persian Empire. At a congress in Corinth in 337 B.C.E., many Greek cities agreed, with whatever forced smiles, to join a league to invade and conquer the Persian Empire. Before Philip and his main force could amplify and join the vanguard already

380. The modern Greek poet Kiki Dimoula (b. 1931) recalls seeing a stork's similarly tall nest near Alexandroupolis, in Thrace, and likens poetry to its nest: "Art is ever-vigilant, elliptical, balancing on one leg. When we write we subtract." Quoted by Cecile Inglessis Margellos in *The Brazen Plagiarist*.

381. Chaeronea seems to have been a convenient rendezvous for battles. It was there that, in 86 B.C.E., Sulla defeated the oriental potentate Mithridates and made sure that the eastern Mediterranean would remain part of *mare nostrum*, our (Roman) ocean.

ashore in Asia, he was stabbed to death, as he walked alone at
the wedding of his daughter to the king of Epirus. The assassin
was a young man called Pausanias who, like the Athenian tyrannicide Harmodius, may have had some sexual affront to avenge.
The killer was quickly cut down; so quickly that it kindled
suspicion that Philip's discarded queen Olympias (the most
memorable and resourceful of his seven wives and many mis-
tresses) was behind a plot to put her son Alexander on the
throne.

60.

It is said, in brief histories, that the succession passed smooth-
ly to the crown prince. The smoothness was quick with the
blood of Alexander's siblings (Philip's latest wife had recently
produced the smallest of them). Olympias no doubt steadied
his resolve, if that was needed. Nero's mother Agrippina came
from the same mold. The ambitions of ancient mothers, Greek
and Roman, for their sons were often fired by a passion that
they were rarely able, or expected, to feel for the husbands to
whom, in most cases, they had been delivered, in early puberty,
as marital merchandise.[382] Olympias was an initiate of the
ceremony of the Great Gods of Samothrace. Alexander became
a fervent, intermittently riotous follower of the peripatetic

---

382. Sigmund Freud's Oedipus complex may be derived, to whatever
small degree, from the particularly close bonds between mothers and sons
as a result of arranged marriages of the kind common in eastern European
Jewish communities, as well as in rich or aristocratic gentile society. Balzac's
novel *Le lys dans la vallée* depicts a pseudo–mother-and-son relationship with
suggestive thoroughness.

Dionysos: drinking parties were a recurrent form of relaxation for Macedonian officers.

As if in tribute to Demosthenes' old opponent Isocrates, who died in 338 B.C.E. at the age of ninety-eight, Alexander advertised his invasion of Persia as the warranted revenge of all good Greeks for the sacking of their cities and temples over a century and a half earlier. When the self-appointed leader of all the Hellenes (except for the Spartans) flung his spear, in conscious reprise of Homer's Protesilaus, into the soil of Asia, the bulk of Alexander's force was composed of Macedonians. He did not care to have it publicized that, as he advanced into Asia, more Greeks fought against his expeditionary force, mostly as Darius's mercenaries, than figured in its ranks.

The Persians had not failed to play economic politics with the Greeks in the intervening period, but Darius II (423–404), who killed his brother Artaxerxes IV to attain the throne, had warned his son and successor, the next and last Darius, never to attack the Greeks since "land and sea are on their side." Out for gold, for praise, and for unmatched glory, Alexander attained them all. Alexander's chivalry (to female members of the Persian royal family) and his leading-from-the-front courage are regularly lauded; his excesses and cruelty are either ignored or attributed to Macedonian celebratory traditions. M. C. Howatson's *Oxford Companion to Classical Literature* says that, after the first victory at the river Granicus, "many Greek cities in Asia Minor opened their gates to him." Not all of Darius III's subjects were so accommodating. Even after Alexander's second great victory at Issus, late in 333, north of today's Beirut, the ancient Phoenician city of Tyre, in its eminently defensible offshore site, resisted bravely. Alexander built a three-kilometer causeway to carry his heavy catapult artillery within range of the walls; he was to be the first over them. Howatson does not mention that some 7,000 of the defenders of Tyre were crucified. After the capture of Gaza, its brave commander, a eunuch called Batis, was dragged to death in the dust behind Alexander's chariot, in gross rehearsal of Hector's fate in the wake of Achilles.

Alexander combined ruthlessness with superstitious caution. On his way through Palestine, a local myth reported that he was affronted when Jerusalem's high priest, Yaddous, failed to deliver the tribute that Darius III usually received.[383] As the Macedonians approached the Jews' holy city, Yaddous came out to meet him (in the Mediterranean world, the man who displaces himself concedes superiority), whereupon Alexander is said to have prostrated himself. He was allegedly rewarded with the oracular promise that he would remain the lord of Asia. In fact, Alexander never went to Jerusalem, nor did he, as reported, commission sacrifices in Yaddous's name, but he did enroll a body of Jewish soldiers. In Babylon, some of them refused to assist in building a temple to Marduk; when they were about to be disciplined, Alexander reprieved them.

Had Macedon's capital, Pella, sat more centrally in the empire that its soldiers conquered and Hellenized, it might have grown fat and metropolitan, as Rome did, on the revenue of success. Its rulers might then have kept control of the finances and administration of the empire their armies had overrun. As it happened, while Alexander's military genius procured territory and booty beyond measure, the sumptuous speed of their acquisition, followed by the king's early death (when he was thirty-two years old), fractured the Macedonian leadership.

383. See Maurice Sartre, *D'Alexandre à Zénobie* (2001).

Alexander's generals—Seleucus and Ptolemy in particular—
became the several tyrannical rulers of the Middle East, and
each other's dynastic antagonists. Alexander's expedition proved
so successful, its fruits so cosmopolitan, that Macedonia itself
lost its charm for those who had tasted and enjoyed the softer
pleasures of Persia. Their homeland's depleted manpower would
render it vulnerable, in particular to Rome.

While Greek became the common language of what had
been the Persian Empire, Alexander's generals proved no more
capable of harmony, or even of mutual accommodation, than
had the city-states of Hellas after Salamis and Plataea. The great
Egyptian city of Alexandria—one of many, all the way to India,
that bore their founders' names—might have furnished the
eastern Mediterranean with a fulcrum from which to operate an
efficient hegemony; but no single candidate among Alexander's
surviving generals, the so-called *epigoni,* was ever strong enough
to impose himself on the totality of the conquered territories.

Before advancing toward the supposed limits of the world,
Alexander had traced the foundations of the greatest of the
cities that bore his name. When its Hippodamian ground plan
was marked out on the Egyptian desert in flour, the birds of the
Nile delta came quickly to consume its tasty outline. Quick-
witted augurs interpreted this to mean the city would prosper,
and its founder be happy as all the people of the world ate out
of his hand. In the event, Alexandria's imported population
failed to foster a reliable model for government, but the great
harbor became a cultural meeting place.[384] Imitated later by

384. The city's five boroughs were designated, unsentimentally, by the
first five letters of the Greek alphabet. The only local hero in Alexandria was
Alexander.

Bologna, Montpellier, Salamanca, and Oxford, it had the first resident, state-subsidized faculty of any university. Thousands of scrolls of Greek texts were purchased, appropriated (from passing merchant ships), or copied. The library's stacks excited both emulation—in the almost equally extensive library at Pergamum, in Anatolia—and, when the Arabs stormed the city in 642 C.E., countercultural incineration. Alexandria's self-advertising Pharos lighthouse shone for over 1,000 years before an earthquake toppled it into the harbor it had served as a beacon.

If all the volumes on the shelves when the willfully abstruse poet Callimachus[385] was the presiding librarian in Alexandria, were still available, classical literature, even without its attendant commentaries and concordances, would burst the bounds of what any single scholar could hope to construe or even list (lists and rankings were a regular byproduct of Alexandria's curatorial zeal). The entire works of all the Attic tragedians alone would fill countless shelves and, no doubt, trail a glossy retinue of textual and grammatical cruxes. The ancient literary landscape without lacunae would be impassably mountainous.

---

385. It used to be said that Callimachus (ca. 310–240 B.C.E.) was the model for many subsequent poets, especially the Roman innovators of the "Alexandrian" school, whom Cicero deplored. While he certainly inspired Catullus (as he did Alexander Pope's *The Rape of the Lock*), some recent scholars have downgraded him to a pretentious maverick.

61.

In his uncompromising pursuit of military and diplomatic purposes, Alexander set an example that the Romans were to follow. When Darius offered to surrender half his empire for the sake of peace, the story is that Alexander's chief of staff, Parmenio, said that if he were Alexander, he would make the deal. "And if I were Parmenio," Alexander replied, "so would I." In 330 B.C.E., a plot to assassinate Alexander was discovered to involve Parmenio's son, Philotas. He was immediately executed. Alexander sent express word that Parmenio himself, who held a key command over the imperial treasury, should also be killed. There was no evidence of his implication in the plot.

Two years later, at the end of a drinking bout in the old Macedonian style, "Black" Cleitus, the veteran general who had saved Alexander's life at the battle of the Granicus, was loud in regretting the Medizing of the Macedonian ranks. In the old bold style of Macedonian generals, he dared to say, in whatever mock-solemn tone, "Poor Greece, how you've fallen!" Alexander ran the old general through with a spear. After a period of remorse, the conqueror's march continued. What began as a band of brothers had become an imperial court; fratricide replaced fraternity.

Alexander marched into the Persian heartland at a speed that Julius Caesar would mimic in his campaigns in Gaul. Darius had assembled a huge army east of the river Tigris, at Gaugamela, but the impact of Alexander's assault shattered its incoherent ranks; the once Great King fled yet again. The road was open to Persepolis, the great capital city infinitely richer and more remote than Susa, to which the Spartan king Cleomenes had declined to trek when solicited by the Milesian Greek Aristagoras at the beginning of the fifth century.

The sack and burning of Persepolis are sometimes passed off as revenge for what Xerxes did to Athens, sometimes as a drunken concession to please a comely whore named Thais. They are more likely to have been calculated to induce shock and awe[386] among Darius's remaining subjects; and they did. They also promised that the Macedonians were in Asia to stay. The palace compound, large enough to house 100,000 courtiers and servants as well as the royal guard of 10,000 "Immortals," can scarcely have been torched as an idle whim. When Scipio Africanus ordered the equally signal destruction of Carthage, he remarked to the Greek historian Polybius (embedded with the Roman forces), "One day will the same thing happen to Rome?"

Babylon, a city four or five times grander than Athens, was astounding (and welcoming) enough for Alexander to leave it intact. The hanging gardens, as if reflecting the heavenly paradise, made it the double of the home of the gods. The regulated irrigation of the Tigris and Euphrates enriched a valley with countless inhabitants. Ziggurats covered with green and blue, yellow and ochre, red and gold tiles seemed to scale the sky. On the sacred way to Ishtar, its walls covered with cyclopean friezes of lions, bulls, and serpentine monsters, Alexander found himself in a setting that must have appealed to his Dionysian image of himself as the master and child of the world, Greek born, but bursting beyond the bounds of Hellas. His Epeirote mother, with her reputation as a sorceress, now had the allure of a successful Medea.

386. The terms in which George W. Bush and his advisers chose to describe their treatment of Baghdad in 2003, when a largely undefended city was bombarded with rockets.

62.

When Alexander caught up with Darius, he found that he had been killed, and succeeded, by his best general, Bessus. The conqueror covered the once Great King's corpse with his own cloak, in humble and presumptuous deference. After an arduous pursuit, Bessus was betrayed to the Macedonians by his rival Spitamenes. His nose was sliced off and he was whipped before being sent for trial before a Persian court whose judges no doubt knew what they had to do. It was as if he had been a traitor quite as much to Alexander as to Darius III. Spitamenes then became the prey. When his head was presented to Alexander by the Scythians, only Oxyartes, the king of Bactria, the last of Darius's satellite monarchs, remained to be subdued.

Oxyartes' mountaintop eyrie was known as Aornos. The Greek alpha privative—*a/ornis*—promised that "no bird land" was too high to nest in. An oracle had promised that it could be captured only by winged soldiers. Alexander ordered 300 mountaineers, originally from Epirus in northwestern Greece, to scale the bluffs and then emerge, waving sheets like white wings, under the walls of the citadel. Thirty fell and died, but the others appeared to fulfill the oracle. Alexander, who had only a small escort with him, received Oxyartes' surrender (and the delivery of a huge cache of booty) in gracious style. When he saw the king's daughter Roxana, he asked Oxyartes for her hand. The wedding festivities lasted a week. The winner of the celebratory games received a crown of palm leaves. Alexander said that the best man could be rewarded only with glory, a pious notion that had small place in his train.

Whatever his original intentions, Alexander evidently did come to believe that he could homogenize mankind, not least in deference to his own genius. Did he find, or need, encouragement in the words of Empedocles:[387] "There is nothing legitimate for some, / Illegitimate for others. /The law covers everything and everyone / Like the air that reigns in the distance / And the infinite light of the sun . . ."? So many Asiatic troops came to be enrolled under Alexander's colors, as he marched east, that Macedonians were no more than a quarter of the force with which he crossed the Hindu Kush toward India. When Alexander promised a local king named Taxiles that he was on "a crusade of fraternity,"[388] Taxiles yielded with tactful immediacy. The Macedonian army marched on and down into the Indian heartland. Before King Porus of the Pauravas was granted a peace of the brave, a set-piece battle had to take place, in which two of his sons were killed. Asked how he wished to be treated, Porus replied, "Like a king"; and so he was: Alexander entrusted him with regency over his lands. Lucian reports that when the Macedonian army embarked on the river Hydaspes, a tributary of the Indus, one of the surviving secretariat took the occasion to recite his wholly fictional account of single combat between Porus and Alexander. Alexander threw the text into the river. "I ought to do the same with you, Aristobulus," he said, "for fighting such duels on my behalf and killing elephants for me with a single spear!"

The core of Alexander's officers had now had enough. Coenus—son-in-law of the dead Parmenio—was deputed by the general staff to declare that, if Alexander wanted to go

387. He might have been set to learn them in his student days with Aristotle.

388. The phrase, whether accurate or not, comes from Jacques Benoist-Méchin's *Alexandre le Grand* (1976). The author was a notorious admirer of Hitler's Wehrmacht. Although not a flagrant collaborator, Benoît-Méchin's notion of a pan-European superpower had fascistic undertones.

further east, he should raise a new army. Alexander replied that those who wanted to go home were free to do so. He shut himself in his tent for three days before taking the omens. They were all bad. He decided to lead from the front, as usual, and crossed the river on his own. No one followed. He came back and conceded, to the cheers of his soldiers, that it was time to turn back. He ordered the construction of twelve towered altars to Dionysos, to mark the limit of his rampaging adventure.[389] He was the last to leave the site.

63.

Not all of Alexander's faith in his ex-enemies was honored. After a protracted march back to the Fertile Crescent, on which more than half of his men died of thirst and disease (and, no doubt, left the desert littered with booty), he learned that his Persian legates and subjects had ignored or suborned the few Macedonian officials left in his wake. The mausoleum of Cyrus the Great had been thoroughly pillaged. Alexander decapitated Baryaxes, a pretender to the throne, and the satraps Orxines and Aspastes. The Macedonian governors of the plundered provinces and 600 of their soldiers were also executed. In practice, as Thrasymachus had told Socrates in the first book of Plato's *Republic,* justice was the interest (*sumpheron*) of the stronger.

Alexander's boyhood friend and trusted treasurer, Harpalus, had already made a smart getaway with enough gold to pay a substantial bodyguard. When he landed in Attica, Demosthenes moved that the absconding treasurer be held prisoner,

---

389. Terence Rattigan's underrated 1949 play about Alexander was entitled *Adventure Story.*

with his stash, on the Acropolis. Harpalus then escaped, leaving a good deal of the gold behind him, the price of his exit perhaps. Demosthenes was accused, not implausibly, of helping himself to a large amount of the treasure. Since the gold was Macedonian, self-interest and patriotism were, by that time, hardly to be distinguished. Demosthenes was convicted and went into exile. Harpalus made off to Crete, where he was murdered by his second-in-command.

As the returning Alexander approached Babylon, the priests of Marduk offered religious pretexts to deny him entrance. The so-called Magi had indulged in peculation on a massive scale. Alexander evicted them and ordered a new temple to be built, with the aid of 20,000 soldiers. On the cusp of summer and autumn in 324 B.C.E., a festival was mounted, by Atropates, the satrap of Media, to celebrate the Dionysia. During its lavish course, Alexander's dearest companion and designated successor, Hephaestion, fell ill and died. Alexander was prostrate for many days, his distress modeled, it may be, on that of Achilles at the death of Patroclus. When he emerged, he put on a great show of renewed energy.

As the new temple was completed, a man was discovered sitting on the throne, claiming to be Dionysos. When the Magi proclaimed that it meant that a madman would succeed Alexander, the impostor had to be executed, if only because Alexander's entourage had been witnesses of the solemn comedy. The joy had gone out of conquest; its duties remained, alleviated only by the traditional Macedonian drinking parties, with a plethora of Banquos in attendance. The dull doggedness of even somewhat honest administration had small place in any post-Periclean Greek's idea of a worthy life.

Alexander died, perhaps of a fever, perhaps from alcoholic poison, if only self-administered, a year after Hephaestion.

As he lay dying, Perdiccas asked him who should succeed him. He responded, "The one who most deserves it." The Roman historian Curtius Rufus reported the most poignant reaction to Alexander's death: Sisygambis, Darius's mother, whose family had been treated with courteous (if calculated) respect, threw herself on the ground, as Hecuba did at the fall of Troy, weeping for her own and her children's misfortunes. The titanic carcass of empire was torn into contending kingdoms by the band of Macedonian brother-generals who now became the vulturous Diadochi (Inheritors). Alexander's corpse was appropriated, en route to Macedonia, by Ptolemy I "Soter" (the Savior), who had quickly made Egypt his own. The casket was prominently ensconced in his capital, as if to certify Ptolemy's majesty.

Demosthenes had retained the affection of enough of his fellow Athenians for them to welcome him back after news came of Alexander's death. For the last time, he convinced a majority to believe that the city-state could recover its glorious independence. At the battle of Crannon, in Thessally, in 322 B.C.E., the Macedonian regent, Antipater, made sure that Demosthenes did not survive his illusions; the great orator took poison to avoid capture. Athenian democracy died with him. Its clever garrulity, but not its capacity for independent action, was diffused among the disputatious writers, poets, and intellectuals whose learned tracts and journalistic wit were to fill the oikoumene with the literary culture, at once elaborate and servile, eventually filed under the rubric of the Second Sophistic. Greece was diffused into the Fertile Crescent. Athens dwindled into a university town; Sparta degenerated into a sort of Club Med for sadomasochistic voyeurs: the ritual flogging that had once served to toughen adolescents before they went into battle became a bloody, sometimes lethal, entertainment.

64.

Alexander had ceased to see himself as a Macedonian. His rapacious successors were left with the richest carcass in history. The generals and despots who, for the next three centuries, lorded it, insecurely, over the Hellenistic world were neither wholly Greek nor thoroughly barbarian. Alike in their divisions, they maintained their authority by force. If they were to endure, they had to deliver both ostentatious amenities to subjects whom they never consulted and wages to the mercenaries on whom, after Gyges, usurpers came always to depend.

Alexandria became the greatest of all monuments to the founder whose will had traced its outline. For three centuries, its Ptolemaic rulers mimicked their predecessors, the native-born pharaohs, in the lordly practice of incest. Indigenous Egyptians were treated as a helot race until, after a long dynastic run, the Ptolemies were supplanted by the exacting Romans. Italy's hunger was thenceforth sated by shipments of Egyptian wheat. Cleopatra, the last of the Ptolemies, still spoke a Greek dialect that originated in the Pindus Mountains of northwestern Greece; she was, however, the first of her line to be able to address Egyptians in their own language.

Alexander had been succeeded on the throne of Macedon by his brother Arrhidaeus, who reigned as Philip III. To secure his tenure, he procured the murder of Roxana and her unborn infant, Alexander Aigos. The stretched Persian Empire remained Hellenic, but it was never even briefly the peaceful, unified federation that Alexander is said, by the British classicist W. W. Tarn and others, to have had in mind. It is probable that, like many conquerors, he dignified his announced purposes in the course of a war primed by vanity, greed, and curiosity. By the time he died, he had been transformed into a restless, androgynous Dionysiac god, of no fixed character or abode. Neither pedigree Greek nor accepted Persian, Alexander elevated himself to be the world's greatest nobody-in-particular: the most successful Odysseus (Outis) in mythistorical antiquity.

Alexander's unmatched triumph has proved an embarrassment to scholars and moralists. His early death failed to serve as a warning against unbridled ambition: rather than being put down by a god, he was assumed to have become one.[390] His successors decked themselves with titles that mimicked his divine authority. The art of the Greeks, once the mark of their liberty, served to gild tyrannical patrons. Democracy had no place in kingdoms whose rulers might appease their subjects with ostentatious luxuries, but were wise not to put arms in their hands. It was safer to employ alien mercenaries who would not be tempted to side with the local population. The Hellenistic kingdoms, for all their splendor, were police states.[391] Their populations, with their various languages and mythologies, had in common only social and economic ambitions. Their most articulate koinē (common language) was coinage; understanding was as much a commercial as an intellectual activity.

Alexander's successors attached his style of divinity to their names in order to procure their subjects' superstitious allegiance. The Middle East became a region in which religious affinities trump nationality and overrun geographers' boundaries, except

390. His restless progress from west to east was a reversal of the route traveled by Dionysos, whose androgynous verve, restless desire for dominion, and bibulous example were rehearsed in Alexander.

391. In Franco's fascist Spain, the Guardia Civil was, in effect, an occupying force. Care was taken that its garrisons came from another, distant province and were immune to local loyalties.

in the case of Judaea. The singularity of the Jewish religion, in the ancient and the modern world, has never solicited proselytes;[392] its strength and its vulnerability are that it generates close, seemingly exclusive, social bonds within a limited community. Tradition claims that Jews had an ethnic affinity with the Spartans. In the time of Herod the Great, a Spartan opportunist called Eurycles took advantage of this supposed link to prevail on Herod, not usually an easy touch, to pay him a lavish fee in order to procure a reconciliation between Herod and Octavian, the future Augustus, after the latter had defeated Herod's patron, Mark Antony, at the battle of Actium in 31 B.C.E.[393]

Since his achievement was undeniable, if not miraculous, Alexander's story was edited to conform to later proprieties. The princely monomaniac was refigured by Plutarch as an evangelist for racial harmony and the "submission of the world to the same law of reason under a single form of government, the whole of humanity a single people."[394] The sexually versatile,

392. The Maccabees are the exception: they conscripted and circumcised the Idumaeans, a tribe living in the south of Palestine, as reinforcements for their war of liberation from the waning Seleucid Empire. The story of the Maccabees became literally apocryphal when the Hebrew bible was edited to confirm the virtues of conformity with imperial and divine purposes.

393. See my *A Jew among Romans*. The Nazis also claimed affinity with the Spartans.

394. Sartre, *D'Alexandre à Zénobie*. Plutarch was modernized by W. W. Tarn in *Alexander the Great and the Unity of Mankind*, published in 1933, just as the futility of the League of Nations was about to be exposed by the Nazi regime in Germany. Hitler was shown the way by Mussolini's earlier unpunished assault on Ethiopia. After World War II, a photographic compendium entitled *The Family of Man* sought to revive Tarn's sentimental notion of universal kinship. René Cassin's notion of "universal human rights" stems from the same magnanimous ambition.

bellicose Alexander became a conjugal example, once he had "settled down" with the beautiful Roxana, and an advocate of universal peace (of which the Pax Romana was a derivative). His sculptured hair style set a standard that Pompey the Great, for egregious instance, was careful to imitate; Julius Caesar was envious of Alexander's achievements,[395] too bald to match his coiffure but tall enough, it seems, not to have to be elevated, as Alexander and Napoleon often were, by being portrayed on horseback.

Alexander's two most powerful successors, Seleucus and Ptolemy, had helped themselves to baggy kingdoms of tempting dimensions and uncertain strength. Neither realized the Alexandrine fantasy of a hybrid population of mixed bloods, united in subservient prosperity. Syria was an ample base from which the Seleucids might dominate the Fertile Crescent, but it was easily permeable by predators. The Ptolemies were better placed for security; their capital, Alexandria, an implantation of Greeks and Jews, grew into magnificence under their pseudo-pharaonic autocracy. The indigenous Egyptians had little part in its social or economic life. The inability of Hellenistic rulers, however impressive their appanages, to foster patriotic loyalty or to eliminate each other, led them to hope that the Romans could be recruited to their own partisan or venal purposes without becoming their rivals. Hellenistic princes grew accustomed to

---

395. That Alexander was so young when he began his victorious ascent has made his success proverbial. In his novel *The Five*, Vladimir Jabotinsky has one young character say to another, "Remind yourself that Alexander of Macedon at your age was already almost twenty years old!" *The Five* is set in prerevolutionary Odessa, a great cosmopolitan port willed into existence by Catherine the Great, as Alexandria was by Alexander. Jews were a substantial minority in both cities.

diplomatic compromises. Their battles were as often theatrical as lethal: their shows of strength led, not unusually, to one or the other side climbing down. They were to learn that the Romans did things differently.

When, in 168 B.C.E. the Seleucid king Antiochus IV Epiphanes (God Made Manifest) sought to visit his majesty on the Romans, who had landed in Alexandria in the wake of their conclusive victory over the Macedonian king Perseus at Pydna, in northeastern Greece, he was put in his place by the local Roman legate. Popillius Laenas drew a circle in the dust around Antiochus and advised him not to step out of it before agreeing to become, in effect, a client of the Senate and the Roman people. God Made Manifest thought about it and then complied. The Romans had come to stay in the Greek world.

On his way home, Antiochus vented his pique on the Jews by having a pig sacrificed on the High Altar of the temple in Jerusalem and by other measures designed to advertise his enfeebled toughness. He was less a prototypical anti-Semite than a sore loser who needed to reestablish his local clout in order to fund the tribute exacted by Laenas.[396] Jews outside Jerusalem suffered no systematic persecution. It is not implausible to imagine that the Seleucid's tantrum was primed by the Jews of Alexandria who had been able, with encouraged impunity, to display their delight at his humiliation.

---

396. See Sartre, *D'Alexandre à Zénobie.*

65.

By extending his empire to the ends of the earth, Alexander—whatever his intentions—had ensured that unelected tyrants would rule the segments they and their armies managed to detach from his legacy. Alexander's affectations of divinity were eagerly cadged by his successors. Indifference to the opinions of their subjects was common to all of them. Outside the now outmoded city-state, democratic politics, with popular votes in the Athenian style, were practically impossible. In a world without press or microphones, ancient speakers, even if they could emulate the volume of Menelaus or even of loud-mouthed Stentor, could never be heard by more than a few thousand people. In the post-Alexandrine oikoumene, the one surviving self-governing democracy was the durable association of three cities on the independent mercantile island of Rhodes.

When their riches were coveted by Demetrius Poliorketes (Besieger of Cities),[397] the Rhodians held out against him for the whole year of 305–304 B.C.E. The Macedonian general then abandoned both his ambitions and his famous siege engines. His bellicose machinery was sold off to fund the Colossus, the gleaming, 33-meter-tall image of their patron god, the Sun, which dominated the entrance to the Rhodian capital's thriving harbor. By clearing the region of pirates and by the efficiency of their merchant marine, the islanders made themselves

397. Son of Antigonus the One-Eyed (382–301 B.C.E.), at first one of the most prominent of Alexander's epigonoi. Antigonus was cut out of his share of the empire by Seleucus and killed at the battle of Ipsus in central Phrygia. In return for ceding some of Alexander's Indian conquests to a local king, Seleucus had been given the elephants which, like tanks in modern warfare, turned the tide of battle. See *Antigonus the One-Eyed* by Richard A. Billows (1990).

welcome wherever they sailed.[398] When rendering commercial services, they were careful not to take sides, especially between Ptolemies and Seleucids. The Colossus continued to advertise their prosperity, until it was toppled by the earthquake of 142 C.E.[399]

Once the influence of Macedon had been eclipsed at Pydna, Roman power sailed unopposed into the eastern Mediterranean. Rhodes stood out as an intolerable example of successful independence. In 168 B.C.E., after Delos had been converted by the Romans from the sanctuary of Apollo to a supermarket for the slave trade and ancillary commercial activities, under

398. A surviving vessel, on show in Bodrum, proves that nervous passengers could entrust their valuables to the captain's safekeeping when going on board.

399. In modern times, the trading fleet of the small island of Castellorizo, once a possession of democratic Rhodes, enjoyed a long period of prosperity, thanks to the large merchant fleet that operated from its excellent harbor. The whole fleet was purchased by the British when they needed troop transports for the Gallipoli expedition, conceived in 1915 by Winston Churchill. The Castellorizans used the British gold to buy new ships and continued to prosper until the outbreak of World War II. In 1943, the British decided to use the island as a base and evacuated all 15,000 islanders, promising to restore them to their property after Greece was liberated. In the event, the island was completely devastated by a fire which, the British claimed, was caused by German air raids. There were, however, no bomb craters. Later investigation suggests that British troops, from various quarters, rioted and destroyed the fine houses owned by Castellorizo's merchant captains. The islanders were made an offer, which they were advised not to refuse, to emigrate en masse to Australia. Few had the will or means to resist. Castellorizo became all but uninhabited, but the emigrants stuck together, mainly in the region of Perth, in Western Australia, where they were known as "Cazzies." Enough were sufficiently successful for some of their grandchildren to return to the deserted island and start to rebuild the ruined houses around the deep harbor. I have heard them talking Greek with an Australian twang.

favorable terms for its merchants, the Rhodians were squeezed into coming to humiliating terms with the new superpower. In 43 B.C.E., the island's still enviable wealth attracted a piratical Roman too strong for the pacified islanders to resist: Shakespeare's "lean and hungry" Cassius Longinus, a leading player in the assassination of Julius Caesar a year earlier, was always notorious for his greed; now in urgent need of the means to raise more troops to confront Mark Antony and Caesar's great-nephew and adopted son, the young Octavian, he helped himself to anything he could take to fund his losing cause.

Soon after Cassius and Marcus Brutus were killed at Philippi in 42 B.C.E., the winning Roman faction, led by Octavian and Mark Antony, imposed a program of more tolerable exactions on the island. Rhodes prospered again, modestly, as an intellectual greenhouse (while attending the lectures of Posidonius, the young Marcus Tullius Cicero had taken a course in rhetorical technique and was infected with a taste for philosophy).[400] In the intervals of a public life both illustrious and, at times, ignominious, as advocate and politician, Cicero managed, almost singlehanded, to transplant Greek thought into Latin terms, some of which he had to compose more or less ab initio. It was a sublime aspect of the arrivisme that drove him, with hectic energy, to the pinnacle of Roman society, and toppled him from it. Cicero's penchant for Greek culture led

400. Posidonius (ca. 135–ca. 51 B.C.E.) was a Syrian Greek Stoic polymath, educated in Athens, and a peripatetic lecturer before he settled in Rhodes. His version of Stoicism, always a matter as much of style (or stylishness) as of doctrine, had a long influence on personal conduct under the confused circumstances of what became the Roman Empire. His cultural curiosity and cross-referential intelligence make him an exemplary figure of "pagan" culture before Christian authoritarianism set out to anathematize heresy.

him to freckle his letters with Greek expressions, "pour faire beau" (to look smart), as Flaubert said of Balzac's penchant for fancy phrases.

Republican Rome was already a hybrid of Greek political styles: like Athens, it had a popular assembly (its powers more influential, as Peter Wiseman has pointed out, than grand historians allow) and two annual consuls who, like Spartan kings, were often at once colleagues and rivals. For three centuries, until the elimination of Carthage, members of the senatorial order, of old families, were content to wait their turn to administer the provinces from which they expected to return with due emoluments. The courts were likely to protect governors wise enough to share the pickings, provided they were not unduly immodest.[401]

The young Cicero made his name by prosecuting the upstart Verres after he had pillaged Sicily so flagrantly that even his patrician friends, the Caecilii Metelli, were unable to protect him. Courtroom triumphs and his improved oratorical brio moved Cicero up the ladder toward the consulship. The radical advocate became a conservative politician. His performances amused and persuaded juries, but the gallery he played to was predominantly of the upper and middle classes. The fate of the nobly born brothers Gracchus and their radical friends, done to death by senatorial colleagues[402] twenty years before

401. Roman sophisticates said that provincial governors had to accumulate three fortunes during their year of office: one to pay their debts, one to bribe the jurors when, on their return to Rome they were charged with extortion, and the third to keep.

402. One of the most implacable of those who instigated the quasi-judicial murder of the Gracchan faction was the same Popillius Laenas who had put Antiochus IV in his place in Alexandria a few years before. See David Stockton, *The Gracchi* (1992).

Cicero was born in 106 B.C.E., was enough to warn all but the boldest or the most desperate against challenging the *mos maiorum,* ancestral custom, and the vested interests of its proponents.

Cicero's crowning glory came during his consulship, in 63 B.C.E., when the great civilian put on a general's breastplate and defended the old order against the reckless insolence of L. Sergius Catilina, the very type of the rogue aristocrat that no provincial could ever hope to be. Cicero's suppression of Catiline's putsch earned him the title of "pater patriae" (father of his country) from the senatorial *boni* (literally, "the good men," certainly the men with the goods), but he was never quite one of them: vesting sentimental hopes in what he took to be the innate qualities of Old Families, he ignored the fact that few of those who applauded his actions had the morals or the muscle necessary to keep the old Republic alive.[403] Marcus Porcius Cato was the priggish exception who, impersonating his severe great-grandfather, Cato the Censor, took pleasure in denying Cicero the endorsement he craved.

403. See, e.g., Arthur Kaplan, *Catiline: The Man and His Role in the Roman Revolution* (1968). Benjamin Disraeli, another arriviste with rare eloquence and even greater panache, played the Ciceronian part by lending his wit to the English Tory party, whose grandees were happy to let him do the hard administrative work for which they had small appetite and to refashion the image of their party in a way that would appeal to the wider electorate. Disraeli, like Cicero, was a performer of the highest quality, but never an accepted member of the class whose interests were served by his sentimental cynicism.

66.

The so-called father of Roman poetry known as Livius Andronicus was born around 284 B.C. and lived till he was eighty. Andronicus sounds Latin enough and wrote for a Roman audience, in the clumping antique Latin meter known as Saturnian. He was, in fact, a Greek, or at least Hellenic. Captured and enslaved when the once Spartan city of Tarentum, which had become a Macedonian thorn in the heel of Italy, fell to the Romans, Livius turned his coat and his talent. The prosaic Flavius Josephus would do much the same thing in 68 C.E., when, as a Jewish general, he surrendered to the Romans and became the salaried historian of Vespasian, whose son Titus uprooted the Jewish state.[404] His literary skills procured Andronicus his freedom from slavery. He not only wrote and acted in tragedies and comedies; by translating Homer's *Odyssey* into Latin, he also made the first, wide bridge across which Greek poetry came to impress and educate the Romans. More than two centuries later, Horace would recall being forced to learn chunks of Andronicus's Homer by heart, just as yesterday's young classicists were set to learn selections from Horace, whose verses were regularly quoted, or misquoted, in the Victorian House of Commons.

Among Rome's first home-grown poets was Gnaeus Naevius. Born around 270 B.C.E., he followed Livius's example in writing for the stage, but he was of Italian origin. As a veteran of the First Punic War (264–241), of which he wrote a verse history, he had the nerve to be outspoken. His stage comedies

---

404. See my *A Jew among the Romans*.

were taken from Greek models, to which he gave Italian settings
and, as it were, dubbed dialogue. The modern privileging of
"showbiz" has old roots. Whoever procures ticketed tears or
laughter can enjoy a well-rewarded life.[405] Condescension from
below is a regular aspect of literary social climbing. When,
however, Naevius went so far as to poke fun at the great family
of the Metelli, their unamused reaction and unarguable clout
lowered the curtain on his career. Both Cicero and Catullus
were to run up against a branch of the same family. Dispatched
into African exile, Naevius died in Utica, in today's Tunisia, not
far from Carthage, which he had helped to defeat.

Utica was to have another poetic connection. The unbend-
ing Marcus Porcius Cato (the younger of that name) committed suicide there, during the Civil War, in 46 B.C.E., rather than
accept Julius Caesar's *clementia* (mercy). A century later, Cato
was the loudly sung hero of the precocious Lucan's *Pharsalia,*
an (unfinished) epic lament for the lost Roman Republic,
written during Nero's reign. Cato's suicide was immortalized
in the famous line "Victrix causa deis placuit sed victa Catoni"
(The gods favored the winning cause, Cato the lost); its composition was followed, not long afterward, by the poet's own

---

405. Noel Coward spoke, if more candidly than most, for the majority
of playwrights when he confessed, unless it was boasted, that his intention
had always been to travel first-class through life. He announced his arrival
by mocking the aristocratic Sitwells, whose literary works were allotted by
the critic Frank Leavis, another outsider, though never an amusing one, to
the history of publicity. Oscar Wilde, a greater wit than Coward, had made
Naevius's mistake and incurred the enmity of an aristocrat, the marquis of
Queensberry, who provoked Wilde into the disastrous legal action that led
to his imprisonment and exile, in Calais. On his deathbed, Wilde found the
wit to say, "I'm dying as I lived, beyond my means."

forced suicide. To kill oneself was never regarded as any sort of a crime in the ancient world. With sad prescience, Cicero suggested that it resembled leaving the theater after one had seen enough.

In the generation after Naevius, the patriotic note was struck, on a more solemn gong, by Quintus Ennius (239–169 B.C.E.), a prodigious producer of verses and plays in a spectrum of styles. The protégé of Cato the Censor, Ennius was a provincial Italian, and he too had served in the army. His *Annales,* in Homeric style, affected to be a history of the origins of Rome. It was cited as authoritative by Cicero and others. What the *Aeneid* would do with sophisticated grace, Ennius did in ponderous measure: supply a foundation myth that gave Roman expansionism the luster of manifest destiny. Most of Ennius's work has perished, but he helped to Latinize Greek meter and set an early example of literary careerism by eulogizing the great Scipio Africanus, whose victory at Zama, in 202 B.C.E., clinched Rome's triumph over Hannibal's Carthage. Ennius established himself as a prolix, allegedly boozy upstart in the Roman style. By his talent to amuse and impress theatrical audiences and by his flattery of the influential, he made himself a patriotic paragon.

Terentius Afer, or Terence, the most elegant of Latin comic playwrights, is said by Suetonius to have been brought to Rome from Carthage as a slave in the 160s B.C.E., in the interval between the Second and Third Punic Wars. Although it is sometimes claimed that he was black, his alleged African negritude may derive simply from his cognomen (family name) Afer. His elegant *fabulae palliatae,* plays featuring Greek characters in Greek dress but speaking Latin, had prompt success, which was as well; he died young on a visit to Greece in 159. His obituary is supplied by his own oddly moving "Hinc illae lacrimae" (Hence those tears).[406] One of his other apothegms, "Homo sum; humani nil a me alienum puto" (I am a man; I consider nothing human foreign to me), was carved in the beam above Michel de Montaigne's desk in the study in his château in the rural Gironde, where the great humanist (and sometime mayor of Bordeaux) wrote his essays. On a decisive whim of his father's, Montaigne learned Latin before he spoke French.[407] It would be a curious, vain exercise to speculate how his cursive thoughts would have come out had Greek been his first language.

67.

As the Romans incorporated the East under their imperium, Greek writers, teachers, and doctors came to instruct them in a cultural and literary syllabus for which military discipline and narrow culture had allowed no time.[408] The Romans were drawn eastward more by the grand folly of Hellenistic rulers than by any Alexandrine curiosity. In 182 B.C.E., after his defeat in the Second Punic War, Rome's greatest enemy, Hannibal, was granted sanctuary by the Seleucid Antiochus III. Once Hannibal's pursuers had seen what the region had on such sumptuous display, the riches of Alexander's heirs provoked predators

406. To be distinguished from Virgil's equally plangent "sunt lacrimae rerum et mentem mortalia tangunt" (There are tears in things and mortality touches the soul), in book 1 of the *Aeneid*.

407. Exiled to Lausanne, the young Edward Gibbon became proficient in French before he scribbled in English.

408. Cato the Censor, who had pressed so monotonously for the destruction of Carthage, remained an unreformed monoglot until, at the age of eighty (in 154 B.C.E.), he decided to discover what all the fuss was about by learning Greek.

whom they, like Darius III before them, were unable to repel. The Greek world was pacified in the Latin style; arrogance and tolerance (of cooperative inhabitants) arrived together. The Romans were both newcomers and, they liked to believe, revenants. Roman myth had it that the Trojan prince Aeneas had escaped from the burning city, carrying his old father Anchises, once the lover of Aphrodite, on his shoulders, on the way to Italy to plant himself and his descendants on the seven hills of Rome.

The fate of Mithridates the Great (120–63 B.C.E.) served as a warning to any further attempt to push the Romans back into the sea that they now claimed as their own. Mithridates, from Pontus on the Black Sea, mounted the first and last strenuous attempt to evict Roman adventurers, tax collectors, and fortune hunters from the eastern Mediterranean. Eighty thousand Latin immigrants were massacred in what came to be called "the Asian Vespers"[409] before the discipline and ruthlessness of the best Roman generals, Lucullus, then Cornelius Sulla, settled matters in the Roman zero-sum manner. When cornered, Mithridates had to order his slave to stab him because he had taken care to render himself immune to arsenic, the ancient poison of choice, by taking small regular doses of it to guard against the possibility that, in the Hellenistic manner, some of those around him might use a large sudden dose in order to supplant him.

409. At Easter 1282, the Sicilians rebelled against the Franks, who had occupied the island, and massacred 3,000 of them, without achieving the independence of which Sicilians have continued, intermittently, to dream. See Steven Runciman, *The Sicilian Vespers* (1958) and, for a modern instance, Gavin Maxwell's *God Protect Me from My Friends* (1956), in which the bandit Salvatore Giuliano is shown to have hoped to attach Sicily to the United States.

Lucullus resented the way in which Sulla had usurped his command. He assuaged his wounded vanity by outdoing Lucius Mummius[410] in the quantity and quality of Greek sculptures and objets d'art that he shipped back to Italy. As the most fastidious, as well as the first, Roman collector of the riches of the Hellenistic East, he looted only the finest pieces. A prototypical Lord Elgin,[411] with gastronomic finesse, Lucullus brought home to the Romans what they had been missing in the way of art and of delicacies, the cherry tree among them. Pliny the Elder alleged that the patrician gourmet committed suicide in rage when his transplanted orchard failed to produce a crop. Imitation of Greek styles became the sincerest form of envy. Roman domestic architecture, however, owed more to the Etruscans, who invented the *impluvium,* the indoor pool filled with rainwater to be found in the lobby of any grand Roman house. As for the priapic figures with bright-red erections that served the Romans as scarecrows, were they Italian natives or cousins of the Athenian herms that Alcibiades and his friends were accused of mutilating?[412]

410. Mummius sacked Corinth in 146 B.C.E. He is said to have stripped the city bare.

411. Elgin was lampooned by Byron for filching the Parthenon marbles and exporting them to London, where they are still on display, despite the vigorous campaign to have them repatriated to Greece. No Greek has solicited the return of the Aeginetan figures filched from Aegina and carefully defaced by the Danish sculptor Bertel Thorvaldsen (who made an iconic bust of Byron) en route to the museum in Munich where they are now on display.

412. Few Greeks of the golden age had grand houses on the Roman scale. Athens had no famous collectors of the order that Lucullus inaugurated and who, in imperial Rome, embellished their private museums in the fashion that Petronius Arbiter satirized in Trimalchio's gross ostentation and Orson Welles in the crated treasures in Charles Foster Kane's Californian Xanadu.

Roman generals and high officials helped themselves, as a matter of course, to whatever in the provinces was portable, even with difficulty. Italy came to be garnished, shamelessly, with looted masterpieces; so did Napoleon's Paris and imperial London. After Christianity became the institutional religion of western Europe, the ubiquitous pagan residue of often erotic Greek originals, their Latin copies, and more recent, seemingly pious allusions to them reminded the baptized of the profane charm that monotheism had displaced but could never quite obliterate.

Marching in Lucullus's bootsteps, with less fastidious tread, Sulla amassed the golden means to return to Rome with an irresistible force of enriched veterans whose allegiance was to their general rather than to the Roman state. Before issuing a formal rescript of the constitution, designed to restore the primacy of the old senatorial order, Sulla became the first Roman magistrate to display in the Forum the names of citizens whose murder would enrich their killers. What became known as proscription was a form of lethal ostracism from which there was no return, except to the murderers. The principal victims were supporters of Sulla's rival and mortal enemy, Gaius Marius—like Cicero, a *novus homo* (a euphemism for an upstart without senatorial pedigree) from Arpinum, south of Rome— who had been scarcely less vindictive, in eliminating aristocrats, when Sulla was away fighting in the East.

Six times consul, Marius had become the leader of the common people. The savior of his country against barbarian invasions from the North, he organized a professional army, with standardized equipment and long terms of service (15 years or more). Detached from family properties, recruits became dependent on victorious generals for the rewards and housing that would give them comfortable retirement. Patriotic courage doubled with partisan interest. While both Marius and Sulla affected to be saving the Republic, each was no more unselfish, and each markedly more vindictive, than Alcibiades.[413]

68.

T. Lucretius Carus was a loner: his unprecedented use of Latin epic for philosophical argument (the Greek philosophers Parmenides and Empedocles had advanced their ideas by similar poetic means) and his unassuming, hermetic life set him apart. Born at the beginning of the first century B.C.E., he died in 55. *De rerum natura*—not so much the *Poem on Nature,* as C. H. Sisson translated it, as *About the Source of Things*—carries no direct reference to the bloody times in which its author lived. Almost alone among Latin authors, Lucretius does nothing to flatter Roman vanities or reproach Roman vices. His small defiance was to begin his poem with "Primum graius homo . . ." (A Greek man was the first . . .), giving pride of place to Epicurus and his humane, godless gospel. Moderation was never more passionately advocated. *De rerum natura* is a sustained polemic in favor of quietism. A. J. Ayer's *Language, Truth and Logic* is a modern, fierce, if prosaic, instance of similar fervor in the presentation of an alien philosophy—Viennese logical positivism—as a "scientific" cure for religious superstition.

---

413. Peter Green's first historical novel, *Achilles His Armor,* was about Alcibiades. His later fiction *The Sword of Pleasure* takes the form of the memoirs of Cornelius Sulla, in the style of Robert Graves's *I, Claudius.* Historical novels on Roman topics are almost invariably more convincing, if only because a certain English style can match the brickwork of Latin prose more closely than it can, for instance, the Corinthian flourishes of the Hellenistic novel. Robert Harris's enjoyable trilogy about Cicero is a recent instance.

Lucretius invited his readers to abandon fears of posthumous punishment or divine sanction. The gods, if they existed, were unlikely even to be aware of mankind. Mortal life was best enjoyed in amiable company and modest comfort, preferably a garden. It was senseless to live in fear of some shadowy or penal afterlife. This benign message came to be reviled by the Christian fathers. St. Jerome either invented or was happy to repeat the story that Lucretius died of a poisoned love philter; others said that he had gone mad, probably a malicious response to the sanity of his militant skepticism. Unlike overheated modern dogmatists, neither Epicurus nor his disciple denied categorically that divinities existed.

Although there is only one mention of his genius in Cicero's extant work, Lucretius may well have been a protégé of the great orator (and less great poet). Cicero's friend, correspondent, and publisher, Pomponius Atticus, spent much of his time in Athens and was himself a businesslike Epicurean.[414] Atticus proved his wisdom not least by taking no loud part in the political contretemps that culminated in the Civil War between Pompey and Caesar, and later between Caesar's murderers—the "Liberators," as they saw themselves—and his young, implacable heir, Octavian. If Lucretius's philosophy was principally Greek, his grandiloquent urgency lent virility to the Latin hexameter, which would be turned to more subtle, and politic, purposes by Virgil, who is said, in line with the coincidental neatness of antique chronologies, to have assumed the *toga virilis*, the

414. Asked what he did during the Roman Civil War, Atticus might have given the same reply as the Abbé Sieyès with regard to the Terror of the French Revolution: "J'ai vécu" (I lived through/survived it).

uniform of manhood, on the very day in 55 B.C.E. on which Lucretius died.

Lucretius stands alone in maverick honesty, a hater of war who confessed—it is typical of his candor—to a thrill of horror when he witnessed bloodshed in gladiatorial shows (which no Greek state is known to have sponsored, or Greek audience to have enjoyed, until the spread of Roman showbiz). Not all pleasures, the poet conceded, had to be good. He honored Venus as the source of life, but he was matter of fact, to the point of clinical, when it came to physical passion. He promoted a public philosophy of tolerance and simplicity: slaves were entitled to respect and no god was worth (or desired) bloody sacrifice. These views are enough to explain why Lucretius had little impact on pagan Rome, for which war was a paying industry, and why he was disparaged by Christian zealots, for whom hellfire was the destination of whoever advocated a philosophy of live and let live.

69.

Lucretius's almost exact contemporary, Gaius Valerius Catullus (ca. 84–54 B.C.E.) has often been regarded as unique among Roman poets, for his passionate feelings and the presumed sincerity of their expression. Lord Tennyson called him "tender"; Harold Nicolson was unable to understand why. Perhaps Tennyson was thinking of the Latin sense of *tener*, which implies thin-skinned, easily hurt, as well as youthful. The uniqueness of Catullus's work lies in the fresh, yet learned[415] variety of his

---

415. Ovid, who was no less clever, addressed him in *Heroides* 15 as "docte Catulle."

elegance, as well as in the Archilochan obscenity of his rage and contempt.

When expressing first love, and later pained and protracted loathing, for Lesbia, his work seems as spontaneous as it is artful. Lesbia was, almost certainly, his pseudonym (in tribute to Sappho, no doubt) for Clodia Metelli, the wife of a consular grandee. Catullus made adultery into the truest love, himself a tortured martyr in its cause. When his fury was directed against friends who had betrayed him or—in the case of Julius Caesar and his (again pseudonymous) henchman Mentula—who had degraded Rome, Catullus could be a master of scatological invective. In either mood, he laced his feelings with allusive, Alexandrian smartness and savage self-mockery.

If he was the greatest of the group whom Cicero called the *neoteroi*, Greek for the younger generation, with overtones of too-clever-by-half avant-gardism, Catullus was one of a self-conscious pack of mutually admiring and competitive aesthetes. Ostentatious Hellenism was at the heart of their willfully pretentious code, as the French symbolists, Jules Laforgue in particular, were for Ezra Pound and T. S. Eliot before World War I. While Catullus and his friends imitated the lyric meters, and sometimes the matter, of Alcaeus and Sappho, their *maître-à-penser* was Callimachus, who lived and taught in the "Museum" in third-century B.C.E. Alexandria. His conceits sprigged with recherché erudition, Callimachus was one of the first academics to use criticism as a way of fortifying his own supremacy.[416] This too

416. Callimachus's verses may have been brief, but his lost *Pinakes* comprised a prosaic critical inventory of the library of Alexandria in 120 volumes. The great classical scholar A. E. Housman (1859–1936) wrote English verse of superb trenchancy as well as, in particular, an exhaustive and erudite commentary on the little read Latin poet Manilius. A master of academic invective,

was imitated by Catullus, in the lampoons that punctured long-winded contemporaries.[417]

What is left of Catullus's work survived antiquity thanks to a single manuscript, discovered during the Renaissance being used as a bung (or wedge) for a barrel of wine. Others of his smart set, who may have been hardly less talented (Gallus and the lawyer Calvus—Catullus's talkative "Little Man"—among them) were not so lucky. If today Catullus stands alone, he was no solitary genius. The neoteroi subscribed to Callimachus's quip "mega biblion, mega kakon" (big book, big crap). They had little use for the inflated epic tradition that made Ennius a bore and infected dear old Cicero with sententious verbosity.[418] Catullus and his friend did, however, exercise themselves in producing elaborate mini-epics. Catullus's own poem 64 compresses, parodies, and embellishes the theme of *Voyage of the Argonauts* by Callimachus's colleague and bête noire Apollonius Rhodius, as well as synopsizing the story of Theseus and Ariadne, seen from the accusing point of view of the deserted princess. Catullus shows knowledge of the killing of Androgeos by the Athenians and of the "cargo of living dead" who had to

---

Housman prepared searing denunciations of other scholars whose names, whatever they might be, were inserted when suitable ineptitudes came up for review. T. S. Eliot's claim that the latter half of the 20th century was an "Age of Criticism" was calculated to mount him and his friends as Callimachan arbiters. Frank Leavis and the *Scrutiny* connections were adjacent pretenders to judicial supremacy.

417. See, for instances, my *A Thousand Kisses,* a radio drama broadcast by the BBC in 2011. Catullus's poem 46 is markedly ambiguous with regard to the old school impersonated by Cicero.

418. Kingsley Amis and Philip Larkin took a similarly naughty-boyish view of *Beowulf,* the Anglo-Saxon epic hallowed by the Oxford English syllabus and recently translated, with renovatory license, into a TV series.

be delivered annually in recompense. Jean-Paul Sartre's play *Morts Sans Sépulture* (Dead Without Burial) depicts hostages awaiting execution by the Nazis. His not very daring play *Les Mouches* was a version of Euripides' *Bacchae*, written—not very daringly—during the Occupation.

Recourse to Greek models on the part of the *neoteroi*, suggests revulsion not only from traditional Roman solemnity but also from the social mayhem and bloodletting that stained the last decades of the Republic. Catullus's father had entertained Caesar (and 2,000 of his men) on his estate at Sirmio, near Verona, when the unprecocious and balding deutero-Alexander passed through on his way to conquer Gaul beyond the Alps for the greater glory of Rome and in order to pay off his overdraft. Was Catullus reacting against his father's deference when he savaged Caesar and his enforcer, Mentula?

70.

The free speech and freer invective on which Catullus and his friends prided themselves were an extension into poetry of the rhetoric practiced prosaically in the courts and in the Curia, the Senate House, where friends (in the Roman sense of social equals who, in other circumstances, owed and did each other favors) often appeared on opposing sides. There they then indulged in rituals of mutual denunciation, which convention required should not foster abiding grievances. In court, English lawyers still refer to opposing counsel, with mordant collegiality, as "my learned friend." The abusive interchanges of Roman attorneys had a pastoral equivalent in the flyting banter of shepherds and other rustics in Theocritan and Virgilian eclogues.

Caesar's triumphs and his place in history, his own versions of it not least, served to make his dictatorial ascent seem

inevitable and even desirable. Inevitable only because it happened, it has been applauded by those who put "order" above
freedom, a common German habit. For most of the upper-class
Romans in whose company the provincial Catullus was eager
to shine, Caesar was an insolent renegade who relied on the
support of the rabble (and his own veteran soldiers) in order
to enrich and empower himself.[419] He could afford to forgive
Catullus his puppy impertinence, and did; Caesar too was a
writer, of whom it was said that, for his literary reputation, it
was his good fortune that his verses were lost to posterity. The
only poet known to have died because of Caesar was the unfortunate Cinna, who had gone to Bithynia with Catullus,
under the patronage of Caius Mummius. Mistaken for one of
Caesar's murderers who had the same name, the lyrical Cinna
was torn to pieces by an enraged crowd.

In treating Caesar as a self-important fellow citizen,
rather than a superior being, Catullus played the Byronic
dandy[420] in the last days before the autocracy which often made
literary outspokenness a life-threatening indulgence. Cicero, in
his turn, was nervously brave enough, after Julius Caesar's
murder, to wage verbal war on Caesar's unsubtle lieutenant,
Mark Antony.[421] The latter responded by having him proscribed,

419. Franklin Roosevelt was so regarded by the WASP establishment,
who had the habit of referring to him as "that man." Their revenge was the
amendment that made it unconstitutional for a president to seek reelection
more than once.

420. Disgusted by—and no doubt envious of—the duke of Wellington,
who celebrated the victory of Waterloo with a ball to which all London came,
Byron remarked of the beau monde, "They will worship any bloody booby
who breaks heads." Translations of Catullus figure among his juvenilia.

421. In Joe Mankiewicz's film of Shakespeare's *Julius Caesar*, Mark Antony
was played by Marlon Brando, who was accused by some purists of mumbling

a death sentence to which Cicero's young friend Octavian was craven, and self-serving, enough to make no objection.[422] For the moment, Caesar's heir needed Mark Antony's support more than Cicero's condescending advice. Thirteen years later, Octavian was sufficiently in control of events to declare Mark Antony an enemy of the Roman people. After the battle of Actium, the date of the latter's birth was "celebrated" as a day of ill omen, but his patrician family prospered under the imperial aegis. Many years later, Augustus came on his grandson reading Cicero. The boy feared reproach, but the emperor commended the patriotism of the man whose death warrant he had initialed. Unchallenged imperium licensed magnanimity.

Catullus almost certainly did not live to see his father's friend Caesar obtain dictatorial power. How or when exactly the poet died is not known. To presume that he faded away, broken-hearted, when not much older than thirty, after Lesbia dumped him, sentimentalizes his passion;[423] if Caesar's enforcer, derided as Mentula (the Prick), was less amused or indulgent than his master chose to be by the poet's provocations,

---

his lines. He was, however, clever enough to pronounce the too well known opening words with an original emphasis: "Friends, Romans, *country*men. ..." The implication was that rustics (and ex-soldiers of Caesar's) had come into town to mourn and/or avenge the lost leader.

422. Cicero's wit was often the making and the undoing of him. Although he had received Octavian amiably in person, he had remarked (probably too often) that the young man was *tollendus,* an ambiguous gerundive which meant that he merited both promotion and/or removal.

423. Peter Green infers from the poet's references to his cough that Catullus may well have been tubercular. His erotic and his sometimes furious verses have something in common with those of D. H. Lawrence, whose great love, Frieda, was another man's wife when he met her. Lawrence died of tuberculosis at the age of forty-five.

that may not be wide of the mark. Peter Wiseman, however, has suggested that Catullus may have renounced lyric poetry and lived a second creative life as a dramatist of the same name, who wrote theatrical comedies that have not survived to allow for philological autopsy.

Since there are so few reliable biographical dots to join up, especially if the "sincerity" of the poems is discounted, Catullus offers tempting opportunities for inventive speculation. The usual biographical line is that the poet quit Sirmio for Rome in order to make a name for himself and then somehow—always a neat bridge over lacunae—fell in with the circle around Clodia Metelli and was drawn into her orbit and her bed. Once enchanted, he discovered that what he had taken for his true love was a mixture of Circe and Medusa. By then he was helpless to escape the consequences and was left to lament his folly in having believed in Lesbia's *amicitia* (a form of bonding usually reserved to males). This is a pretty reading of what may just as well have been purposeful, if not cynical, social climbing. To have found his way into the bed of a consul's wife and a woman of renowned sexual independence is unlikely to have been due only to the fervor or sincerity of his passion. A tender heart is not incompatible with an eye for the main chance.

Writers and scholars have varied greatly in their view of Catullus's work. C. J. Fordyce, whose edition was published in 1960, was so scandalized by the several scabrous or scatological poems that he either excised them from the corpus or rendered them into Italian. Even Peter Wiseman declared, at the age of forty-two, that he was getting too old to handle Catullus, quite as if Catullan exercises made physical demands on his critics. Catullus is the Latin poet whom people most regularly take personally.

The notion that sincerity is a warrant of merit is so obnoxious to some sophisticated critics that they are tempted to claim that all Catullus's work is as Alexandrian as Callimachus's factitious lament for Berenice's lost locks. In literary criticism, scheme both neatens and distorts. Common sense suggests that Catullus's exquisite folly was to fall in love with his own fancy; his mundane mistake was to imagine that his mistress and his best friend would honor his illusions. In an early version of an old, old story, while Catullus was away from Rome, in Bithnyia, in the suite of his patron Mummius, the wit and fellow dandy Caelius Rufus supplanted him in Clodia's bed. Since Caelius was a friend of Cicero's, as was Catullus to some degree,[424] some of his lively correspondence is extant. It may be that neither Clodia nor her new lover guessed, or cared, how badly Catullus would take their casual treachery, or how memorably he would pillory them.

71.

When Caelius was accused of complicity in the murder of a Ptolemaic diplomat, Clodia's brother subscribed, in both the literal and the technical sense, to the prosecution. This gave Cicero, as Caelius's counsel, the chance to besmirch both Clodius, a populist politician whom he hated and feared, and his sister Clodia's reputation (he procured cheap laughs by "apologizing" for referring to her as Clodius's wife). Caelius was acquitted, but he later disappointed Cicero's fond expectations

---

424. Catullus's tribute to Cicero (poem 49) can be taken as either flattery or mockery, or both. See Frederic Raphael and Kenneth McLeish, *The Poems of Catullus* (1978).

by rallying, with unconcealed opportunism, to Julius Caesar's
disreputable partisans.[425] After being elected praetor (a senior
magistrate, below the rank of consul), he made a fatal mistake.
In defiance of the consul and in association with Clodius's
enemy (and Cicero's friend) Milo, he advocated a popular
scheme for debt relief of the kind proposed by his boyhood
friend Catiline. When they attempted to make themselves important political players by raising a rebellion among the rural
poor, both were killed.

The end of the old Republic had been presaged by Sulla
when, on his rich return from the East in 83 B.C.E, he embraced
the young Gnaeus Pompeius as "Magnus," the Great. Pompey
was to honor the title (probably bestowed with a measure
of sarcasm) with a swathe of victories. His greatest achievement,
after pacifying the East, was to emulate the Hellenistic Rhodians,
on a much greater scale, and clear the Mediterranean of the
pirates whose privateering threatened trade. Success enabled
him, as it had Sulla, to dominate the Senate, whose members
accepted the provincial swaggerer as one of their own. With
typical ambivalence, Cicero feared and patronized him.
Social insecurity had something to do with Pompey's willingness to make common cause, in what came to be called the
First Triumvirate, with Julius Caesar and the multimillionaire
Lucius Crassus. In taking control of the state, the three men
had little in common except the ambitions that would separate
them.

425. Among his clever letters to Cicero is one that takes delight in avoiding
the smallest affectation of principle in giving his reasons (which he urged on
Cicero himself) for siding with Julius, the likely winner.

Caesar, an impoverished aristocrat turned populist, had been a youthful member of Gaius Marius's party. He had the Odyssean cunning to lie low when Sulla was culling his more obstreperous enemies. Thirty years later, Caesar's success in the Civil War was crowned by his being presented with his ex-son in law Pompey's severed head when he landed in Alexandria. No loser in ancient history had more successes or received more insincere eulogies than the unlucky and unloved Gnaeus Pompeius. Even at the peak of his powers, he misjudged the mood of the people by staging triumphal games in which, as a novelty, he had elephants done to death, for fun, in the arena. The animals' pitiful bewilderment at the cruelty visited on them excited the pity of the usually callous Roman plebs; Pompey was hooted for his generosity. Not one of the many writers who looked back with nostalgia at the old Republic (and its well-distributed dividends) referred with respect or affection to the sorry figure who died friendless and unadmired, the leader of a caucus of aristocrats whose authority he had, in the days of the first triumvirate, disempowered. Pompey's reputation never received as much as a quotable epitaph.[426]

In 46 B.C.E., on his return to Rome after pacifying the Middle East,[427] Caesar was so singularly powerful that, during the public celebrations, Marcus Antonius offered him the crown, in a charade rigged to allow the dictator graciously to refuse

426. Lucan did his best with "Stat magni nominis umbra" (There stands the ghost of a great man). Pompey's best apologist is Peter Greenhalgh, whose 1980 biography is subtitled, with almost ironic effusiveness, "The Roman Alexander the Great."

427. He took the opportunity to report his achievement with laconic vanity: "veni, vidi, vici" (I came, I saw, I conquered).

what Roman mythology regarded with abhorrence.[428] Caesar's murder in 44 B.C.E. led, by bloody steps, to the very thing that Brutus and his friends had plotted to prevent—the institution of a single, arbitrary ruler. In *The Roman Revolution,* in which he broke with a long tradition of homage to Caesarism,[429] Ronald Syme likened Roman emperors to mafia capos, ruthless in disposing of potential rivals, including their own close relations. After the first Christian emperor had established a second, eastern Rome in Constantinople, Byzantine kings came to display Christian charity by blinding rather than killing competitive siblings.

During the more than four centuries of the Roman Empire, electoral formalities continued to be observed and ancient titles, including that of consul, to be bestowed,[430] but there was recurrent

428. Caesar had the prudent grace not to celebrate too loudly his triumph over other Romans. Perhaps he recalled how Elpinike, Cimon's sister, had reproached Pericles for giving himself heroic airs after his bloody treatment of Athens's Samian allies. The upstart emperor Vespasian knew no such modesty when, after reducing the revolt of Judaea, a Roman province, he mounted a triumphal procession through Rome. No one before him had celebrated "victory" in what amounted to a glorified police operation. Even Caesar had not been universally applauded when he made a great deal of his Gallic triumph.

429. Theodor Mommsen was the greatest of Julius Caesar's admirers. The imperial German use of the title Kaiser to dignify their leader was a tribute to the Roman style which, in other respects, the Germans were proud to reject (Luther's Reformation was nothing if not nationalistic). Both Mussolini and Hitler paraded Caesarian conceit. Syme, a New Zealander, lacked the European inclination to antique homage. His seminal *The Roman Revolution* was published, with pertinent punctuality, in 1939.

430. Gaius Caligula had the satirical wit and disdain for aristocratic office seekers to declare his favorite horse his fellow consul. Caligula's egotism, wit, and profligacy, during his short reign, excited admiration of a kind in Albert

fighting, to the death, between imperial candidates. The emperors' private regiment, the Praetorian Guard, whether of Roman or other origin, was as good, or as bad, as the mercenaries whom Pisistratus rented to secure his leadership in Athens: their loyalty depended on their deal, and on the inability of anyone else to better it. When, during the reign of Domitian, in the second half of the first century C.E., Juvenal wrote the much quoted line "Quis custodiet ipsos custodes?" (Who will guard [or guard us from] the guardians themselves?), he was thinking less of Plato's ideal ruling class than of the Praetorians who, like the Janissaries in Ottoman Constantinople,[431] could determine who gained or kept supreme power. After Nero's death, in 68 C.E., the insufferably proper Galba became emperor, but lasted no longer than his old-fashioned determination not to give fat bonuses to the Guard. The mos maiorum had had its day.

72.

Looking back on Roman literature, in the first century C.E., the first great literary critic Marcus Fabius, born in Spain and generally known as Quintilian, remarked, "Satura quidem tota nostra est" (Satire at least is entirely ours). That sighing "quidem" conceded that the Greeks had been pioneers in every genre except the scurrilous, seemingly improvised, versified or prosaic riffs, often peppered with malice, which Ennius and Lucilius put

---

Camus and other modern writers. Gore Vidal wrote the script of a film that centered on his bisexual debaucheries.

431. Their long and insolent power was ended only when an 18th-century reforming sultan used the army to disband the presumptuous and undisciplined parasites, many of whom were bundled into sacks and drowned in the Bosphorus. See Mansel, *Constantinople.*

together in the second century B.C.E. In truth, Roman satire too was influenced by Greek originals, Parian Archilochus the first. Contempt for *graeculi*, Greeklings, especially philosophers and pedagogues, paid wincing tribute to how much Rome owed to Hellas. Virgil and Horace, Catullus, Ovid, and Sextus Propertius (who inspired Ezra Pound's exhortation to "make it new") were all in unconcealed fee to ancient Greek models: for Pound, as for many others, Sappho's work and the lacunae in it doubled for the pool of Narcissus.[432] As Plutarch enjoyed showing, in *Parallel Lives,* Greece and Rome produced many men of remarkably comparable qualities.

In the foundation myth of Rome, Romulus played a role similar to that of Theseus in Athens. Both were outsiders: the bastard Theseus grew up fatherless in Troezen; Romulus and Remus were foundling brothers who survived only because they were said—perhaps in tribute to Sparta's legendary Lycurgus—to have been suckled by a wolf.[433] Romulus proved his manliness by killing his brother after the latter skipped over the line of the city walls that Romulus had traced, forbiddingly, on the ground. Fratricide did more to establish Romulus's virtue as a leader

---

432. For a quiver of delightful, often fanciful, sometimes protracted glosses on Sapphic models by poets down the ages, see Margaret Reynolds's *The Sappho Companion* (2000). By contrast, Jeffrey M. Duban's *The Lesbian Liar* (2016) is an immodest, articulate, and timely reaction to wishful translations of Sappho and others.

433. Archimedes' lever has political analogues in the actions of outsiders whose alien leverage changes, renovates, or ruins a targeted society: King David comes from obscurity to replace Ahab, Oedipus from presumed orphanage, Philip and Alexander from marginal Macedonia, Marius (and Cicero) from provincial Arpinum, Jesus from Galilee, Napoleon from Corsica, Stalin from Georgia, Hitler from Upper Austrian poverty, Charles de Gaulle from marginal Lorraine.

than to blight his reputation. In Genesis, although Cain was branded for killing his brother Abel, it proved no obstacle to his going on to become a wealthy landowner and paterfamilias. Romulus continued to be honored in Roman myth; the monarchy that he had instituted did not. When a single man did indeed come once again to rule Rome, Octavian took clever care to preserve republican forms by accepting the deferential, but never regal, title of Augustus. The Thucydidean antithesis "logō men, ergō de" continued to distinguish between what was posited in theory and what was true in fact.

Augustus's house poet Virgil became first a classic (as a model for schoolboys), later something of a saint. His "messianic" Fourth Eclogue, which predicted that a new world would come into being, was later dressed in the lineaments of Christian redemption. In the sixth book of the *Aeneid,* he suggested that an embryonic infant (Augustus's nephew Marcellus[434]) was destined to be the savior of the world. In 1820, Jean-Auguste Ingres painted a portrait of Octavia, Augustus's sister and mother of the infant, who fainted as Virgil declaimed the ominous lines. Sitting in the shade behind Octavia, Ingres portrayed Augustus's wife Livia, who is often assumed to have procured the death of a potential rival to her son, Tiberius Claudius Nero, by her first husband. Whether by chance or through her machinations, Tiberius survived his several potential challengers to become the cheerless successor of the great Augustus.[435]

---

434. Who died very young.

435. After being obliged by Augustus to divorce the wife he loved, Vipsania Agrippina, in order to marry the emperor's daughter, who soon died in childbirth, Tiberius remained a sulky, if dutiful, servant of the regime. He spent time in semi-exile on Rhodes and, after acceding to the purple, soon

If Rome had its own folklore,[436] its formal literature was rooted in Greek originals. Many of the city's early wars were against the Hellenic settlements in southern Italy. Until the early third century B.C.E., the Italian Hellenes were backed, for no sentimental reason, by the ambitious King Pyrrhus of Epirus. His victories over the Romans became so expensive in men and material (including eight elephants) that he declared that he could not afford any more of them.[437] The Romans had overrun the ancient, long-buried Etruscan civilization, north of their city, with less difficulty.[438] The assimilation of Etruscan and

---

absented himself from Rome and lived on the island of Capri, where, according to the gossipy but well-informed Suetonius, he consoled himself with a retinue of underage sexual placebos.

436. Peter Wiseman's *The Myths of Rome* (2004) is a rich compendium of instances. The elegiac verses of Ovid's *Fasti* made the Roman religious calendar as enjoyable as anyone possibly could.

437. Pyrrhus was a top-of-the-range Hellenistic predator. He died in Argos in 272, after being hit on the head by a tile thrown from a roof. If the reaction of the women of Plataea to the Theban attack on their city in 427 B.C.E. offers a precedent, the missile may well have been launched by a female hand.

438. Maecenas, who began as Octavian's not very scrupulous but very efficient fixer, became minister of culture when Augustus assumed the purple. Maecenas was of Etruscan origin, from Arretium (modern Arezzo), near the Etruscan city of Bononia, today's Bologna. As the archetypal artistic patron, he advanced the careers of Virgil and Horace. His taste in literature seems to have been better than his performance: he is said to have been a very pompous prose writer. Etruscan civilization is now generally regarded as a mixture of indigenous and Hellenic elements. Herodotus quotes a claim that the Etruscans were originally emigrants from Lydia. In *Sketches of Etruscan Places,* D. H. Lawrence makes a forceful, if never scholarly, case for the uninhibited vitality of pre-Roman Etruria and its art (literally buried, until quite recently, in sites such as the domed tombs near Cerveteri, north of Rome). The dignity of Etruscan art is displayed in the museum in the Villa Giulia in

Hellenic elements supplemented their claim to a fundamental place in the Mediterranean mythology. Virgil's *Aeneid* was the superb, fabricated certificate that not only were the Romans descended from the Trojans, but also that they now had a national poet whose hexameters chimed worthily with those of Homer.

Poets and comic dramatists enjoyed a measure of the renown in Roman society that tragedians had in Hellas. Under unpopular emperors, theatrical audiences expressed their displeasure by cheers and applause for lines that could be given a topical relevance. Unlike the Great Dionysia in fifth-century Athens, however, the drama never supplied a unifying quasi-religious climax to Rome's festive calendar. The Roman theatrical repertoire was largely of remakes of Greek models. Literature and the theater were the main means, apart from money, by which ambitious outsiders, including ex-slaves, could make names, and places, for themselves.[439] Poets might be commissioned to edify the public with anthems in honor of Rome's civilizing mission, or they could set out, in proud and hungry isolation, to amuse or pique a coterie. Only Nero's aristocratic minister of culture, the dandy Petronius Arbiter, had the nerve to say that the Pax Romana had been procured by turning the world into a graveyard and calling it peace. Like the long-winded Livy, historians could gild or—like the underrated Sallust and

---

Rome, notably in the funeral sculpture known as *The Happily Married Couple*, a nice instance of what was no doubt a standard trope.

439. This may have been true even in 5th-century Athens. Nicias is said to have freed one of his slaves after his performance as Dionysos won wide applause. Paul Cartledge regards this alleged geniality as "implausible if not impossible."

the epigrammatic Tacitus—darken reputations. How writers expressed themselves, at various stages of Roman social history, was a function of talent, audacity (the equivalent of Athenian tolmē), and opportunism.

Horace and Sextus Propertius were alike in advertising their reluctance, if not their inability, to tackle epic themes. Describing himself as "Epicuri de grege porcus" (a pig from Epicurus's herd), Horace preferred, so he said, to loiter in his rural villa in the Sabine hills. His farm was a luxurious second edition of the smallholding in Apulia from which his father had been evicted when the young Horace rallied to Marcus Brutus, whose military tribune he was, very briefly, before— *more Archilochi*—he threw away his republican shield and agreed to be Octavian's domesticated rhapsode. While refusal of public commissions (*recusatio*) could advertise the value a poet set on his own independence, a cynic—echoing the duc de la Rochefoucauld—might say that he who refuses a commission asks to be commissioned twice.

Horace's rustic attitude was akin to wariness, but it was marked by gratitude, especially to his patron Maecenas, Augustus's intimate friend and diplomatic enforcer, until he fell from grace in 3 B.C.E., perhaps on account of some whispered conspiracy, perhaps only after offering ill-received advice. Maecenas was an Etruscan of royal blood (or so his protégés chose to say). Even before his patron's not very heavy fall, the pressure brought on Virgil to undertake the *Aeneid* may have been Augustus's feline way of reminding his Etruscan friend who was in charge of Rome's literary caucus. When he declined an official position as Augustus's secretary, Horace managed to do so without offending Rome's *capo dei capi*. He genuinely admired "gentle" Virgil (five years his senior) and envied neither his genius nor his grand house. For all his rural modesty, the adroit Horace remained urbane enough to pay his respects to Augustus by writing the elegant, if little-loved *Carmen saeculare,* an anthem composed to advertise the epoch-defining advent of a stately morality imposed by an emperor whose serenity was the result of having eliminated all his enemies and rivals.

When Virgil agreed, with whatever misgivings, to compose the *Aeneid,* perhaps the least spontaneous masterpiece in the history of literature, he embraced both a big opportunity and the big rewards, which included a mansion on the swank Palatine. The story that the dying poet asked his friends to burn the manuscript of the *Aeneid* was romanticized by Hermann Broch, in his 1945 novel *The Death of Virgil,* as a signal instance of belated recusatio. Broch imagined the remorseful genius to have been ashamed of having accepted the propagandist's role. It is more probable that Virgil, no less obsessive than his friend Horace, did not want to have his masterpiece published without the final touches that perfectionism required. During the reign of Nero, Petronius Arbiter, no mean poetic *pasticheur,* crowned Horace with "curiosa felicitas": the painstaking effortlessness which arranged that no word was ever awkwardly placed or tritely chosen. It is senseless to bless such immaculate verses with sincerity (rarely an ingredient of great art). Like Fabergé's jewels, they were calculated to amuse and amaze. L. P. Wilkinson chose to compare Horace's odes to Giorgione's paintings, in which a seemingly serene setting seems to convey intense, immaculate fragility.[440]

440. In 1924, the dying Franz Kafka asked his friend Max Brod to destroy the unfinished text of *The Trial.* Brod took loud pride in not having honored the request. A meta-psychoanalytic reading might say that Virgil's obsessive perfectionism had at least something to do with the effacement of a guilty conscience at having served a tyrant.

While no ancient artist achieved supreme power, unless Nero was an artist, important Romans were sometimes poets, often writers: Nero's intimates, Seneca and Petronius Arbiter, were granted consulships, though not for literary reasons. At once aesthete and megalomaniac, Nero—like the more prosaic Hadrian—was an unceasing admirer of Greek culture. In 67 C.E., while giving a curtain speech, as it were, after a performance at the Isthmian Games, Nero made the magnanimous gesture of giving Greece its freedom, essentially from taxation. His successor (after the extinction of two intermediate emperors), the fiscally prudent, unfailingly mundane Vespasian,[441] reimposed Greece's tributary obligations.

73.

Catullus, whose provincial family (in Cisalpine Gaul) was well off, was adept at impersonating penniless condescension.[442] As the young Virgil suggested in urbane verse, tradition insisted that rural tasks were healthier and more honest than metropolitan socializing. Nostalgia for country life was as persistent

441. Although he played the imperial game with an immutably straight face, Vespasian had no divine aspirations. Nothing if not mundane, he installed public urinals in Rome. When this was done in 19th-century Paris, some public official was enough of a classicist to call the conveniences *vespasiennes*.

442. While affecting to have nothing in his wallet but a dead spider, Catullus was the last Roman writer to presume that all citizens had the right of free speech (what the Athenians had called *parrhesia*). Like Archilochus's on Leophilos, Catullus's attacks on Julius Caesar (his father's friend) were without nuance. Caesar took the poet's remarks in good part and asked him out to dinner. The "Caesars" who ruled imperial Rome had little sense of tolerant civility. All criticism was soon treason; all individual dissent disloyal.

among the Roman upper classes as it was among the British, for whom hunting, shooting, and fishing were more noble, and manly, than stockbroking or even than running the empire. What Thorstein Veblen called "conspicuous consumption," and its accompanying snobberies, made good taste the cover for acquisitive enterprise. As he rose in the social scale, Cicero became an ostentatious collector who could not resist a notoriously expensive table made of lemon wood. He also claimed, like an old-fashioned grandee, to love to get away from the city to one of his several country places. He rarely stayed very long, however, in case he missed something, not least the sound of his own voice in the Senate or in court. As a young magistrate *en poste* in Sicily, Cicero had discovered that to be out of sight of the Roman élite was to be dismissed from their minds.

In time, imperialism both supplanted and mimicked the *respublica,* if only in the titular distribution of now more or less hollow honors. Emperors came to own everything and to be the objects of universal veneration among their subjects. Even after victories in which they played no brave part, they alone could celebrate public triumphs. Monotheism, transplanted from Jerusalem, came to supply a sublime version of the rule of a single, omnipotent being. By his conversion to Christianity, Constantine the Great incorporated the unique godhead in himself. He showed little sign of abasing himself to the God under whose lineaments he hoped to unify his disparate subjects: soon after his public embrace of Christianity, the emperor authorized the construction of a temple in honor of himself and his family.[443]

---

443. James Carroll's *Constantine's Sword* is a Roman Catholic's honest account of the calculations and perversions of doctrine and meaning that

Country life was a recurring Roman literary topic: Cato the Censor and the prolific Marcus Terentius Varro wrote treatises on farm management, following the example of the prosaic Xenophon in fourth-century Greece. Landowning was the only virtuous form of wealth in both Greece and Rome. Virgil's *Georgics* were a smart handbook for country dwellers, even if those who read it were likely to have second homes considerably fancier than those of the beekeeping smallholders whom Virgil sentimentalized. The same poet's *Eclogues* crowned a tradition of poetic dialogues in which shepherds and yokels exchanged compliments and insults, often in the cocky hope of winning sexual favors.

Virgil had a third-century B.C.E. Greek model in the versified banter of Theocritus. Nostalgia for peaceful rural simplicity begins with Hesiod and in some of Homer's similes and the scenes described on Achilles' shield. The decline of Athens encouraged the long tradition of Hellenic pastoral, of which the *Iliad* itself could be said to be an example: the warfare it depicts is of a heroic age, with an anachronistic spectrum of weapons and attitudes. In the first century C.E., Dio Chrysostom, from a rich Greek family in Bithynia, sited his seventh oration, the *Euboicus,* among rural hunters, true Greeks living in the middle of unspoiled, unlettered Euboea (Palamedes' island). The *Heroicus* of Philostratus (about heroes of the Trojan War), written in the third century C.E., portrayed the archetypal Hellenes as coming from rural backwaters. A character in Philostratus and Eunapius's *Lives of the Sophists* decries

---

accompanied Rome's symbiotic merger with Christianity. Evelyn Waugh's historical novel *Helena,* which exalts Constantine's mother and her pilgrimage to recover the True Cross, is a skimpy work of pious mythologizing.

the corrupt and barbaric language to be heard in central Athens.[444] Theocritus struck his bucolic attitudes not on the blue remembered hillsides of his native Sicily but in cosmopolitan Alexandria, the capital of the Ptolemies who ruled Egypt after the death of its founder, Alexander the Great. Only the last of them, Cleopatra, was fluent in the local language; her Greek retained the accents of the Macedonia that she never visited. Alexandria remained polyglot and cosmopolitan until President Gamal Abdel Nasser expelled foreigners in 1956. The Ptolemies founded the "Museum" (home of the Muses), which became the first university with a comprehensive library of some 200,000 volumes. By the second century B.C.E., Alexandria was the literary capital of the Mediterranean, rivaled only by the intellectual and cultural kudos of Athens. Pericles' shining city crumbled and shriveled, slowly. By Byron's time, it was little more than a village.

444. Whitmarsh, *The Second Sophistic,* cites the speaker's name as Agathion. It is tempting to see this as an ironic pun on that of Agathon, satirized by Aristophanes as the type of artificial metropolitan. John Constable recalls hearing a yokel saying, as he paddled across the river from rural Suffolk to hardly less rural Essex, "Goodbye, old England, when shall I see you again?" Thoreau's *Walden* (1854) caps a very old, often sentimental, notion of pastoral (past/oral) life. Implicit in the tradition is distrust of central governments, cosmopolitan moneyed interests, and tyrannies too powerful to be challenged directly. William Empson's 1935 *Some Versions of Pastoral* is the classic study. Showbiz violence is a more modern version of pastoral: James Bond is a solitary, handsome hero who seems able, singlehanded, to rid England of whatever might threaten her sleep; in the TV series *24,* Jack Bauer, with the same initials, plays an American Achilles who always survives to save the world again, if that is what the viewers want.

74.

After Caesar's murder, in 44 B.C.E., Octavian's progress to the mastery of Rome required him (he was no older than Catullus had been when he "conquered" Clodia) to make his first moves through a sequence of tactful alliances. None lasted longer than would serve the merciless purpose that he dignified as piety.[445] His most important temporary associate was Mark Antony, whom Octavian had earlier denounced as a menace to the Republic. Marcus Antonius had the military nerve and experience that the young pretender lacked. Once the "Liberators" (Brutus, Cassius, and their followers) were disposed of, Octavian could afford to turn on his ally. Antony was accused, with good reason, of the equivalent of what fifth-century Greeks called Medism, oriental self-indulgence. He was eliminated at the battle of Actium in 31 B.C.E., along with his wife, the diabolized Cleopatra, the queen of Egypt whom Octavian's "father," the "divine Julius," had fancied almost, but not quite, to the point of folly.[446]

445. Virgil, in Homeric homage, repeatedly used a conventional epithet, *pius,* to grace Aeneas's respect both for his old father and for the destiny that required him to renounce personal happiness in order to honor his divine mission. Augustus became a model of uxorious fidelity, but not before time. Piety involved observing rules of conduct, not specifically religious practices.

446. The Jewish princess Berenice would play a somewhat similar role in the life of Titus, the son of Vespasian, who seems to have had a genuine passion for the oriental beauty whom he brought home with him from Judaea to Rome. It was evidently made clear to him that a second Cleopatra would not be an acceptable Roman empress. He banished her with pitiless regret. Racine's 1670 play *Bérénice* has an exquisite farewell scene between Titus and his (considerably older) lover. It ends with the single word "Adieu," implying precisely that they would meet again only in heaven.

Without his uncle's genius as a soldier (or wit as an orator), Caesar's nephew was his master in measured generosity. As Cato had dared to say, what Caesar paraded as clementia (mercy) was no more than sugared ruthlessness: he forgave those who conceded his right to make (and break) the laws of the Republic. In one of history and morality's coincidences, the notion of "forgiveness" became central to the Christian notion of the divinity. Hebrew scripture had made morality and the observance of the law all but identical: a Jew was defined by his habits and devotions. The lordship of the Trinity declared itself not least in the abject deference of the individual sinner before the throne of God. Apocryphal Jewish literature has instances where God's people, especially learned rabbis, have a certain license to disagree with His judgments and decisions. Such insolence became unthinkable in the face of the triune deity to whom Christians bent the knee, just as it was in the conduct of Roman citizens, of whatever degree, in the face of the autocratic justice of the emperor, whether amiable, capricious, or malign.

If only for the sake of convenient delineation, historians have given the impression that a new institution called the Empire succeeded the Roman Republic. Autocracy is said to have been a pragmatic necessity in view of the huge expansion of Rome's territorial conquests, acquisitions, and bequests.[447]

---

447. Syme's *The Roman Revolution* was cardinal in debunking the noble version of Augustus's motives in creating a "constitutional" tyranny. John Buchan's *Augustus* was a 1930s encomium which, in the nicest British style, endorsed the autocracy that Mussolini, in particular, impersonated. Buchan (later Lord Tweedsmuir) was the author of, among other thrillers, *The Thirty-Nine Steps*. His recurrent hero, Richard Hannay, was the prototype of James Bond.

In fact, no new constitution was ever drafted; nor was the Republic ever officially disbanded. After the assassination of Caligula in 41 C.E., the Senate had the chance, but not the nerve, to declare that it had had enough of institutional megalomania. Nevertheless, no reliable system was ever set up to regulate the succession of one emperor by another. Roman emperors were seldom as secure as even the most confident of them appeared.

Augustus had not been joking when, at the end of his life, he compared himself to an actor who had kept a straight face over a very long period of imposture. On his deathbed, Suetonius reports that the dying emperor remarked to his entourage:

Epei de panu kalōs papaistai, dote kroton,
Kai pantes hēmas meta charas propempsate. . . .[448]

The dying grandee had ample reason for self-congratulation in the Greek style. His long run as leading actor restored superficial harmony to a schizoid state. Many had died in the years of civil war; survivors were glad to survive; and almost all Romans agreed to play along with the imperial charade, especially if offered juicy parts. This was as true of poets as of bankers, administrators, men-about-town, and tax farmers.

448. "Since my part has been beautifully played, give me credit / And send me, all of you, on my way with applause."

75.

Sextus Propertius (who was born sometime between 54 and 47 B.C.E. and died about 2 B.C.E.) exemplifies a more modest form of recusatio not unusual among poets who rated private emotional states above grand public themes and sentiments. Propertius's father had lost his property after backing the losing side in the wars preceding Augustus's monopoly of power. If, unlike Horace, the poet did not cause his father's impoverishment, he felt it more enduringly. Never reconciled to the Princeps, he expressed hostility not only by what he said, albeit obliquely, but also by what he would not say or applaud. In this he was braver than Horace, if less felicitous.

Ezra Pound's *Homage to Sextus Propertius* was published in the grimmest days of the Great War and seems to excuse Pound's own sense of alienation from patriotic rhetoric.[449] Propertius claims (somewhat like Horace, whom he disparages) to have gifts too delicate and a heart too tender for martial themes; but his timidity is close to defiance. His surviving four books of elegiacs have as their central theme the poet's disastrous passion for Cynthia, the pseudonym (in homage to Callimachus) for an older woman, said to have been a certain Hostia, who was possibly a courtesan somewhat like Dumas *fils'* "Dame aux Camélias," but with a harder heart and better lungs.

Propertius mimics Catullus in his dolorous recital. Unhappiness in love was common among elegiac poets; only

---

449. Sullivan's *The Poet as Translator: Ezra Pound and Sextus Propertius* (1964) was the first book to explore the affinity of the two poets, without remarking that Pound later blundered willfully into applauding and endorsing the tyranny of Mussolini and the murderous ideology of Hitler.

doomed passions suited their muse. Propertius's rancor, however mitigated, did not lack political undertones. The protraction of his desire for Cynthia and his refusal to consider marriage to anyone else entailed refusal to comply with Augustus's new conjugal code, which required bachelors to marry and—as Byron would put it—propagate their kind. Rome's upper classes had been depleted by mutual slaughter. When Virgil makes Aeneas abandon his passionate love for Dido in order to fulfill his role as a man of destiny, he was promoting Augustus's civil code: duty to Rome had to be placed above personal feelings. For Propertius to publicize his anguished romance with an older courtesan and to make it the spine of his entire poetic corpus verged on defiance. His tortuous obscurities can make reading Propertius a testing trip, but they are typical of the ways in which intellectuals encode their dissidence to deceive censors. Jorge Luis Borges was not alone in remarking that dictators force writers to be more subtle than is necessary in a permissive society.[450] Brave words are easy when they carry no penalty.

Publius Ovidius Naso (43 B.C.E.–17 C.E.) seems to have had a tranquil middle-class childhood despite all the public upheavals. He completed his education with a Greek tour rather more luxurious than Horace's. He embarked on, but

---

450. Borges's own dissent from the usurping putschists in his native Argentina was so nuanced as to be all but indiscernible. Boris Pasternak was similarly quiescent under Stalin, unlike his friend Osip Mandelstam, whom he failed to support when it might have saved Mandelstam's life. Pasternak was scorned for his cowardice by Stalin himself, but survived to win the Nobel Prize for *Doctor Zhivago*, which Vladimir Nabokov despised as he did all accommodation with the ideologists and fellow-travelers whose jargon had debased the great Russian language.

soon abandoned, the routine political career available to him, in order to follow his frivolous muse. Unlike those of Propertius, his elegiacs are not stressed with grievances; his mellifluous wit never makes awkward waves. He took the early years of Augustan society as he rejoiced to find it: sophisticated, amoral, and ostentatious. As readable as he was prolific, he gladly and glibly undertook the role of sexual mentor to a hedonistic society, eagerly forgetful of the horrors of civil wars. Ovid's erotic manuals—the *Amores* and its sequel, the *Ars amatoria*— were the talk of the town, and the boudoir. His wit secured a place in the fast set around Augustus's daughter Julia, who took naughty pleasure in rebelling against her father's new, tediously middle-class morality. Ovid's iambic love affair with the shadowy, perhaps fictional, "Corinna" lacks the bruised sincerity that has often been said to dignify the loves of Catullus, Propertius, and the tripping Tibullus, whose Delia was courted with what became textbook propriety.

While making salacious play with the liaisons dangereuses that were part of the protoypical dolce vita, Ovid—like Oscar Wilde—never guessed that he himself might be in danger. André Malraux's dictum that eroticism is a way of escaping one's epoch ignores the provocation that such escapism can offer to a dictatorship such as that of Augustus. Once established as *primus inter pares*—the first among equals wise enough not to proclaim their parity—the emperor imposed conjugal propriety on Rome. His politic purpose was to halt the demographic decline that civil wars, not least those he himself had waged, had caused in the upper-class male population.[451]

451. Augustan legislation was more purposeful than moral: Rome needed men who were men. Homosexuality was not improper unless it demeaned

The precise cause of Ovid's thumping fall from imperial favor, in 8 B.C.E., remains uncertain. Did his happy incitements to erotic fancy infuriate an emperor vexed by his own daughter Julia's adulterous frivolity? Was there a serious plot to unseat Augustus, in which some of Ovid's grand friends were complicit? Was Ovid aware that something seditious was being talked about, and did he then choose to go on being sociable? His fame (like Wilde's) made him an exemplary victim of the new, prim morality. At one moment he was the guest every Roman hostess wanted at her party; at the next he was served with imperious notice of exile. Neither tears nor fame procured reprieve. Unlike Propertius, Ovid was married (for the third time) and had at least one child (a daughter who herself had children). He was forced to leave them all in Rome.

Ovid's exile in Tomi, today's Constanta on the Black Sea (where a handsome statue pays tribute to the city's most famous, and most reluctant, inhabitant), was lamented at lachrymose length in his unfailingly well-turned *Tristia*, with never anything but a disyllable as the last word of a pentameter, and in his no less sorry letters from the Black Sea. Augustus never relented. The poet who had reveled in metropolitan promiscuity was reduced to a woeful absentee. Not even Tiberius, when he assumed the purple, had the small grace to recall him. The once cynical amorist was left to weep away his last years in solitary uxoriousness. Society, Somerset Maugham once said—thinking of Wilde, and of himself unless he was careful—may tolerate

---

a free (young) citizen by turning him into a passive victim. The seduction of a (free) virgin, male or female, might be an offense, never a sin. Tiberius's conduct on Capri, where—according to Tacitus's *Annals* (book 6) and Suetonius—the sour emperor defiled innocent children, was iniquitous because tyrannical.

you for a long time and then, when you least expect it, crumple you like a piece of waste paper and toss you away. History has never been short of examples. At the height of his early fame, Byron too had to go into exile from Regency England because of his flagrant infidelity to his wife Annabella, whom he satirized, between apologies, as the Princess of Parallelograms. Embracing his Venetian exile, he wrote *Don Juan,* toyed with revolution, and, in the end, which came in his thirty-sixth year, embraced the cause of Greek liberation and died, as the result of medical incompetence, at Missolonghi in 1824.

Ovid is the first great writer to be scorned by critics because he was both prolific and a best seller. His industry matched but never debased his rare facility: he not only wrote immaculately turned elegiacs but, in the *Metamorphoses,* which fascinated Renaissance artists, he leavened the hexameter with a dexterity that all but mocks Virgil. If there is a certain monotony in effortless excellence, who but a prude or a killjoy can deny genius to "Ovid Venus-clerke" (as Chaucer called him)?

76.

There were poets at work in Rome in the period after the golden age of those who benefited from Augustan patronage, but neither Tiberius nor his successor Gaius "Caligula,"[452] a charming prince whom power transformed into a rabid psychopath, offered incentives to writers to seek anything but prudent obscurity. Caligula's

---

452. Gaius's nickname "Little Boot" was given him as a small boy by legionaries who kitted him out when on active service with Caligula's father Germanicus. As a glamourous monster, Caligula made an apt subject for both Albert Camus, who wrote a play about him, and Gore Vidal, who wrote (and later repudiated) Bob Guccione's quasi-pornographic 1979 film *Caligula.*

successor, Claudius was a doddery antiquarian eccentric who had fully expected the Praetorian Guardsmen who had dispatched the emperor to do the same to him. For whatever motive, probably job security, they hailed him as Caesar. Quick and clever enough to offer prompt donatives, he proved a more efficient, hands-on emperor than anyone could have imagined.

Even more than his predecessors, Claudius relied on the services of freedmen. A new caste of increasingly powerful administrators, manumitted slaves became the preferred ministers of the emperor. Clever ex-slaves (not unusually of Greek origin) were favored because they had no connections outside the imperial household. Their authority depended entirely on imperial favor. There were fortunes to be made by serving him well; no appeal against deserved or capricious dismissal. The more his instruments were hated by the old patricians, the better it suited the emperor. Freedmen in imperial Rome resembled "the king's Jews": a privileged fraction of an otherwise despised and powerless caste. As long as they spoke with the emperor's authority, they were dangerous to cross and important to know. Many became rich; few were interested in culture. All were suspicious of anyone, especially of the old patrician class, who by his intelligence or sophistication entertained or instructed the emperor.

Claudius loved Roman history and arcane precedents. He liked to play the sagacious judge in legal cases, but he was a fool with women. His two wives, Messalina and Agrippina, were notorious for their manipulations and infidelities. He was also gullible enough to entrust state business to freedmen such as Polybius, who probably had a hand in decreeing the exile, in 41 C.E., of Annaeus Seneca (the famous son of a philosopher of the same name) to Corsica. The formal charge was adultery with Julia Livilla, the sister of the now-dead Caligula, but Polybius took pleasure in keeping Seneca at a distance for nine years, despite the great man's dismal and prolonged pleading. Seneca was a provincial, from today's Cordoba in southern Spain, but he belonged to a rich family and had influential connections. The closer such an amusing and urbane man might get to the emperor, the less secure Polybius was likely to be.

Seneca's ambitions were so grand, both in politics and in literature, that he could not resist their incautious expression. At the same time, he was morbidly conscious of the risks of conspicuousness. In his youth, he offended Caligula by outsmarting the emperor, but he had the adroit charm to make his mark with the younger Agrippina, the mother of Nero, a woman of ruthless and unquenchable ambition. Having replaced the lascivious Messalina in Claudius's bed, her supreme aim was to put her son on the imperial throne. When the moment seemed auspicious for Nero to succeed his stepfather, whether or not she poisoned him, Agrippina did not strive officiously to keep Claudius alive when he had one of his epileptic fits. She served notice on Polybius and his greedy associates by having Seneca recalled to serve as tutor to the sixteen-year-old Nero. After the succession had been confirmed, Agrippina did away with Nero's only plausible rival, the tragic Britannicus,[453] Claudius's short-lived son by Messalina.

77.

Vilified by posterity for a variety of reasons, including several good ones, Nero was, for much of his principate, widely applauded. Applause being his drug of principal choice, he

453. Jean Racine's second great tragedy, *Britannicus,* was produced in Paris in 1669. Seneca is a notable absentee from the cast list.

particularly relished the effusive style in which Hellenic fans greeted their stars. Nero's uniqueness as an emperor lay in his vision of himself as, above all, an artist; and as an artist above all others. Having inherited an empire at peace, with stable boundaries and no looming barbarian enemies, Nero proposed to enjoy the arts of peace. In this he was honoring Seneca's tuition in what was meant to be mature statesmanship. Seneca urged the young Nero to respect the Senate (of which he was a member) and to adhere to a program calculated to win popular support: games and circuses, but also public works. The common people had no practical vote, but their support would inhibit any ambitious senator from overthrowing a princely distributor of conspicuous favors.

Seneca could not have had the influence that he did had he not recruited Burrus, the commander of the Praetorian Guard, as friend and colleague. Their tandem strengthened Nero's hand against Polybius and other hated freedmen left over from the previous reign. Within a short time, they were executed to cheers from the public. Agrippina, Nero's formidable mother, now showed every intention of being her (for the moment) docile son's regent. Both professor and pander, Seneca encouraged Nero's emancipation from his mother's exclusive love by a liberating affair with a beautiful freedwoman called Acte. Nero was to be damned in the eyes of posterity—and of not a few contemporaries—by the (at first ludicrously botched[454]) murder of his mother, but Agrippina was a monster who, in the

---

454. The original plan was to stage an accident in which Agrippina would be drowned in a collapsible boat, off fashionable Baiae on the Bay of Naples, but she managed to get back to shore, where she was stabbed. A collapsible boat figures in Jacques Tati's 1953 film *Monsieur Hulot's Holiday.*

words of a modern classicist, "had it coming" to her.[455] Agrippina's death was commissioned in 59 C.E., five years after her
son's accession to the purple.

Seneca cannot be blamed for everything that went wrong
with Nero; nor can he be absolved. The Spaniard was a versatile
writer, not only of tragedies that verged on Grand Guignol, but
also of squibs such as the scurrilous *Apocolocyntosis,* a Hellenic-
style lampoon written for Nero's entertainment immediately
after the death of Claudius. The late emperor seeks entrance to
Olympus but is deemed by the gods to be ineligible for divinity and turned into an immortal pumpkin. In public, the dead
emperor had to be solemnly deified and, as custom now required, praised by his successor. This formal obituary too was
composed by the versatile Seneca. As Nero's official friend, he
had to amuse and instruct without either boring or patronizing
the young Princeps. He also had to keep Burrus on side and not
alienate the new intake of freedmen who, like them or not, were
crucial to the administration. They soon became rich and
powerful.

Nero's reign supplies a grimly entertaining instance of the
collision of poetry and power. Nero hoped to impersonate both.
The arts festival of the Neronia inaugurated what he meant to be
a new stage in Roman social life, the union of politics and poetry,
Greek and Roman culture. While Seneca was a dominant figure
in the emperor's life, the former's nephew Annaeus Lucanus, the
precocious author of the *Pharsalia,* and the worldly Petronius
Arbiter were more congenial company. Both Seneca and Lucan
were of Spanish origin; neither could have become famous

---

455. The phrase was used by the bold classical scholar Mary Beard with
regard to the Americans immediately after 9/11.

anywhere but in Rome, where all great careers had to be made. We hear only of rare cases of stay-at-home Iberian intellectuals, such as Pomponius Mela from what is now Algeciras, a travel writer of the first century C.E. with pronounced sympathy for the vanished Carthage from which his family had emigrated.

Petronius—a man of consular rank and remarkable swagger—was at ease with, if he did not condescend to, Roman high society. Nero so admired the Petronian swagger that he made him his *arbiter elegantiae,* the decisive judge in matters of taste. He combined a wit's punctuality with the courtier's discretion. Like Sir Walter Ralegh, poet, adventurer, and Queen Elizabeth's one-time favorite, Petronius so outshone others (not least Burrus's replacement as commander of the Praetorians, the unamused Tigellinus) that he made enemies even of those who laughed at his jokes, and wished they could be as quick. When Ralegh was asked why he bothered with court life and all its risks, he replied, "For gold, for praise, for glory." It was always tempting to lose one's head for such ambitions, and Ralegh did. He patronized Robert Cecil, Elizabeth's chief of staff, and called him "little man." Ralegh was tall and Cecil was not. One can imagine Petronius being equally condescending to Tigellinus, whose height we do not know but who was never known for lively banter.

After Burrus died, in 62 C.E., Seneca thought it prudent to retire from the imperial service. He was apprehensive of Nero's now uncontrollable rage and rich enough to guess that the spendthrift emperor might covet his wealth. Seneca had more caution, if no better luck, than the young Louis XIV's finance minister, Nicolas Fouquet, who hoped to impress the new monarch with his magnificence. He did; and was dispatched to the Bastille. Seneca offered to cede his entire, very large fortune to Nero, but the emperor both refused it and took offense. Seneca's fate, if delayed, was sealed by his withdrawal from the palace, leaving the ruthless freedman Crescens and the upstart Tigellinus to do their insidious stuff. While enjoying, or trying to enjoy, his ostentatious obscurity, Seneca was always conscious of what people might say or think about him. Happy to ride in a peasant's cart, as a good Stoic should be, he confesses that he hid under some straw lest he be seen, in reduced circumstances, when a rich friend came along the same road in a fine conveyance.

Petronius was an Epicurean; Seneca affected the Stoic's unperturbed, essentially solipsistic attitude to life's vicissitudes; Lucan was a handsome, smart young man in an undiplomatic hurry to be famous. His unfinished *Pharsalia* was an elegy, in elaborate hexameters, for the Republic put to death, in effect, at the battle of Pharsalus in 48 B.C.E., when Julius Caesar defeated Pompey. Lucan's lament for pre-imperial Rome brims with paradoxical impertinence: he presumed that looking back, brilliantly, would not be offensive to Nero; nor was it, until it was. Lucan was not some reckless Alexis de Tocqueville, wishing that he still lived in the ancien régime, but a coiner of dazzling phrases. The silly danger that he and Petronius incurred was that the competitive emperor admired them so much that envy sapped affection.

When Calpurnius Piso, a senator with wide connections in patrician circles, decided that Rome had had enough of a matricidal lunatic who insisted on performing on the public stage like some self-infatuated Dionysos, a conspiracy was instigated that embraced a caucus of famous names. Was Petronius involved or merely, as he liked to be, au courant? He was most probably amused; that was his response to most of life; neither art nor society was to be treated with portentous solemnity. Lucan was probably at least a passive sympathizer with Piso. Seneca may well have thought that his one-time pupil had gone too far; it is unlikely that he had an active hand in the plot.

Guilt and innocence were decided not on evidence but on the emperor's whim. Seneca, Lucan, and Petronius were ordered to commit suicide on suspicion of sympathy with treason. If only to upstage the long-faced Seneca, Petronius disdained to comply with time-honored gravity. His friends were invited to his death-day party. He sustained his dandy pride by opening his veins in the bath and then binding them up again, to give himself time to enjoy another glass, to praise or punish a slave, or to make one more joke. His last action was to smash a pitcher of great value that he knew Nero coveted; he also made public a list of Nero's sexual partners (of both sexes) and detailed the emperor's riper fetishes. He then broke his signet ring, so that nothing to implicate others could be forged under his seal. Young Lucan imitated his hero, Cato, and made suicide into a gesture of contempt for autocracy. Seneca's end was a dignified salute to the Stoicism that never quite healed all the splits in his personality. It lacked the panache that the bibulous Petronius displayed in his red bathtub.

78.

Like Nero's trio of poetic victims, Martial (Marcus Valerius Martialis) was Spanish. He was born in Bilbilis, in what is now the northern province of Aragon, around 40 C.E. He traveled to Rome to make a name for himself as a composer of erotic, often scabrous squibs, as well as of prudently occasional verses. Although he benefited from Seneca's generosity and Lucan's

friendship, he avoided the Icarian fate of his high-flying compatriots. Never a grandee, he made his amusing way into smart
circles and found favor with the Flavian emperors who succeeded Nero, the last of the Julio-Claudian dynasty. Titus was
the most amiable of Martial's patrons, though the poet always
affected poverty, in the usual way of Bohemians who like to live
in funded independence.

The danger of saying the wrong thing, or the right thing
in the wrong way, continued to threaten the careers of those
who could not resist the limelight. Martial had to play a clever
game in order to gain social promotion during the reign of the
malign Domitian; he did so with flatteries that were promptly
reversed once the tyrant was dead and officially anathematized.
Unlike Catullus, Propertius, Ovid, and Tibullus, Martial makes
no parade of his romantic attachments, real or fancied. Unlike
Petronius and his circle, he retained a sentimental attachment
to his native Spain, to which he returned toward the end of a
rackety life, at the beginning of the second century.

On paper at least, Martial's attitude to women is more
prurient than affectionate. He gives a sour twist to the sentimental connection between elegiac versifiers and the female
sex. Martial's friend Juvenal, of whose personal life almost
nothing is known, announced indignation to be the fuel of his
verses. Did his parade of outrage at Rome's decline bear witness
to a moralist's severity, or was it a liberating affectation? Disgust
at the degeneracy of today's world, whenever that may be, is a
regular literary trope. Juvenal claimed that in his Rome it was
impossible to be anything but a satirist. Unlike Martial (who
regularly remarked on the evidence of oral sex), Juvenal controlled his scatological scurrility; he saved his disgust for Jews,
Greeks, and other impertinent social intruders. As for women,
Juvenal went to great lengths, in his notorious Sixth Satire, to

depict Roman wives as whores and vampires. Fear of women runs, like the fabled river Alpheios, under the surface of ancient life. It is as if the repression of the female required that all women should be seen as uncontrollable menaces. This tendency had its modern equivalent when Winston Churchill's grandson, Nicholas Soames, described Princess Diana as "a loose cannon," where the word "loose," applied to a woman, carries telling ambiguity.

Running beneath much of Roman poetry is the uncertain role of what Byron called "the sex." The attitudes of poets to their art and to society can be measured, to a degree, by the extent to which women are (or are said to be) determinant in their lives. When Aeneas turned his back on Dido, he enacted what Rome's destiny (and Augustus's social morality) required; he also impelled the queen of Carthage to die, by her own hand, after she has prayed that some avenger would arise from her bones. In her stored resentment, Dido stands for women in general: who knows what they might not do, or—as Freud never ceased to wonder—what they really want? Roman women were chattelized when docile and ruthless when, like Nero's mother, they had occasion to assert themselves.

Roman poetry turns sour with Juvenal; he finds no joy in public or in private life. The hexameter in which, from Ennius to Virgil, Rome's poets had celebrated her history became, with Juvenal, the vessel of scorn for the stinking masses and of disgust with the idle rich, including the emperor (once he was safely dead). There is, however, perennial pleasure to be derived from Juvenal's resourceful indictments of almost everything. He has the rampant rhetoric of an Old Testament prophet denouncing the scandal of the times, but his satire changed nothing and had nothing to commend: he had no God to whom he could urge the people to revert in pious orthodoxy.

79.

In 98 C.E., Cornelius Tacitus, a young patrician who would mature into the archetypal stylish historian, wrote a prolonged essay entitled *Germania*. It affected to show knowledge of the lives and virtues of a congeries of barbarian tribes, out of the Roman orbit, on the far side of the Rhine. Julius Caesar had failed to subdue those he catalogued under the generic name of "Germani." They never called themselves by that title; nor was there a single country whose citizens knew it as Germania.

For the Romans, those sunless, beery, northern regions beyond the Alps and across the Rhine remained terra incognita, full of somber menace. The only serious attempt to enroll them into the Roman Empire came in 9 C.E., during the reign of the emperor Augustus. His legate, Quinctilius Varus, advanced with three legions into the Teutoburg Forest. Gulled by promises of a friendly welcome, he was ambushed by the native leader (and ex-legionary) Hermann, whom Tacitus called Arminius (his name is inscribed on a bleak woodland canvas by Anselm Kiefer). The Roman expeditionary force was annihilated. Augustus decreed that there should never be another attempt to recruit the Germans into the civilized world. During the following centuries, there was copious trade with the boozy and bellicose inhabitants of the far side of the Rhine. Fractious with each other, the Teutonic tribes were united only in being alien to Rome.

Tacitus never went near them. Read in his original trim Latin, the *Germania* is a work of fanciful anthropology, more like Jonathan Swift's *Gulliver's Travels* or Montesquieu's *Persian Letters* than Lévi-Strauss's *Tristes tropiques*. It purports to be about unspoiled tribesmen who have none of the Romans' sophistication and—more important—remain immune to Mediterranean decadence. Somewhat in the manner of Kevin Costner's film *Dances with Wolves*, Tacitus contrasts the good faith and honesty of natural men with the urbane Romans who affected to be superior to them. Thickened with a sediment of old soldiers' tales, the *Germania* was an early essay in the mythology of the Noble Savage. Like Jean-Jacques Rousseau's Natural Man, Tacitus's unwashed, unspoiled tribesman was a utopian fiction. He lived close to the soil but left it to his faithful women to till it, while he did virile things, mostly boozing and brawling.

It can hardly have occurred to Tacitus that anyone north of the Alps would ever read his book. It was intended to amuse and alarm an audience of hedonistic metropolitans whose prime activity was to toady to the emperor in order keep their family fortunes immune from confiscation. In stylish contrast, Tacitus's German clansmen had no such timidity: fierce egalitarian warriors, they served no tyrant and owned no possessions but their simple crofts and their sharp weapons. Modern opinion-mongers, such as Mary McCarthy and Susan Sontag, made similar paragons of the North Vietnamese and an exemplary template of Mao's China, to put down the comfortable readers of the *New York Review of Books*. Neither gleeful Cassandra was ever up to her ankles in a paddy field.

How did the *Germania* come to be described as a "most dangerous book"[456] and why, almost two millennia later, did

---

456. Christopher Krebs attaches that title to his scholarly and informative 2011 account of the Nazi appropriation of Tacitus's mordant "history" of the Germans as forerunners of Rousseau's fantasy of the Noble Savage.

the hunt for a rare fifteenth-century manuscript (the Codex Aesinas) become an obsession of Reichsführer S.S. Heinrich Himmler? Himmler was a prim provincial schoolmaster, dressed as an unconvincing Aryan warrior in a uniform designed by Hugo Boss. Craving authenticity as well as power, he was known to declare that he was really a farmer, like Tacitus's Germans of old; it just so happened that he didn't have a farm. The mechanization of Germany in modern times went along with the Nazi sentimentalization of the pastoral life, which Tacitus was held to idealize.

Hence, in 1943, as the Third Reich was beginning to founder, a detachment of S.S. men was sent to a villa not far from Ancona, in central Italy, to purloin what amounted, in Himmler's crackpot estimation, to a holy book, the scripture that supposedly confirmed that the Germans were literally a race apart, sprung from the soil on which they had always lived, their homogeneous blood untainted by non-Teutonic dilutions. What was "dangerous" about Tacitus's book was not what he actually said in it, but what German historians, philosophers, and ideologists could claim that he had. *Germania* was the only quasi-biblical source for those who wanted to idealize the blond, blue-eyed ancestors who left no literature, no art, no laws, and no monuments.

For some fifteen centuries, the *Germania* was a neglected classic. Hence the rareness of that manuscript, on which, in fact, Himmler never laid his thieving hands. Its alleged contents became central to the aspirations of German-speaking central Europeans only after Martin Luther pinned those 95 antipapal theses to the doors of Wittenberg Cathedral in October 1517. There would be no unified German state for more than three and a half centuries. In 1871, Bismarck's imperial dream was realized, after Prussia's victory in its war with France. Until then, as Friedrich Nietzsche put it, "to be German meant to wonder what it was to be German." In the swell of German self-esteem, Tacitus—falsely construed and ingeniously emended—was held to enshrine the age-old answer: it was to be magnificently unlike anyone else.

Martin Luther's rebellion against Rome was theological in form, nationalist in spirit. Luther's ranting defiance found popular backing because the Catholic Church had turned into another Roman invasion: papal legates and officious priests took the place of legions and generals. The outlandish Germans were expected to pay excessive tribute to the Vatican in return for being absolved of their sins by unmanly, Latin-speaking professional pardoners. The Reformation was a colonial revolt in theological costume. In the late 1800s, Bismarck's Kulturkampf was another round in the rejection of Rome's intrusive moralizing. In the late 1930s, Pius XII's concordat with the Nazis was a feeble attempt to stay in spiritual business north of the Alps. For German purposes, Tacitus supplied the chauvinists' gospel. It was taken to be especially valuable because it was written by someone on the other side. Commentaries tacked onto it by tendentious scholars and romancing philosophers veered further and further from the original text. Irony proved, as usual, untranslatable. Misreadings and falsifications abounded to validate racial conceits; blended with Lutheran anti-Semitism, the *Germania* was conscripted into the Aryan ideology of Alfred Rosenberg and his like. In 1937, Thomas Mann, who was raised as a Lutheran, endorsed Nietzsche's sardonic view of the Germans: "The prominence of Hitler," Mann said, "is not a case of rotten luck, but directly in line with Luther and so *a truly German phenomenon.*"

Racism is a way of defining who you are by proclaiming who you are not. Resentment of Napoleon's conquest of Prussia, and his attempt to unify Europe under his own rational despotism, made not being French an early element in being a German. The Nazi philosopher Carl Schmitt insisted that political seriousness was a function of having an enemy against whom one's own society could then be engaged in a righteous fight to the death. The Persians served in that role for Alexander the Great, the Carthaginians for Cato the Censor. Christianity's displacement of the Jews as God's supposed favorites provided a singular target. With a common fiendish enemy, all manner of people might be united in vindictive superiority. For Germanic racial fantasists, fear that Jews too had "unpolluted blood," as a result of their endogamous habits, made them an ideally dangerous Other. In the chorus of Wagnerian conceit, the *Germania* was taken to prove that the Germans were always harmonious, folk-singing people.

In the hope of preferment, divines, philosophers, professors, and mountebanks (Martin Heidegger's name fills a number of these boxes) twisted the *Germania* into a gospel bestowing quasi-scriptural authority on Teutonic supremacy. To avoid inconvenient blemishes, they suppressed Tacitus's mention of recourse to human sacrifice, although they endorsed it in practice. Passion for antique origins was not limited to the Germans: echoing Virgil's *Aeneid,* many Europeans had an appetite for Homeric ancestry. Francus, a Trojan prince, was said to be the forefather of the French kings; Britons and Normans made similar claims.

In fact, Tacitus wrote, even tribal kinsmen could hardly share a meal without brawling among themselves. He prayed that their discords would continue, since "fate could provide no greater favor" to Rome. In this he presaged the views of François Mitterrand and Margaret Thatcher; neither was in any hurry to have the two Germanies unite after the fall of the

Berlin Wall. Ancient texts, of which the Bible is only the most durable instance, are regularly contorted to certify whatever pretensions a powerful hierarchy or vainglorious patriotism can get away with. In 1632, Justus Georg Schottelius, the erudite tutor to the son of Duke August the Younger of Brunswick-Wolfenbüttel, claimed that German was spoken by those constructing the tower of Babel.[457] Noah's alleged adoption of "Tuisto" as his son was taken to make the "earthborn god" of ancient Germanic songs into the eponymous (if you worked at it) promise of Teutonic superiority. Others chose to announce that they were of Spartan stock: Goebbels's catchphrase "make way, you old ones!" was a parody of an old Laconic round-song.

Only a few honest men equaled the great Latinist Eduard Norden, who in 1920 dared to say that the virtues supposedly specific to Tacitus's Germans were, in truth, "wandering motifs" that other ancient writers had attached to Egyptians and Scythians. There were also brave priests, such as the cardinal archbishop of Munich, Michael von Faulhaber, who, on New Year's Eve 1933, denounced the folly of "Nordic or German religion" and praised the people of Israel for possessing "the noblest religious values." He even dared to deride the loutish pre-Christian Germans, citing Tacitus's description of their drunken carousals. The Nazi Security Police reported that the cardinal had excited a good measure of popular support. Imagine if Pope Pius XII had done as much, instead of so little.

---

457. Maurice Olender's 2009 *The Languages of Paradise* shows how the face-off between Aryans and Semites was pushed back, by inventive etymologists, to the dawn of mankind and furnished another warrant for supposititious ideologues.

Is there a contemporary moral to be drawn from how Tacitus was hijacked, deformed, and misused? It is that intellectuals, however good their intentions, cannot be trusted to give an unvarnished account of the foreign texts they claim to be teaching. In modern universities, students tend to rely on translations of classics and of the Bible and the Qu'ran. How many have the linguistic competence to verify the accuracy of an assigned translation? The more refined a version is, the less likely is it to give an untainted account of the original. Three centuries ago, after reading Alexander Pope's now-classic version of the *Iliad*, Richard Bentley remarked, "It is a pretty poem, Mr. Pope, but you must not call it Homer." When we talk or write about the ancient Mediterranean world in modern terms, we should be aware that its inhabitants would not be at home in what wishful ingenuity or tendentious hindsight chooses to parade as the restored face or translated logos of antiquity.

Index

Rogatianus, 117
Roman Catholic Church, 44, 81,
    155n246, 160, 179, 250, 336
Roman Curia, 297
Rome: consular model of, 206–7n;
    country life in, 314–15; as empire,
    313, 317–18; founding of, 306; and
    Hellenistic empire, 183, 191, 217, 279,
    281–82, 289; military-political
    strategy of, 200–201, 217–18; poetry
    of, 285–301, 309, 319–23, 330–31;
    politics in, 302–4; slavery in,
    114–22
Romilly, Jacqueline de, 50n88, 70n121
Romulus, 306–7
Roosevelt, Franklin, 209, 298n419
Rorty, Richard, 80n135
Roscius, 136n226
Rosenberg, Alfred, 336
Rousseau, Jean-Jacques, 334, 334n
Roxana, 270, 275, 278
Rudbeck, Olof, 41
Rufus, Caelius, 166n258, 301–2,
    302n425
Rufus, Curtius, 274
Russell, Bertrand, 16, 104, 104n181
Russia, 221–22
Ryle, Gilbert, 8, 8n14; *The Concept of
    Mind*, 170n261

Sabine women, rape of, 114
Sacred Band, 46n82
sacrifice: animal, 9, 13, 128; human,
    13, 34, 46, 46n83, 58–61, 126–27;
    rituals of, 126–28
Salamis, 169, 187, 197–98, 233
Sallust, 309
Samos, 146–47, 202, 211, 212, 218, 225,
    240–41, 246n
sandals, 58
Santorini, 39–40
Sappho, 81, 98n169, 122–24, 295, 306

Sartre, Jean-Paul, 79n134, 180n;
    "Erostrate," 261n379
satire, 305–6
satyr plays, 159
scapegoats, 46n83, 61n, 127, 131,
    164n
Schiavone, Aldo, 43–44n77
Schiller, Friedrich, 108
Schliemann, Heinrich, 75
Schmitt, Carl, 337
Schottelius, Justus Georg, 338
science, 16, 21, 50n87, 81, 100–101,
    208–9n307, 219–20
Scientology, 47, 150n
Scipio Aemilianus, Publius, 217
Scipio Africanus, 269, 287
Scrutiny (journal), 296n416
sculpture: Cycladic, 38–39; by
    Phidias, 43–45; by Praxiteles,
    44n79; *xoana*, 11, 11n
Scylax, 23–24
Scythians, 195
Seaford, Richard, xiv, 85n, 100, 105,
    108, 173n266, 179, 250n359
Second World War, ix, 51, 62n105
Seferis, George, v, 19n39, 29, 126,
    137, 165
segulah (characteristic), 83n142, 156n
Seleucids, 278, 281
Seleucus, 266, 278, 280n
Semele, 2n3, 10, 10n, 27n56
senators, Roman, 129n214
Seneca, 117, 118–19n199, 312, 324–30,
    325n; *Apocolocyntosis*, 327
sexuality and eroticism, 6, 6n9, 7n13,
    8n14, 36n, 48, 85, 85n, 90–91, 250,
    308n435, 321–2n, 321–22. *See also*
    homosexuality; incest
Shakespeare, William, *Julius Caesar*,
    298n421
Shapiro, Karl, 229n335
Shelley, Percy Bysshe, 83n142